CRITIC

C000145717

The Life and Work of

Benito Mussolini

Alan Axelrod, Ph.D.

ALPHA

A Pearson Education Company

For Anita.

L'amor che muove il sole e l'altre stelle.

Copyright © 2002 by Alan Axelrod, Ph.D.

International Standard Book Number: 0-02-864214-7
Library of Congress Catalog Card Number: 2001093558

04   03   02   8   7   6   5   4   3   2   1

Interpretation of the printing code: The rightmost number of the first series of numbers is the year of the book's printing; the rightmost number of the second series of numbers is the number of the book's printing. For example, a printing code of 02-1 shows that the first printing occurred in 2002.

Printed in the United States of America

Publisher:
Marie Butler-Knight
Product Manager:
Phil Kitchel
Managing Editor:
Jennifer Chisholm
Senior Acquisitions Editor:
Randy Ladenheim-Gil
Development Editor:
Lynn Northrup
Senior Production Editor:
Christy Wagner

Copy Editor:
Cari Luna
Cover Designer:
Ann Jones
Book Designer:
Sandra Schroeder
Production:
John Etchison
Tricia Bronkella

CRITICAL LIVES

Benito Mussolini

Foreword

Alan Axelrod's study demonstrates that violence was Mussolini's constant companion and support, the common denominator of virtually every aspect of his public life. The Duce was not a man of ideology or of ideas, even as he traversed all the ideologies of his age, from anarchism to socialism to fascism, each in the service of his drive for and retention of power. Power was the prize, not the fulfillment of ideology. One would search in vain for a rational, evolutionary pattern to his development, given his frequent ideological zigzags and blatantly contradictory statements and positions.

Indeed, for Mussolini, contradiction was not to be explained, but celebrated. "Illusion is the sole reality of life," he proclaimed, and he lived his maxim to the fullest. Images were what counted, images of war, struggle, combat, heroism, and danger. Mussolini's fascism as an ideology consisted essentially of action words stolen from the socialist left and nationalist right, making it an unstable yet powerful "doctrine" with a radical veneer, ideally suited to the multiple crises that boosted him to power in 1922. Fascism promised an ordered life, social discipline, economic development, imperial destiny, and, most critically, an authoritarian state. Achievement of these goals required obedience and allowed for the most ruthless suppression of individual rights and public liberties. Thus everything about Mussolini's Italy was tinctured with the language of violence, including "battles" for wheat and births.

In the pages that follow, Alan Axelrod offers a succinct and insightful account of Mussolini's life and work, from his rude childhood to his execution at the hands of resistance partisans in 1945, when he had become the most hated man in Italy. As an adolescent, Mussolini played the bully, a role so congenial that he never abandoned it as he became a teacher, then insurrectionary, politician, and ultimately dictator. A socialist in 1914 on the eve of World War I, violent in word and deed, Mussolini may have understood that the war opened an uncommon opportunity for revolution. That revolution, however, required jettisoning old ideas and comrades, and Mussolini's path to power was strewn with renunciations of his past. Axelrod quite rightly argues that Mussolini's manipulation of men and events was an artful balancing act in bringing about his elevation to power, that he realized that threat was more potent than irreversible action, and that lies were a most valuable part of his repertoire.

Similarly, as the Duce, Mussolini manipulated a generation of Italians, even as he was a genuinely popular leader, providing all the rewards of victory without risking European conflict. Mussolini appeared to erase Italy's past failures: Economic development, social peace, imperial conquest, rapprochement with the Catholic Church, and a key role in European affairs, all were partially won, with the only cost the loss of freedom. Foreigners, including Churchill and Hitler, admired the Duce, and the Nazi leader hailed him as "my mentor." Yet it was the fatal attraction of Mussolini to Nazi power that led to his downfall in the midst of a disastrous war; illusion then yielded to the brutal reality of weakness, Mussolini's and Fascist Italy's.

Nathanael Greene
Nathanael Greene is Professor of History at Wesleyan University, where he teaches European history and has served as Vice-President for Academic Affairs. His major scholarly interests are the history of France, Spain, and Italy in the twentieth century. Professor Greene has published studies concerned with fascism, European and French socialism, and with France during the years between the world wars. He is a reviewer of books for several journals and has held Fulbright and Guggenheim fellowships.

Introduction

Man and Monster

"He has not only been able to secure and hold an almost universal following; he has built a new state upon a new concept of a state. He has not only been able to change the lives of human beings but he has changed their minds, their hearts, their spirits. He has not merely ruled a house; he has built a new house." The subject of this paean is not Caesar Augustus, or George Washington, or even Napoleon Bonaparte. It is Benito Mussolini, in 1928, six years after he became prime minister of Italy. And it goes on: "It is one thing to administer a state. The one who does this well is called statesman. It is quite another thing to make a state. Mussolini has made a state. That is superstatesmanship."

The assessment comes not from a member of the Italian Fascist Party, nor even from an Italian of the period, but from Richard Washburn Child, who had served in the early 1920s as the U.S. ambassador to Italy. He wrote it in the foreword to the autobiography he proudly claimed credit for having persuaded Mussolini to write. "For his autobiography I am responsible," Child crows, and, like so many of us, he takes delight in having recognized greatness and celebrity from the beginning, before almost anyone else: "I knew him before the world at large, outside of Italy, had ever heard of him; I knew him before and after the moment he leaped into the saddle and in the days when he, almost single-handed, was clearing away chaos' own junk pile from Italy."

The ambassador from the sweet land of liberty was hardly alone in his admiration of a man who came to power by intimidation, beatings, and murder and who maintained power by offering order in exchange for nothing less than freedom. Leading French and English diplomats praised him, sometimes lavishly, though sometimes with reservations, as a welcome if not entirely wholesome alternative and antidote to anarchy and "bolshevism." In the early 1930s, President Franklin D. Roosevelt expressed approval, while Eleanor Roosevelt despised him from the very beginning. In the mid-1920s, Clementine Churchill wrote to her husband that Mussolini was "most impressive" and possessed of "beautiful golden brown piercing eyes which you can see but can't look at." Winston Churchill replied to Clementine with sly reserve: "No doubt he is one of the most wonderful men of our time," then qualified this judgment by quoting a contemporary liberal politician: "It is better to read about a world figure than to live under his rule."

Those of us who read, write, or even talk about history enjoy the privilege of being amused or appalled by the opinions of those who actually lived that history. Time confers on the audience a perspective the actors do not have. "I remembered [British foreign secretary] Lord Curzon's impatience with him long ago, when Mussolini had first come into power, and Curzon used to refer to him as 'that absurd man,'" Ambassador Child wrote. "Time has shown that [Mussolini] was neither violent nor absurd. Time has shown that he is both wise and humane." Of course, we see now that, in 1928, it is precisely time that Child lacked to reach a sound verdict. It is the difference between passing judgment on a new movie twenty minutes into it and waiting, instead, for the end.

Twenty years into the twentieth century, the world was a disappointing and terrifying place. It had fought a "Great War" of unprecedented destructiveness and heartbreak. It killed almost twenty million men, women, and children. The world's democracies salved themselves with the words of America's Woodrow Wilson, that all the sacrifice would "make the world safe for democracy" and that this terrible war had been a "war to end all wars."

But even before the war had ended, a new ideology burst onto the shell-shocked world: Soviet communism—or, as it was commonly called at the time, bolshevism. To a rapidly growing minority of the planet's people, communism seemed a salvation, but to the stunned majority, it was terrifying, a threat to wealth, to religion, to individuality, to the human spirit, a threat, when all is said and done, to the accepted order of things. For most of the world, communism loomed as the coming terror of the postwar era. And if the terror was debilitating, the disappointment that accompanied it was desperate. For it looked as if all that sacrifice had gone for nothing and worse than nothing. A war to make the world safe for democracy seemed to have become a war to make the world safe for bolshevism.

Blind fear, like blind admiration, is not of time, but of the moment. It precludes and prevents perspective. As the cliché goes, a drowning man grasps at straws. To a world at the burnt-out end of the Great War, a man like Mussolini seemed very much more substantial than a straw. To some, like Richard Washburn Child, he appeared to be a genius and a savior. To others, he merely seemed a better alternative than the likes of Vladimir Lenin or Josef Stalin. And among this latter group, there were many people willing to persuade themselves that Mussolini added up to more than just the lesser among evils. Yes, they admitted, he was a dictator, in whose name people were imprisoned, beaten, intimidated, even sometimes killed. But this all seemed very little compared to the twenty million human beings who had been blasted apart, gassed into suffocation, and shot to pieces during the late war. To a world and nation threatened with burial under "chaos' own junk pile," order, productive order and discipline, seemed more important than liberty—at least for the time being.

In time, people let themselves believe, there would be time for such luxuries as freedom, but, for *now,* the need was for the order and discipline and sacrifice Mussolini promised. And so Italy accepted fascism, Hitler in Germany took inspiration, and the rest of the world watched, often with approving smiles.

This book presents the life of Benito Mussolini. It begins with the birth of a son to a socialist blacksmith, who worshiped Garibaldi and revolution, and an indulgent schoolteacher mother, who worshiped the Virgin Mary, the Church, and her new little boy, Benito. He grew into a precocious, curious, vicious problem child, one who liked to get into fights and who was expelled from school for knifing another student. The narrative goes on to account for the political influences by which young Mussolini grew into both a Marxist and an advocate of violent reform. It tells of his relationships with a variety of women, two of whom served as his political and ideological mentors. It then recounts his abrupt about-face from Marxism that turned him from an antiwar journalist to an enthusiastic recruit in World War I and, after the war, drove him to create the fascist party, with which he promised to remodel Italy as nothing less than the nucleus of a new Roman Empire. And then the narrative turns to the personal magnetism that propelled Mussolini, at age thirty-nine, into the office of prime minister, the youngest in Italian history.

If Mussolini had been a conventional political figure, this first part of his life story would be, conventionally enough, the story of his "rise." But conventional Mussolini never was. He did not so much develop politically and ideologically as he swam about in a sea of politics and ideology, sometimes drifting with the changeable currents, sometimes fighting vigorously against them. A political journalist before he became a politician, he did not so much *rise* to power as he was suddenly *elevated* to it, as if, by his journalism, he had come upon just the right combination of words to create the mystical incantation that thrust open all doors.

Mussolini's political "development" was no conventional rise to power, yet the conventional reason for writing the life of Mussolini is to present the story of the man who created fascism, one of the two horrific ideological forces (the other was communism) that, between them, seduced, subjugated, and even destroyed much of the world in the last century. As fascism's architect, Mussolini shaped, however grotesquely, the destiny of millions, and for this reason alone his deserves to be called a "Critical Life."

Yet Mussolini's life work, fascism, the reason for our interest in him, proves to be a highly elusive subject. During much of his two decades as Italy's *Duce*—absolute leader—Mussolini kept a small army of scholars busy inventing an ideology for fascism. They never finished their work. For this great and powerful antagonist of communism had, in the end, no ideology. Back in 1928, the starry-eyed Richard Washburn Child intuited as much: Mussolini "has kept his faith in an ability to build up a machine—the machine of Fascism—the machine built not on any fixed theory but one intended by Mussolini to run—above all, to run, to function, to do, to accomplish, to fill the bottles with wine first, unlike the other isms, and put the labels on after."

Fascism was a machine, not an ideology. Fascism was an idol, not a religion. Fascism was the power by which Mussolini acquired—power. At the core, however, it was quite empty. As the distinguished historian A. J. P. Taylor put it in *The Origins of the Second World War* (1961), "Everything about Italian Fascism was a fraud. The social peril from which it saved Italy was a fraud; the revolution by which it seized power was a fraud; the ability and policy of Mussolini were fraudulent. Fascist rule was corrupt, incompetent, empty ..."

Empty at the core—and, for that reason alone, fascism was perhaps the most chilling object to which a mass of humanity ever sacrificed its treasure, ideals, and life. It was an avatar of that very heart of darkness into which Mr. Kurtz, emissary of modern civilization, gazes at the conclusion of Joseph Conrad's great and prescient novella of 1902 and about which he can repeat only a single phrase, "The horror, the horror."

Adolf Hitler's Nazi Party was inspired by the example of Mussolini's fascism. Even after he had attained power, Hitler continued to see his National Socialism as of a piece with fascism, and it is common for us to identify Hitler and Mussolini as the two leading fascist dictators of the twentieth century, without necessarily distinguishing Nazism from fascism. Yet we do tend very decidedly to distinguish Hitler from Mussolini. Hitler is evil incarnate, the creator of the Holocaust, a twisted political genius, a psychopath and serial killer on a planetary scale. But Mussolini, with his shaved and shiny block of a head, his pouting lower lip, pugnaciously out-thrust chin, his bantam-rooster stance, arms akimbo, chest and belly straining against a uniform blouse fit for an operetta hero, these do not seem the features of evil so much as of low comedy. In most of us, the figure of Mussolini somehow fails to stir visions of bona fide horror. It is not that we are unaware of the bad things he did—rising to power and maintaining it through conscienceless brutality, devastating far-off Ethiopia, bombing women and children in Spain, dragging his people, unprepared and unnecessarily, into a war that nearly destroyed them, and in cowardly desperation selling out his nation's Jews to the Holocaust—but that we tend to think of Mussolini as a kind of second-string Hitler, a wanna-be military genius, and, ultimately, a failed dictator.

The fact is that Mussolini is both worse than this and far more important precisely because he built the edifice of his particular horror upon the emptiness of deception, delusion, and fraud. World War I shattered the faith of many, it is said, creating a "lost generation" that believed in nothing, that trusted nothing, that accepted nothing on faith. Coming of age in that generation, Mussolini understood, in a way that a handful of catastrophically powerful modern men understood, that no ground is more fertile for the growth of illusion than the soil of shattered illusions.

Part One

---◆◇◆---

Blacksmith's Forge

Chapter 1

"A Sulphurous Land"

Whatever else he would become in the wider world, the boy born at 2:45 P.M., Sunday, July 29, 1883, in the remote hamlet of Verano di Costa, in the parish of Predappio, not far from the town of Forlì, in the Romagna region of northeastern Italy, would be almost always and above all a liar. He would lie to lovers, to his wife, to officials of his government, to the Italian people, to foreign diplomats and heads of state, to allies, and to enemies. His lies led him to power and led hundreds of thousands directly—and, indirectly, millions more—to their deaths. Among the less destructive of his myriad fantasies was a claim to have read the Greek and Roman classics in their originals, all of Dante, and every word written by William Shakespeare. Even the most fantastic lies typically harbor a grain of truth, and perhaps Mussolini was actually familiar with the question posed in Act II of *Romeo and Juliet:* "What's in a name?"

Plenty, his father must have believed.

Alessandro Mussolini named his firstborn Benito Amilcare Andrea, after his personal trinity of radical revolutionary heroes.

The fortress Rocca di Caterina Sforza, a landmark in Mussolini's home district of Forlì.

(Image from ArtToday)

Benito was Benito Juárez, the man who had led Mexico's most important revolution. Like many Italian socialists, Alessandro hailed Juárez's victory over Catholic conservatism and, even more, his triumph over Maximilian of Austria, the puppet emperor Napoleon III had sent to Mexico. Not only did the forces of Juárez overthrow Maximilian's government, but they tried Maximilian himself on charges of treason, found him guilty, and stood him up before a firing squad. It may not have been the shot heard 'round the world, but it certainly reverberated through the hidebound royal courts of Europe, terrifying the aristocrats and thrilling the revolutionaries. Northern Italians chafing under the yoke of Austrian domination, men like Alessandro Mussolini, celebrated the execution of the brother of Austrian emperor Franz Josef, oppressor of Lombardy, Venetia, Trieste, and the Trentino.

Amilcare Cipriani was the right-hand man of the great Garibaldi, Italy's most dynamic and revered revolutionary. Cipriani fought by Garibaldi's side in the attempted liberation of Rome in 1862. Following this, Cipriani fought for the Paris Commune in

1871, survived the Communards' massacre by French troops, but was apprehended, tried, and exiled to a brutal penal colony on the remote Pacific island of New Caledonia. He languished there, a living martyr to the cause of revolution, for nine years, gaining his release in the general amnesty of 1880. He returned to a hero's welcome in Italy, just three years before Benito Mussolini's birth.

When he returned to Italy, Cipriani joined the Internationalists, the worldwide socialist movement that sought to end nationalism and, instead, unite the proletariat of the entire world. Andrea Costa, another leader of the Internationalist movement, was even more radical than Cipriani, his ideas crossing into the realm of anarchy. Of young Mussolini's three namesakes, Andrea Costa was, for the people of the Romagna, the most immediate presence. In the summer of 1874, he had led the Internationalists in the formation of the Italian Committee for the Social Revolution, which resolved to launch a great revolution in Bologna, the chief city of the Romagna. The plan was for an army of three thousand men to muster at Imola on the night of August 7 for the march on Bologna. Alessandro Mussolini personally led forty-nine local socialists from Predappio parish to advance directly on Bologna, where he expected to join the thousands who had marched from Imola.

For Alessandro Mussolini, the Bologna uprising promised to be the high point of his life. He had been born a poor peasant in Montemaggiore, Romagna, in 1854. It was, in those days, an especially backward region of Italy. "A sulphurous land," Benito Mussolini called it in *My Autobiography* of 1928. The Appenine Mountains ran through it, and mineral hot springs, redolent of sulfur, percolated up through the ground in numerous places. It was a hard, stony land, good for growing grapes that made a pungent wine, but good for little else. The Pope, who controlled this region at the time, was determined to keep the peasantry docile by keeping them ignorant. Education was actively discouraged. Little more than one quarter of the population was literate, government posts were restricted to members of the priesthood, and, while the rest of Europe was developing a network of rail transportation, the Pope explicitly barred railroad construction in the Romagna lest the new machines convey new ideas, ideas of reform and revolt, to the villages.

Cut off from the world at large, Alessandro apprenticed to a blacksmith and, as a teenager, moved from Montemaggiore to set up a smithy of his own in the village of Dovia, Predappio parish. By this time, Romagna was no longer one of the Papal States, but was now part of the newly formed Kingdom of Italy, and it lay very much in the path of revolutionary winds.

These were not the comparatively gentle socialist breezes that wafted through Germany in the mid nineteenth century, where socialism followed the intellectual pattern of Karl Marx, took the form of the German Social Democratic Party, and established itself lawfully in the Reichstag, the German parliament. In Italy, especially the Romagna, socialism was driven not by the intellectual Marx, but by the more visceral Russian anarchist Mikhail Bakunin, who inspired Garibaldi and his radical Red Shirts, imbuing Italian socialism with a policy of militant action rather than parliamentary reform. In the "Red Romagna," the revolutionary wind came with the force of a gale, hot, violent, well suited to a long-oppressed region of bitter soil and boiling sulfur springs.

As he pounded on his blacksmith's forge, Alessandro Mussolini also expounded to all who would listen the doctrine of violent socialism. Whether or not his propaganda penetrated the minds of his customers at the forge, his presentation was sufficiently effective to keep them listening. People liked the socialist blacksmith of Predappio. He must have imagined that he could, indeed, become an important revolutionary leader, a man at the head of proletarian legions. The revolution set to launch in Bologna would be the start for him. Bakunin himself had traveled secretly from exile in Switzerland to take personal command.

Alessandro Mussolini had reason to believe his dream of socialist glory would become reality. But reality turned out to be something else. Instead of the three thousand that were to assemble at Imola, a mere two hundred showed up. Mussolini, at the head of forty-nine marchers bound for Bologna, was intercepted by the police, who managed to arrest thirty-two of his men, while he and seventeen others escaped. Thus Alessandro became a fugitive, but when he discovered that no jury would convict those who had been arrested, he came out of hiding and returned to Predappio. There he continued to pound and expound until October 1878, when he was served with an order of *ammonizione*. A legal innovation introduced by Italy's minister of the interior, Giovanni Nicotera, an order of *ammonizione* was served, without hearing or trial, on anyone suspected of revolutionary activity. The order required the person to report to the police every Sunday morning, to remain within the confines of the town or parish in which he lived, to attend no meetings of any kind (other than church), to visit no cafés or places of public entertainment, and to observe a curfew commencing daily one hour after sunset and ending at dawn. It was, in effect, an extended form of house arrest, and its term was indefinite, entirely at the whim and pleasure of the minister of the interior.

Primed for violence, animated by revolutionary dreams, Alessandro Mussolini nevertheless yielded to the confining reality of *ammonizione*. He dared not risk a violation that would land him in prison or a penal colony, without trial, for anywhere from three months to five years. But *ammonizione* did not prevent his falling for the local schoolmistress, Rosa Maltoni. She was an enlightened woman, born in nearby Forlì, and selflessly committed to lifting the children of Predappio out of ignorance and illiteracy. She was, however, no socialist, but rather a devout Catholic. It is a testament to the strength of her feelings for the atheist and anti-Catholic Alessandro—and to his feelings for her—that the two not only fell in love, but, over the objections of Rosa's father, married. Alessandro even compromised his politics and wed his bride before a priest in church, on January 25, 1882. The next month, he appealed to local authorities to lift the *ammonizione*. Recognizing that Mussolini was now a respectable married man—his wife no less than the kindly village schoolmistress—the Predappio council intervened on his behalf, and the *ammonizione* was lifted in October.

The three names Alessandro bestowed on his firstborn less than a year later are evidence that, despite his compromises, he had not forgotten his political dreams. Benito Juárez was, among other things, violently anti-Catholic; Amilcare Cipriani embodied the Red-Shirted spirit of Garibaldi; and Andrea Costa was a living symbol of out-and-out anarchy. Yet, wed in a church, Alessandro Mussolini now allowed his thrice-named son to be baptized in that church. In this gesture, it seems, he had moved beyond compromise to outright contradiction.

Whatever else characterized the world into which Benito Mussolini was born, contradiction was omnipresent and would sound throughout his life and career as its keynote. Alessandro held extreme socialist ideas, but he was willing to suppress them for the sake of personal freedom and marital harmony. There is no evidence that he found such compromise of principles particularly difficult or painful, for the fact was that the ideas were never as important as the violence associated with them. This, too, would mark Benito Mussolini for life. For him, political ideas were not only inseparable from the violence used to implement them, but were, in fact, less important than violence itself. The rising dictator Mussolini would compromise and contradict virtually every ideological position he ever advocated, but to violence he would remain forever faithful.

And so it is not surprising to read in My Autobiography that Mussolini deemed his father a better man than himself, a man who combined humanity, altruism, honesty, courage, and idealism, when the reality was that Alessandro Mussolini was a failed socialist revolutionary, hopelessly in debt, a heavy drinker, and a notorious womanizer, who read excerpts of Marx's Das Kapital to Benito, even as he allowed the boy's mother to take him to church every Sunday. In the end, all the words the boy would hear—humanity, altruism, honesty, courage, idealism, socialism, Catholicism— mattered far less in his upbringing than the heavy leather strap his father wielded without reference to any ideas of revolution, reform, or social justice.

Chapter 2

Mama's Bad Boy

Facts are hard to come by in the early life of Benito Mussolini. The recollections in his autobiographical writings, as well as those written by his political associates, are self-serving or, more to the point, self-mythologizing. Mussolini was eager to paint his childhood in hues that presaged his rise to power, as if that rise had been foreordained and inevitable.

Authorities differ on whether the Mussolini cottage in Verano di Costa, a tiny hamlet just above Dovia in the parish of Predappio, consisted of three or four rooms. They agree, however, that one of the rooms housed the village school, of which Rosa Mussolini was mistress. While some of Mussolini's biographers refer to the cottage as Alessandro Mussolini's house, it actually belonged to Predappio and came with the position of schoolmistress. The hard-drinking Alessandro, whose work habits were erratic, could not provide his family a home. His wife had to.

The house was sparsely furnished. The three children—Benito, the eldest, Arnaldo (born 1885), and their sister, Edvige (born 1888)—slept on iron-framed beds Alessandro had pounded out on his forge. Only two pictures hung on the wall: a portrait of Garibaldi, cherished by Mussolini's father, and an image of the Madonna of Pompeii, the object of his mother's worship.

Giuseppe Garibaldi, whose portrait hung in the Mussolini home.

(Image from the author's collection)

In My *Autobiography*, Mussolini remembered his father as a "dark-haired, good-natured man, not slow to laugh, with strong features and steady eyes." Others recall him as affable, but undependable and often brutal. Was he any more brutal than the typical, financially pressed village father of the time? We do not know. "My greatest love," Mussolini declared in the 1928 autobiographical volume, "was for my mother. She was so quiet, so tender, and yet so strong. … My mother not only reared us but she taught primary school. I often thought, even in my earliest appreciation of human beings, of how faithful and patient her work was. To displease her was my one fear." Others corroborate the picture of the gentle, doting Rosa. Mussolini believed that his mother had faith in her son's ultimate greatness: She "had a phrase which remains in my ears: 'He promises something.'"

Benito and Arnaldo Mussolini shared one of the iron beds Alessandro had forged. The brothers remained close all their lives. After Mussolini was firmly established in power, Arnaldo took over his brother's political newspaper, *Il Popolo d'Italia* (*The People of Italy*), and may even have ghost-written *My Autobiography*.

The narrow and shallow Rabbi River ran just outside the cottage window. "With my brother," Mussolini recalled, "I used to try my skill as a builder of dams to regulate the current." Thus Mussolini (or, perhaps, the ghostwriting Arnaldo) portrayed himself as a builder, even from earliest childhood a person determined to bend to his will the course of nature itself.

In the next sentence of this passage from *My Autobiography*, Mussolini writes of having been "a frantic hunter" for bird's nests "with their eggs or young birds. I was passionately fond of young life; I wished to protect it then as I do now." This from the dictator who would enthusiastically advocate criminal assault and murder as necessary and even desirable adjuncts to attaining and maintaining political power, who would spend the 1930s spoiling for war, and who would use poison gas and bomber aircraft in his 1935–36 war against Ethiopia. Yet, could it be that, as a boy, Mussolini really was made of gentler stuff? Perhaps. Others, however, reported that little Benito amused himself by tearing apart live chickens and by putting out the eyes of captive birds. Such assertions came from sources unfriendly to Mussolini. Were they true nevertheless?

Mussolini himself did admit to being "not a good boy." Others, including Mussolini's own partisans, have been more specific, portraying him as a violent bully. In church, he pinched other boys hard enough to make them cry. A childhood friend recalled that he was always ready and eager to start a fight and that he "sought quarrels for their own sake." In 1925, Mussolini's mistress and early political mentor, Margherita Sarfatti, wrote *The Life of Benito Mussolini*, in which she reported that five-year-old Benito terrorized the children in his mother's school. He targeted in particular a pretty seven-year-old girl, whom he frequently ambushed on her way from school, pulling her hair, forcing his kisses on her, then riding her as if she were a horse. When he had had enough, he summarily ordered her home. At age nine, when he was packed off to a boarding school run by Salesian fathers, Mussolini stabbed a fellow student with a knife and was expelled. Later, at another boarding school, he was suspended, again for stabbing a classmate.

> *Out of those distant memories [of my childhood] I receive no assurance that I had the characteristics which are supposed traditionally to make parents overjoyed at the perfection of their offspring. I was not a good boy, nor did I stir the family pride or the dislike of my own young associates in school by standing at the head of my class.*
>
> *I was then a restless being; I am still.*
>
> —*Benito Mussolini,* My Autobiography, *1928*

Understandably, Mussolini mentioned none of this in his autobiographical writings. When he (or, perhaps, Arnaldo) did portray the violence of his childhood, it was always to draw from it a greater significance:

> *Without knowing why, I found myself wishing to attend school—the school at Predappio, some two miles away. It was taught by Marani, who was a friend of my father. I walked to and fro and was not displeased that the boys of Predappio resented at first the coming of a stranger from another village. They flung stones at me and I returned their fire. I was all alone and against many. I was often beaten, but I enjoyed it with that universality of enjoyment with which boys the world around make friendship by battle and arrive at affection through missiles. Whatever was my courage, my body bore its imprints. I concealed the bruises from my mother to shelter her from the knowledge of the world in which I had begun to find expression and to which I supposed she was such a stranger.*

Here Mussolini portrays himself as violent indeed, but no bully. Instead, he appears as the persecuted outsider—no helpless victim, though, but someone who always gave as good as he got. Significantly, this scene from childhood is not so much about fighting to avenge injustice or fighting to stand up for oneself as it is about fighting, period. At an early age, Mussolini discovered a love of battle and violence. He equates it here with "friendship" and "affection" and does so, moreover, as if such an equation were perfectly normal and natural: "The universality of enjoyment with which boys the world around make friendship by battle and arrive at affection through missiles." Perhaps even more telling is his further equation of violence with "expression." Grown to adulthood, Mussolini would begin to make his mark on the world as a political journalist, a user of words. Words—persuasion and propaganda— were essential to the political brainchild he called fascism, yet words were never as basic to fascism as fists, bludgeons, and bullets. Mussolini's politics would express itself, first and last, through violence.

Was young Mussolini actually persecuted as an outsider? Very likely he was, but it also seems clear that he brought this on himself and, indeed, even cultivated it.

As an infant, Benito was a late talker, so late that his parents feared he might be a mute. His mother patiently coaxed speech from him, however, and it soon became evident that he was quite bright. Yet he also proved increasingly difficult to control, and when the Mussolinis had had enough, they sent their son to the Salesian boarding school at Faenza. The boy regarded this as a rejection, an exile, and a punishment. That impression was amplified by his being consigned at mealtimes to a special table reserved for students whose parents could not afford to pay the full tuition. If this school policy was particularly insensitive, the rest of the regimen was downright penal. Absolute silence was always enforced during meals and was the rule at *all* times during the week preceding Easter. Hot baths were available only during the coldest part of winter. Children rose at five in the morning during the summer, and at six in wintertime. Disciplinary measures included the liberal use of corporal punishment and, even more brutal for a child, solitary confinement for extended periods.

Far from taming young Mussolini, the treatment he received at the hands of the Salesians made him even more defiant. He often resisted compulsory attendance at Mass and had to be dragged to chapel by force. In 1893, his second—and final—year at the Faenza school, Mussolini, aged ten, organized a revolt against the quality of the school's vile food. Yet Mussolini was no natural organizer. If anything, he preferred being treated as an outsider. Although violent, he was also bookish, typically choosing books over human companionship.

After his expulsion from the Salesian school, Mussolini spent some time reading at home. Although the rising dictator liked to portray his childhood as impoverished, the hard life of a rural Italian peasant, the Mussolini cottage was amply stocked with books one hardly expected to find in a rural Italian village. There were, chiefly, political writings and history. After a time, the boy enrolled in another boarding school, at Forlimpopoli, this one not run by priests. Here the treatment was far more humane, yet, here, too, Mussolini brawled with and generally terrorized his classmates. As an adult, Mussolini claimed that he had excelled at Forlimpopoli, but, in fact, the headmaster recalled him as a mediocre student. Yet both he and the school persevered through six difficult years, and Mussolini graduated in 1901 with an "educational diploma" entitling him to teach school. Having attended school to his eighteenth year, Benito Mussolini, in many respects still a country bumpkin, was better educated than all but a small minority of Italian young men of his day.

A pair of milestones marked the last two of his six years at Forlimpopoli. By age seventeen, he discovered sex, something about which he could never resist boasting—even after he had begun promoting a straitlaced, ascetic sexual morality as part and parcel of fascism. His sexual appetite appears to have been both casual and voracious. He frequented the brothels of Forlì and Folimpopoli, but he also cultivated relationships with nonprofessionals, both girls his age and women considerably older, a number of whom he described with the word *fiancée*. He seems, indeed, to have had multiple "fiancées" at any given time.

Mussolini especially enjoyed making conquests among married women. In her *Life of Benito Mussolini*, Margherita Sarfatti quoted his account of a 1902 affair with the young wife of a soldier away on active duty: "I accustomed her to my exclusive and tyrannical love; she obeyed me blindly, and let me dispose of her just as I wished."

Should the odd villager venture to criticize Mussolini's arrogant and licentious behavior, a flash of the brass knuckles he took to carrying was usually sufficient to silence any complaints. Sarfatti also reported that he had knifed a girlfriend. Whether this last report is true or not, the picture that emerges of Mussolini in his late teens is of a young man who associated sex not with love, but with domination and power, and who, in turn, achieved domination and exercised power through violence. The association of sex with violence was a louder echo of his earlier equation of friendship with battle. The salient point is this: For Mussolini, the common denominator was always violence, no matter what area of life or sphere of activity was at issue.

Mussolini's second milestone during this period came after the death, in January 1901, of the great composer of Italian opera, Giuseppe Verdi. The schoolmasters at Forlimpopoli selected Mussolini to make a speech memorializing Verdi at an assembly in a local theater. The customarily misanthropic and tight-lipped young man welcomed the chance to praise before an audience a composer who not only wrote music that he loved, but music that was in sympathy with the Italian struggle for nationhood and liberation. It is hardly unusual for a turn-of-the-century Italian to love music, especially the opera; yet it is no accident that Mussolini turned the Verdi memorial into an occasion for his first public speech and, what is more, his first political speech.

Although he seems never to have received professional instruction, Mussolini was a lifelong amateur musician and became a creditable self-taught violinist, who later amassed an impressive collection of fine antique instruments. Fiddling would become a favorite mode of relaxation, an escape from politics. In Italy, however, opera *was* politics, and, for Mussolini in particular, politics was opera, opera in the grand Italian manner of bigger-than-life gestures played out against a backdrop of intense passion and histrionic violence. His Verdi speech, a prelude to his operatic politics, was enthusiastically received by the small audience in Forlimpopoli and was praised by his schoolmasters.

Except for exercising his sexual aggression to attract a string of women (if his own accounts are to be believed), Mussolini went out of his way to avoid most human contact. He boasted in later years that, as a young man, he had no male friends, and he did acquire the local reputation of being a nighthawk, one who ventured out of doors only after dark. At the time of his graduation, he had thoughts of pursuing a literary career. He wrote poetry, which he tried, without success, to get into print. In later years, when his political star was well on the rise, Mussolini dressed with meticulous care and the pompous over-formality of a dandy. Later still, after he was firmly ensconced as Italy's sole dictator, he wore elaborate tailor-made uniforms, chosen from a wardrobe of more than twenty different varieties, depending on the occasion. In 1901, however, he was careless in appearance, disheveled if not filthy, doubtless intending to appear bohemian, but succeeding only in looking the shabby, shiftless, and unemployed youth that he was.

If he had imbibed from his father a politically connected need to rebel, he also inherited Alessandro Mussolini's taste for strong drink and his distaste for steady employment. Only when he had become absolutely penniless did Benito Mussolini decide to make use of his educational diploma and, in 1902, was turned loose upon the students of an elementary school in the village of Gualtieri, near Parma, about a hundred miles from Predappio.

Chapter 3

Wander-Life

The administration of the village of Gualtieri was largely socialist, so the eighteen-year-old radical was more or less tolerated
in the community. Even so, his appointment was only as a temporary substitute teacher. At that, Mussolini was fortunate that most
people chose to see him as nothing more threatening than a run-
of-the-mill socialist. In truth, while most of his associates were
socialists, his own ideological orientation was only vaguely connected with any particular movement. Had he lived in the 1950s,
the young Mussolini might well have identified with the motorcy-
cle gang leader Marlon Brando played in the film *The Wild One.*
"What are you rebelling against?" the Brando character is asked.
"Whadda ya got?" he replies. Or perhaps he would have accepted
the label of another film of the period: *Rebel Without a Cause.*
Mussolini's father had been—and still was—much the same way.
Nominally a socialist, he was, in fact, a rebel, hungering for revolution not so much in the name of socialism, but in the name of
revolution itself. For both Benito and Alessandro Mussolini,
socialism was little more than a convenient hook on which to
hang a revolution.

What, then, did this make Benito Mussolini? If anything, he
was really an anarchist at a time when anarchy was virtually synonymous with assassination. Sadi Carnot, president of the French
Republic, had been assassinated by an anarchist in 1894; Prime
Minister Antonio Canovas del Castillo of Spain had fallen to an

anarchist in 1897; Austrian empress Elizabeth had been stabbed to death by an anarchist in 1898; and King Umberto of Italy was killed by an anarchist's bullet on Mussolini's seventeenth birthday, July 29, 1900.

In 1902, an anarchist would have been hard pressed to find a job, even as a *substitute* teacher, so it was just as well that Mussolini was labeled a socialist. In any case, the parents of Gualtieri's students were less disturbed by Mussolini's politics than by his reckless, raucous, and licentious behavior. He drank heavily and, with what little money he earned, he gambled incessantly. It was in Gualtieri that he had the affair with the wife of a soldier away on military assignment, and he made no secret of that relationship, nor of his brutality toward the faithless young wife, often abusing her in public.

Politically and personally anarchical, Mussolini nevertheless drifted into more conventional socialist circles during his time in Gualtieri. He joined a local socialist group and became its secretary, then made his initial forays into political journalism, writing several articles for leftist periodicals. He also found occasion for public speaking and drew considerable admiration for a ninety-minute address, entirely improvised, on the subject of Garibaldi. That speaking engagement, on June 2, 1902, the anniversary of Garibaldi's death, was entirely accidental. The scheduled speaker was a no-show, and the chairman of the meeting, thinking of Mussolini as a likely last-minute replacement, knew exactly where to find him—at the local inn, drinking and playing cards. Without a moment's hesitation, the young man agreed to speak. Thus, in Gualtieri, Mussolini was discovering two important things about himself: First and foremost, he was an instinctive rebel and revolutionary; second, he was a natural speaker and rabble-rouser.

One thing he was not was a born teacher. When his temporary teaching job ended in June, Mussolini felt no regret. He decided to go to Switzerland rather than return home to Predappio. In his 1928 My *Autobiography*, he explained that "in Predappio one could neither move nor think without feeling at the end of a short rope. I had become conscious of myself, sensitive to my future. I felt the urge to escape."

But escape what? My *Autobiography* does not mention that, for a young man nearing his twentieth birthday in Italy at the time, compulsory military service loomed. To go back to Predappio would almost certainly have meant getting drafted. Nor did Mussolini note that his father, at this time, had been arrested in Predappio and was being prosecuted for inciting a riot and violating election laws. When it had become clear to Alessandro Mussolini and his socialist colleagues that their candidates were being defeated by the Conservative Clerical Party in a local election, they broke into the polling place, assaulted the polling clerk, seized the ballot box, and scattered the ballots to the winds. Alessandro's son showed no desire to come to his father's aid and, indeed, probably wanted to avoid any entanglement in his father's prosecution. (Tried after being held in prison for six months, Alessandro Mussolini was found not guilty.)

If the draft and his father's legal troubles weren't reason enough to escape to Switzerland, there were a number of love affairs gone sour and a pile of back rent left unpaid. None of these mundane motives found their way into My *Autobiography*. Instead, Mussolini chose to dramatize his escape as a momentous and deliberate step in his personal and political development:

> *Money I had not—merely a little. Courage was my asset.*
> *I would be an exile. ... It was in this wander-life, now*
> *full of difficulties, toil, hardship and restlessness, that*
> *developed something in me. It was the milestone which*
> *marked my maturity. I entered into this new era as a man*
> *and politician. ... To this day I thank difficulties. They*
> *were more numerous than the nice, happy incidents. But*
> *the latter gave me nothing. The difficulties of life have*
> *hardened my spirit. They have taught me how to live.*

His self-mythologizing notwithstanding, Mussolini lied to his mother, telling her that he had lined up a job in Switzerland, in order to extract from her the price of a railway ticket—her entire month's salary. This must have been a particular hardship inasmuch as her husband was being held in jail at the time. Nor would it be the last money he would "borrow" from Rosa Mussolini.

My *Autobiography* speaks of the hardship of Mussolini's Swiss "wander-life" as if it were some great burden imposed on him by society. The truth was that Mussolini had no taste for hard work and was incapable of holding a steady job. He found work in Yverdon as a bricklayer building a chocolate factory, carrying a hod of bricks up two flights of stairs one hundred twenty-one times (so he recorded) in an eleven-hour workday for the wage of thirty-two centimes per hour. Of the miserable salary his capitalist employer paid him, Mussolini later wrote in dramatic self-reproach, "What should I have done? Kill him. What did I do? Nothing."

> My stay in Switzerland was a welter of difficulties ... I knew hunger—stark hunger—in those days. But I never bent myself to ask for loans and I never tried to inspire the pity of those around me, nor of my own political companions. I reduced my needs to a minimum and that minimum—and sometimes less—I received from home.
>
> —Benito Mussolini, My Autobiography, 1928

Nothing indeed. Rather than allow himself to be "humiliated" by capitalist exploitation, he turned to begging for food, and when charity was not forthcoming, he stole what he needed or menaced reluctant givers until they gave. He lived mostly in flophouses, but was so revolted by the presence of fellow tramps that he often slept in the street. What little money he managed from time to time to scrape together, from panhandling, from an odd job or two, or from his mother, he spent on wandering. If he could not pay for a railway ticket, he walked or hitch-hiked, and in this way he visited Lausanne, Geneva, Berne, Zurich, Fribourg, Basle, Neuchâtel, and Ticino, the Italian-speaking Swiss canton. His pockets were never completely empty, for he carried with him a nickel medal stamped with the likeness of Karl Marx.

Karl Marx: A medallion stamped with his image was often the only thing in young Mussolini's pocket.

(Image from the author's collection)

Wherever Mussolini went, he attended radical meetings and lectures, and he engaged in lively, even violent, discussion and debate. He quickly acquired a reputation as an extremist. Because of his itinerant ways, that reputation became widespread throughout Switzerland. Moreover, his eloquence wasn't confined to Italian. With a natural talent for languages, he readily became fluent in French and soon also developed a respectable command of German. He never became as fluent in the latter as in French, something that would create a problem later on. In his meetings with Adolf Hitler before and during World War II, Mussolini stubbornly disdained to use an interpreter. The result was highly imperfect communication.

By 1903 Mussolini's reputation was widely enough broadcast that one of his namesakes, Amilcare Cipriani, living in Paris at the time, invited him to visit. Broke, of course, Mussolini could not afford the fare, so he decided to walk. Along the way, he met a Russian anarchist whose appearance was even shabbier and more fearsome than his own. But he made good company—or so Mussolini thought. At this point in his life, Mussolini took no care over how he looked. Concern over appearances he scorned as a bourgeois obsession, and if his looking like a tramp offended others, well, so much the better. But he was about to learn a lesson in the value of appearances, for the wild eyes and matted black beard of his Russian companion inevitably drew the attention of the police in one of the villages through which the pair tramped. The Russian was arrested, and so was his companion.

Although Mussolini was not held long, the arrest itself was sufficient to discourage him from continuing his pilgrimage to Cipriani. He traveled back to Milan and then returned to Switzerland, where he continued to establish himself among the growing colonies of Italian radical refugees. He began to contribute articles and political poems to socialist journals, writing both in Italian and French. One piece that drew particular attention was titled "The Sport of Crowned Heads" and was a thinly veiled call to political assassination. On the eve of visits to London and Paris by Vittore Emmanuelle III, who had succeeded to the Italian throne after the assassination of Umberto I in 1900, the article ridiculed the Republican government of France for betraying the French revolutionary spirit by extending a warm welcome to the monarch. The founders of French republicanism had, after all, distinguished themselves not by welcoming a king, but by beheading one.

The article was typical of Mussolini's politics at the time and, really, typical of Mussolini's lifelong approach to politics. Clearly, Mussolini was an intelligent young man, who had read Marx and other political philosophers and who distinguished himself in political debate. Yet for all his immersion in the verbal stream of radical socialism, he was never really a man of ideology and ideas. If there was any political theory in "The Sport of the Crowned

Heads" it was simply this: Modern republics had betrayed their revolutionary roots because they failed to assassinate royalty and other authority wherever and whenever they encountered it.

When pushed, Mussolini described himself during this period as an "authoritarian communist." But that had little meaning. More clear was Mussolini's insistence that socialism would never succeed in a parliamentary or democratic framework. In Germany, socialists were winning influence by gaining seats in the Reichstag. What good was that? Mussolini asked. Working within the system, socialists could achieve at most some mild increment of reform, but this was hardly revolution. Socialism, Mussolini argued, must have nothing to do with parliaments, except to bring to pass their destruction. Parliaments were about one social class collaborating with another. Mussolini advocated class struggle, not class collaboration. At most, conventional socialism proposed civil disobedience to gain particular ends. If workers wanted higher wages, the conventional socialist prescribed a general strike. As Mussolini saw it, this was a tepid approximation of what was really required: not merely a strike, but mob violence and terrorism. Why settle for a strike when one could have a full-scale social revolution?

For young socialists grown restless with endless tactical and theoretical discussion, Mussolini's violent rhetoric was both invigorating and intoxicating. European politics was a knot whose Gordian complexity had been accumulated by tying and retying over several centuries of incomplete revolution and distressingly complete counterrevolution. Seeing his socialist colleagues scratch their heads over how to untie the knot once and for all, Mussolini proposed Alexander the Great's solution: a simple blow of the sword. In article after article and discussion after discussion, he honed the blade, which became shinier and increasingly appealing to greater numbers among revolutionary circles.

Of course, in advocating violent revolution, Mussolini also drew the attention of the police. Would-be revolutionaries from Russia and Italy gravitated to Switzerland because it was much more tolerant of radical discussion than the governments of czar and king. But there was a limit to the tolerance even of the Swiss. When hotel workers and workers in the tourist trades, generally low-paid immigrants, began listening to Mussolini's advocacy of violent labor action, authorities feared an impending attack on a mainstay of the Swiss economy. Mussolini was promptly arrested in Berne on June 18, 1903, held for twelve days, then served with an order of deportation from the canton. Officers escorted him across the Italian border at Chiasso in July.

Mussolini had no desire to return to Italy, especially not at this particular time in his life. In January, he was scheduled to be called up for the draft. Was he afraid of military service? Probably not. Despite accusations from political enemies throughout his career, Mussolini cannot be written off as a mere coward. Did he find the prospect of military service distasteful? Almost certainly, but whether this distaste was due to an instinctive revulsion from authority or the product of political idealism is impossible to say. Mussolini had proclaimed himself an international socialist, and he declared on more than one occasion that he was not prepared to fight for "his" country.

Whatever his reasons for wanting to avoid conscription, he returned to Switzerland, going to Lausanne, where his deportation from Berne was not in force. The expiration of his passport was a minor inconvenience he overcame by forgery, changing the document's expiration date to 1905.

His movements at this time are not well known. He may have lived briefly in France, and he may even have completed a walk to Paris. On one occasion, Mussolini even recalled that he made a living by fortune telling. He seems to have visited Germany and Austria and to have worked in a distillery and an agricultural machinery factory. He spoke at public rallies and socialist meetings, his subject matter at this period turning increasingly to the denunciation of religion, in addition to advocacy of violent social revolution. He had no patience with socialists, who proposed working within the political system to attain reform, so he denounced those who called religion a matter of individual conscience. Religion, Mussolini declared, was a disease and contagion that no socialist could afford to contract, lest he infect others.

The young agitator, who was having a number of love affairs in addition to apparently indiscriminate sexual encounters at this time, seems to have confessed to having another kind of infection, syphilis. At least that is what he told Angelica Balabanoff, a well-known Russian socialist he met on March 18, 1904, when she spoke at a meeting in Lausanne commemorating the thirty-third anniversary of the Paris Commune.

It was a peculiar thing to tell a woman with whom Mussolini was about to have an affair and a woman on whom he would rely for a time as a political mentor. Additionally, Mussolini may have told her that his father was both syphilitic and a hopeless drunk. Interestingly, a postmortem examination of Mussolini's brain performed during a 1945 autopsy revealed that he did not have syphilis. Could he have been misdiagnosed in the early 1900s? Maybe. As a promiscuous sexual aggressor, did he have a hypochondriacal fear of venereal disease? Perhaps.

It is also possible that Balabanoff, who turned against Mussolini after he broke with socialism to create fascism, made up the story in an attempt to smear the rising dictator's reputation. If so, the effort was misguided. For it is just as likely that *Mussolini,* not Balabanoff, manufactured the diagnosis as a way to boast of his eminently unbourgeois sexual prowess. Perhaps he even added the material about his father to show that he was a chip off the old block.

Separating truth from character assassination from self-mythologizing in the life of Benito Mussolini is often an impossible task. For example, on March 19, 1904, the day after he first met Balabanoff, Mussolini attended a conference of the Union of Italian Socialists in Zurich. Vladimir Ilyich Lenin was living as an exile in Zurich at the time. In 1932 Mussolini told his German biographer, Emil Ludwig, that he "did not remember" meeting Lenin. He told his sister, Edvige, the same thing. Yet Mussolini's wife believed that he had met Lenin, and, in 1945, the dictator himself regaled two German officials with accounts of lengthy discussions with Lenin. Where is the truth to be found in this?

Neither bold rhetoric about the violent overthrow of monarchs, government, and society itself, nor personal boasts, self-mythologizing, and out-and-out lies could alter the hard fact that, in 1904, an Italian court tried Benito Mussolini in absentia for desertion because of his efforts to evade conscription. Under sentence, he was now a fugitive from Italian justice. In Switzerland, various courts and magistrates had declared him a public menace and an undesirable alien, and he was expelled from canton after canton. Desperate, he hatched schemes to flee to such disparate destinations as Madagascar and Vermont, both of which harbored radical socialist colonies. From Italian socialists in New York came an offer to join the staff of the radical weekly *Il Preletario*, to which he was already an occasional contributor. Mussolini seriously considered it.

In the end, however, he didn't have to resort to fleeing Europe. Late in 1904, when Mussolini was twenty-one, the Italian government declared a general amnesty for deserters and the many young men who had variously evaded the draft. Mussolini may have been tired of living as a fugitive. He may have been homesick, sick of living as an exile. It is also true that his mother had taken ill. Although Mussolini had never before played the dutiful son, he decided to take advantage of the amnesty, to return to Predappio, and to give the faltering Rosa Mussolini some relief from her teaching. The scruffy atheist, anarchist, sexual libertine, deportee from several Swiss cantons, and draft dodger now replaced his pious mother at the head of a village primary school class.

In January 1905 Mussolini obediently left Predappio to join the Italian regiment to which he had been assigned. A month later, he received word that his mother, who had contracted meningitis, was near death. Some sources report that Mussolini attempted to gain early release from his military obligation and was denied; however, he did get compassionate leave and arrived home shortly before Rosa Mussolini's death, at age forty-six, on February 19, 1905.

Again, the self-mythologizing went into operation. In subsequent years, Mussolini repeatedly recalled and revised his recollection of his mother's final hours. He reported that he arrived just in time for her to recognize him and bid him farewell. He also reported that he could not work up the fortitude to enter the house and that he hid outdoors until his mother had died. At one point in his career, desiring to sanitize his image, Mussolini spoke of how even his "profound religious faith" proved unable to relieve his great grief.

Anyone who delves into the life of Benito Mussolini soon grows accustomed to such self-contradictions in the history of a man for whom politically expedient expression was a coin of far greater value than fact, truth, or sincerity. In Switzerland, Mussolini had made the beginnings of a reputation denouncing God and country, refusing not only to fight for any nation, but encouraging other young men to do likewise, to evade conscription or, if already serving, to desert. Now, in response to a letter of condolence he received from his commanding officer, Capt. Achille Simonotti, Mussolini replied that he intended to honor his mother's memory by doing his duty as an Italian citizen and an Italian soldier. That he would pledge his utmost in particular to defeat any threat against Italian nationhood from the perennial oppressor, Austria.

Had his mother's untimely death suddenly transformed the anarchist into the patriot, the prodigal son into the dutiful child? Or was his reply to Simonotti merely an early example of the skill, thoroughness, and ease with which Mussolini could tell a lie, brushing aside for the sake of pragmatic convenience the most extreme principles so often passionately expressed? Whether or not the response to Simonotti was sincere, the remarkable fact was that Benito Mussolini served out his twenty-one months of compulsory military service not grudgingly, but with zeal, efficiency, and, it seems, even with pleasure.

In his 1933 *Talks with Mussolini*, Emil Ludwig reported Mussolini's assertion that a man had to learn obedience in order to learn how to command. Any lessons of obedience would evaporate soon after he left the army in September 1906. Command, however, would prove another matter altogether.

Part Two

Romance and Revolution

Chapter 4

Angelica and Rachele

Like most of the women to whom Mussolini was attracted, Angelica Balabanoff was no beauty. Heavy, round-faced, weak-chinned, her wavy hair pulled back in a severe bun, she looked older than her twenty-six years when Mussolini met her in Lausanne at the March 18, 1904, commemoration of the Paris Commune. Yet there was much that the twenty-one-year-old exile found alluring about her. In contrast to Mussolini's humble background, Balabanoff was the daughter of wealth. Whereas Mussolini had been bred to socialist rebellion by his father, Balabanoff's family were substantial Ukrainian landowners and resolutely reactionary. In her 1938 memoir, *My Life as a Rebel,* Balabanoff recounted her shame at how her father's tenant farmers prostrated themselves before him, kissing the hem of his coat whenever he returned to his estate after a prolonged absence. She wrote, too, of her revulsion at her well-meaning mother's charitable efforts, the distribution of cheap gifts to the peasantry she and her husband oppressed. Whereas Mussolini rebelled against that vague entity called society, Angelica Balabanoff rebelled most directly against her own family and less directly against the society they represented. She fled the family estate for study in Brussels, London, and Leipzig, where she took her degree from the university. Her rebellion did not preclude her accepting an allowance from her father when she decided to settle among the Russians of a socialist refugee colony in Switzerland, although she also earned money on her own as a radical journalist.

Mussolini was drawn to Balabanoff by her natural rebellious-
ness, her intellectual intensity, and her eager willingness to introduce him into the higher levels of the Swiss socialist movement.
She also encouraged Mussolini's general intellectual development.
It was during the period of their liaison that Mussolini delved more
deeply into Marx and was introduced to the work of Georges Sorel,
a French social philosopher who promoted syndicalism, the control of government by organized bodies of workers. Any other form
of government, Sorel held, was inherently oppressive and had to be
destroyed. Sorel enthusiastically advocated violent strikes and
other labor actions, for, as he saw it, violence was the sovereign
"creative power of the proletariat capable of overcoming force, the
coercive economic power of the bourgeoisie."

Whether or not it was Balabanoff who introduced Mussolini to
the philosophy of Friedrich Nietzsche, it was at this time that he
found himself drawn to the exponent of the "superman." The
supreme egoist whose overmastering "will to power" was sufficient
to brush aside such dull, oppressive, and mediocre forces of bourgeois morality as Christianity, charity, resignation, and "goodness."
For Mussolini, Nietzsche reinforced Sorel, who differed from anarchists, socialists, and Bolsheviks in his belief that true social revolution was not the product of the will of the masses, but of the
masses bending their collective will to that of an intellectual elite,
in effect a body of supermen or, perhaps, even the will of a single
superman.

Did Mussolini naively show Angelica Balabanoff the medal of
Karl Marx he carried with him? Or had Sorel and Nietzsche displaced Marx in Mussolini's philosophical pantheon by this time? In
discussing Mussolini, it is always dangerous to look for a rational,
evolutionary pattern in his intellectual development. As always,
ideas were important to him, yet not so much as the carefully constructed framework for a revolution or even as the goals toward
which a revolution might be aimed, but as fuel to power the violence of revolution. Never very particular about the contents of
that fuel, Mussolini seized and used ideas as they came along, often
espousing one point of view on Monday and then a contradictory

notion on Tuesday. Mussolini did not need to reject Marx. Instead, he took from Marx only what most appealed to him—the admission that violence was necessary to social change—and modified whatever else got in his way. Namely Marx's concept of historical determinism, the notion that historical process conforms to laws that make certain events necessary or inevitable: "Men make their own history," Marx wrote, "but not just as they please." Bringing to bear on Marx his own reading of Sorel and Nietzsche, Mussolini resolved that *he* would not conform to historical necessity, but would fashion, through overwhelming force of will, whatever history he desired.

Did Balabanoff help Mussolini massage Sorel and Nietzsche into Marx? We do not know precisely what Balabanoff discussed with her protégé-lover during what was for him an intellectually formative time. But it is clear that her demonstrated attraction to him was valuable to Mussolini inasmuch as she gratified his ego and reinforced his growing self-identification as a Nietzschean superman. In one of her early memoirs, Balabanoff recorded her first impression of Mussolini. He was dirty, but his intelligence was keen and his eyes piercing and hypnotic. Their physical affair seems to have been sporadic, but Balabanoff, one of the leading figures in the Swiss-Italian socialist movement, remained intellectually attached to Mussolini even after their affair ended. She led him into greater prominence among the socialists until he became a member of the Italian Socialist Party's Central Committee and, in 1912, editor of its principal publication, the daily newspaper *Avanti!* After the October Revolution of 1917 in Russia, Balabanoff returned to her native land to work for the Bolsheviks. By that time, Mussolini had renounced socialism, and Angelica Balabanoff turned bitterly against him.

The romantic and intellectual ferment of his time in Switzerland seems to have been completely suspended for the twenty-one months Mussolini served in the Italian army. He did not return to Switzerland upon his release from the army in September 1906, but took a job as a schoolmaster near Venice in the little town of Tolmezzo. His love life picked up there when he had an affair with the wife of the owner of the rooming house at which he boarded. When the lady's husband discovered the relationship, he punched Mussolini in the nose—but did not kick a paying guest out of his boardinghouse.

Early in 1907 Mussolini also resumed his life as a socialist, apparently picking this up pretty much where he had left it before entering the army. On February 17, 1907, he made a rousing speech concerning the martyrdom of Giordano Bruno, who had been burned as a heretic on that date in 1600 for having had the temerity to declare (among other things) that the earth revolved about the sun and not, Scripture to the contrary notwithstanding, vice versa. Mussolini regaled his audience with the kind of speech he loved to give—nothing that reflected his reading of political philosophers, but a bare-knuckled attack on religion in general and the Catholic Church in particular. He delivered a variation on this theme in a speech given on the twenty-fifth anniversary of Garibaldi's death, June 2.

As Mussolini must have expected they would, his inflammatory speeches drew the attention of local police, and he was soon aware of being continually under observation. As for his teaching career, the would-be superman was intensely disliked by the forty or so primary school students in his charge. They called him "the Tyrant," and yet he was so inept at maintaining order in his classroom that he resorted to bribing the children with sweets. In this we might discern a foreshadow of the bribes he would give to Ethiopian leaders in 1935 and Albanian generals in 1939 to pave the way for invasion of those countries, and, again, the monies with which he would—unsuccessfully—ply Greek commanders before attacking Greece in 1940. The man of force believed in stacking the deck whenever possible before he made an aggressive wager.

When he was not teaching (or trying to teach), when he was not speaking at some socialist meeting, and when he was not cavorting with the boardinghouse keeper's wife, Mussolini drank and gambled. Reportedly, he also attended outdoor drinking parties in a local cemetery at night. At one of these, fellow merrymakers were amused by the spectacle of Mussolini making speeches to the dead—in the hindsight of history, another grim foreshadowing.

The parents of Tolmezzo did not long tolerate Mussolini's behavior, and his teaching contract was not renewed. On the death of Rosa, Alessandro Mussolini had been obliged to leave the house attached to what had been his wife's schoolroom. He found a new place to live in nearby Forlì, and Mussolini moved in with him after he lost his teaching post. Much as he had found it easy to turn his back on radical socialism and serve as a model soldier in the Italian army, so now this carousing anarchist demonstrated an earnest desire to advance himself in his teaching career. Perhaps what amounted to his dismissal from the Tolmezzo position had abashed and sobered him. Whatever his reasons, he now took lessons in Latin and French as preparation for an examination that would confer on him the title of "professor" and allow him to teach in secondary school. He qualified to teach French, but was unable to pass the German exam. Vowing to renounce political agitation altogether, he appealed to local authorities to expunge his police record. The appeal was denied, but in February or March 1908, he accepted a teaching position in the town of Oneglia on the Italian Riviera. No sooner had he arrived in Oneglia than Mussolini plunged again into the radical politics he had just forsworn and began to write and edit a socialist journal called *La Lima*. Within four months, he lost his latest teaching post and was headed back to Forlì.

During his first sojourn with his father at Forlì, Mussolini renewed an acquaintance with Rachele Guidi. He had first met her in 1900 when he was helping his mother in her classroom and Rachele was an eight-year-old student. In 1908 she was sixteen, fatherless, and working as a live-in maid in a well-to-do Forlì household. With Rachele living in her employer's house, Alessandro Mussolini, shortly after he moved to Forlì, invited her widowed mother, Anna, to live with him as his housekeeper. This eventually provided enemies of Benito Mussolini with the spurious basis for a story that Anna had been Alessandro's mistress, Rachele their bastard daughter, and Benito Mussolini's wife, therefore, his half-sister.

Rachele Mussolini, neé Guidi, pictured early in her years with Mussolini.

(*Image from ArtToday*)

In fact, the relationship that developed between Mussolini and Rachele gave no occasion for scandal. The promiscuous, brutal, licentious Mussolini behaved with great gentleness toward Rachele Guidi, courting her quietly, always escorting her home to her employer's house. She was a sturdy peasant girl, quite plain, except for her striking platinum-blonde hair, which she usually wore in gleaming plaits. She was very different from the worldly and intellectual Angelica Balabanoff, but she had solid good sense and, all who knew her reported, a powerful personality.

When Mussolini returned to Forlì from Oneglia, he began to speak of marriage. Rachele's employer, adopting the role of substitute father, warned her against a union with a notorious atheist, socialist, and all-round agitator whose political and professional prospects were dismal indeed. As if to confirm this dire caution, Mussolini soon got himself in trouble with the law.

The "Red" Romagna was swept by labor disturbances and agricultural riots during the summer of 1908. On July 13, the socialists of Predappio held a demonstration in support of workers striking against a local threshing machine factory and also against scabs who had been brought in to take the strikers' places. The socialists organized an impressive rally of some seven thousand demonstrators, who took over the town until a large contingent of armed troops cleared them out. Five days later, with emotions still running high, Mussolini encountered Emilio Rolli, the manager of the factory. As Rolli rode by on his bicycle, Mussolini, brandishing a cudgel, called out a threat to the effect that he would give him a good beating. Rolli pedaled faster.

Later that same day, July 18, Mussolini was arrested and held in prison to await trial on a charge of having threatened assault. Found guilty on July 22, he was given the stiff sentence of three months' imprisonment—doubtless because of his lengthy police record. He appealed to a higher court and was released on July 30, pending the appeal. In a November hearing, the court upheld the conviction, but reduced his sentence to the time he had already served.

If Mussolini's reputation could land him in jail for the mere threat of violence, it also attracted the admiring attention of the socialists of Trent, a major hotbed of Italian socialism. Trent was the chief town of the Trentino, which, with Trieste and Istria, had not been liberated by the Seven Weeks' War of 1866 and was still under Austrian rule. Although mainstream socialism was in essence international, the nationalist issue in the Trentino gave the local movement added passion and urgency. Party leaders wanted a fiery editor for their weekly newspaper, *L'Avvenire del Lavoratore* and they offered Mussolini the job. Leaving Rachele behind but promising to write her faithfully, he accepted and moved to Trent on February 6, 1909.

> The Seven Weeks' War, or Austro-Prussian War, was fought between
> June and August of 1866. In it, Austria and most of the German states
> were pitted against Prussia and Italy. Prussian Prime Minister Otto von
> Bismarck used the war to force Austria out of the German Confederation
> and to make Prussia the dominant power in Germany. The new kingdom
> of Italy, looking for a way to wrest Venetia from Austria, entered the war
> on the side of Prussia. By the Peace of Prague, which ended the war on
> August 23, a humiliated Austria yielded Venetia to Italy, paid an indem-
> nity to Prussia, and was greatly diminished as a power in German affairs.

In hiring Mussolini, the Trentino socialists got even more than they had hoped for. They found an editor capable not only of churning out rabble-rousing rhetoric, but also of massaging the expression of socialist policy to satisfy simultaneously socialism's international orientation and its support, in the case of the Trentino, of Italian nationalism. Mussolini structured an editorial position promoting the movement of national liberation from the oppressive rule of Emperor Franz Josef, but he insisted that the socialists of Italy would never support a bourgeois Italian war against Austria. Thus Mussolini tapped into the energy of Trentino's nationalist fervor without alienating socialist colleagues in Austria.

It was a talent Mussolini would hone and develop over the entire course of his political career: the ability to express, passionately and with apparent but deceptive clarity, opposing points of view simultaneously. Not that he always made use of this remarkable facility. While he simultaneously stirred and salved nationalist passions in the pages of L'Avvenire del Lavoratore, he let loose in only a single direction the invective of atheism. Under his leadership, the weekly paper became a much-read vehicle of anti-Catholic diatribe. At first, the articles were didactic, lambasting theology and Church policy, but soon they took the form of personal attacks on particular priests. Apparently in response to an article in Il Trentino, the paper of the Catholic party, libeling the reputation of the wife of Cesare Battisti, Mussolini wrote a scathing attack on the morals of a certain politically active priest. For this, he was tried on May 29, 1909, on a charge of libel and was fined thirty crowns in lieu of a prison term of three days. He paid the fine, only to turn around and contribute an article to the Trent socialist daily *Il Popolo* accusing three priests of sexual misconduct and embezzlement. This time, both Mussolini and Battisti were charged and tried. Found guilty of libel, Mussolini was sentenced to three days' imprisonment, and Battisti, editor of *Il Popolo,* was sentenced to seven. Mussolini successfully appealed his conviction.

Mussolini's accusations of sexual misconduct were hardly issued from the moral high ground. Still professing his unofficial engagement to Rachele Guidi, he had a passionate affair in Trent with a married woman, Fernanda Oss Facchinelli, an activist at the headquarters of a trade union. She gave birth to Mussolini's child, a son, who died after only a few months. Facchinelli herself succumbed to tuberculosis shortly after this, and Mussolini, adhering to a strange code of morality, maintained contact with her mother for years afterward. Once he had established himself as Italy's "Duce"—its supreme leader—Mussolini saw to it that the old woman was given a pension. And while Mussolini was unfaithful to Rachele with Fernanda, he was, in turn, unfaithful to Fernanda with another mistress, Ida Irene Dalser, the lively but high-strung twenty-six-year-old daughter of a Sardinian innkeeper.

As frenetic as Mussolini's romantic life seems to have been in Trent, his political life became equally pressured, as police continually harassed him. Local authorities appealed to the Austro-Hungarian minister of the interior, Baron Haerdti, to issue a deportation order against Mussolini. The minister demurred, but finally agreed that he would issue an order if Mussolini took any action sufficiently serious to warrant it.

Mussolini was prosecuted for organizing a demonstration specifically to protest police harassment of himself and Battisti. Subsequently, he was also prosecuted for having denounced, in print, a Catholic priest as a "dog with hydrophobia." Given a seven-day sentence for this latter offense, Mussolini politely thanked the magistrate for affording him the opportunity of a week's rest. He may actually have been more sincere than sarcastic. Released from jail on August 20, Mussolini was rearrested on

August 31, for abuse of freedom of the press. This time, the sentence that followed the guilty verdict was an order of deportation. Despite protests from socialist deputies in the Parliament at Vienna and demonstrations staged by local party members in Trent, Mussolini was escorted to a railway station at Mori on September 26 and put on board a train bound for Forlì.

Back in his father's house again, Mussolini feverishly wrote two books. The first was a novel, which he ground out in the hope of making some quick cash, while roasting the Church in the bargain. *Claudia Particella, the Cardinal's Mistress* is the story of an ambitious courtesan who enthralls a cardinal and other aristocrats in seventeenth-century Trent. She meets her end at the hands of the cardinal's secretary, Father Benicio, who poisons her because she will not yield to his sexual advances. Mussolini's potboiler has reminded some scholars of *Clelia*, a novel Garibaldi wrote toward the end of his life. It was also directed against the Church; however, Garibaldi's heroine was no courtesan, but an innocent and a virgin, who was imprisoned and molested in the Vatican by a lecherous cardinal. While both Italian revolutionaries took pleasure in skewering the Catholic Church, they presented sharply differing views of women.

At about the same time as he wrote his novel, Mussolini dashed off a work of nonfiction, *The Trentino as Seen by a Socialist*. Coming from the pen of Mussolini, this is, if anything, even a stranger work than *Claudia*. Instead of what one would expect from Mussolini, a violent polemic advocating the liberation of the Trentino from Austria, Mussolini merely presented a study of conditions in the region, arguing that the area was divided between Italians and Germans, that the Italians there were quite distinct from those of Italy proper, and that they even spoke a local dialect different from mainstream Italian. Mussolini implied that Italian annexation of the Trentino was not really desirable. Moreover, war with Austria might well prove a losing proposition for Italy. If so, not only would the Trentino remain Austrian, but Venetia and the other Italian provinces that had been won in the Seven Weeks' War of 1866 might also be lost. *The Trentino* was indeed a curiously cautious, noncommittal book, which hardly seems the work of the future dictator who would one day lead Italy headlong into a cataclysmic alliance with Adolf Hitler to fight a titanic war for which the nation was not even remotely prepared.

It was not only authorship that absorbed Mussolini on his return to Forlì. He was delighted to see that Rachele, now seventeen, had waited patiently for him—even though he had not written her once from Trent—and it was not difficult to persuade her to live with him as his common-law wife. Persuading his father and Rachele's mother was another matter altogether. Both were opposed to their children living together, Anna Guidi on moral grounds, and Alessandro Mussolini out of a sense of guilt; he did not think his son should inflict on Rachele the hardships he had inflicted on Rosa, namely the burden of marriage to a radical socialist.

As Rachele recounted it in a later memoir, Mussolini persuaded the parents—who lived together, Anna as Alessandro's housekeeper—by showing up at the house with a revolver and threatening to shoot Rachele and himself if they were thwarted. As a dictator, Mussolini would discover that an outrageous threat could be remarkably effective. Certainly, as a suitor, this particular threat served him well. The parental objections dissolved, and, on January 17, 1910, Benito Mussolini and Rachele Guidi began living together. In contrast to Alessandro, Benito Mussolini did not compromise his radical principles by submitting to a church wedding—nor even a civil one. In contrast to Alessandro's bride, Rachele did not insist on such a wedding. In any case, Rachele may have felt that time was of the essence. She was pregnant with a daughter, Edda, who would be born little more than seven months later, on September 1, 1910.

Mussolini was now—more or less—a married man. Two additional profound changes followed. Just ten days after Benito Mussolini began living with Rachele, his father fell ill. He was hospitalized, then sent home on February 9, 1910. Over the next nine months, Alessandro Mussolini's condition steadily deteriorated, and, at the age of fifty-six, he died on November 17.

By this time, Mussolini was launched on a new career. The socialists of Forlì decided that they wanted their own newspaper, and Mussolini was asked to found and edit it. At last, he had the opportunity to create his own paper from scratch, impeded by the policies of no one. He decided to call the periodical *La Lotta di Classe, The Class Struggle,* and, in the very first issue, January 9, 1910, he sounded a call for combat of "class against class—a struggle that culminates in total revolution."

Chapter 5

The Class Struggle

From the beginning, *La Lotta di Classe—The Class Struggle—* advocated the most extreme form of socialism. Socialists, Mussolini wrote, must abandon any notion of working within the existing system. Their goal should not be attaining seats in parliament, but tearing down all parliaments. Parliaments promoted nationalism, whereas socialism should transcend nationhood. It should be an international movement uniting the proletarian class, regardless of nationality, against the class of capitalist oppressors, regardless of nationality. "The national flag," Mussolini wrote, "is for us a rag to be planted on a dunghill."

At a socialist youth meeting, Mussolini spoke of abolishing the Italian army, and in the pages of *La Lotta di Classe* he proclaimed himself and his paper resolutely "anti-patriotic." He wrote: "We will not defend our country because we have no country to defend." Nationhood—the "Motherland"—he labeled a "lying fiction that has had its day." In the event of war, in case the "Motherland" should call for "sacrifices of money and blood," Mussolini declared that socialists must "reply with a general strike. The war between the nations will then become a war between the classes."

Although Mussolini, at this stage of his career, advocated abolishing the military, he was no pacifist in any traditional sense. His journalism and his speech-making were filled with images and metaphors of war, struggle, combat, and battle. At the bottom, the most radical aspect of his socialism was his complete lack of interest in the movement's positive aspects—rebuilding and restructuring society. And his all-consuming engagement with its negativity: the abject defeat of one class by another, the dissolution of nationhood, the destruction of government, the death of monarchs, and the dismantling of capitalism. That negative phase, the demolition, not the construction, was Mussolini's chief concern.

At this time in his life, he departed further from Marx and Engels, the builders of socialism, and embraced with increasing enthusiasm the Russian anarchists, especially Mikhail Bakunin and Piotr Kropotkin. As mentioned in the previous chapter, he was also drawn to the French social thinker Georges Sorel. But he now read Sorel with an increasingly narrow focus. Political historians discuss Sorel as the leading exponent of syndicalism, a doctrine holding that the means of production and the government properly belong in the hands of a proletariat organized into labor unions. By the time he was editing *The Class Struggle*, what most interested Mussolini about Sorel was his idea that the masses, of their own volition, were actually hopelessly incapable of revolution. Required was an elite, a class of Nietzschean supermen, to lead the masses. One of Mussolini's English biographers, Jasper Ridley, speculates that, at this time, Mussolini must also have read one of Sorel's important sources, *La Foule*, by Gustave Le Bon. *La Foule—The Crowd* or *The Mob*—was a pioneering work on mass psychology. It argued that masses of people were not great collective agents of democracy, but, rather, dangerous forces propelled by emotion instead of reason. The mob, according to Le Bon, was essentially capable of only two actions: It was "always ready to revolt against a weak ruler," but, just as true, it was always ready "to bow down slavishly before a strong one." The mob, like any weapon, was dangerous. Properly directed by a strong ruler, however, the very elements that made a mob dangerous also empowered it to take heroic and highly effective revolutionary action.

Whether these ideas took immediate root in Mussolini's mind or developed in his thinking over time, they would form part of the basis on which he finally began the *building* phase of his revolution, namely the concept of absolute dictatorship. In the 1920s, when Mussolini organized the Fascist Party, Sorel's elite would become what Mussolini called the *gerarchia*, a class of "born leaders" who formed the leadership of the party and, ultimately, the leadership of the Italian government. Their job was to awaken, then harness and direct, the force of Le Bon's mob. Within a few years of the establishment of fascism, however, the *gerarchia* diminished in importance as Mussolini himself assumed more and more of its role, creating himself as, in effect, a *gerarchia* of one—Il Duce, the supreme leader.

> *Still it is already clear that on whatever lines the societies of the future are organized, they will have to count with a new power, with the last surviving sovereign force of modern times, the power of crowds. On the ruins of so many ideas formerly considered beyond discussion, and to-day decayed or decaying, of so many sources of authority that successive revolutions have destroyed, this power, which alone has arisen in their stead, seems soon destined to absorb the others. While all our ancient beliefs are tottering and disappearing, while the old pillars of society are giving way one by one, the power of the crowd is the only force that nothing menaces, and of which the prestige is continually on the increase. The age we are about to enter will in truth be the ERA OF CROWDS.*
>
> —Gustave Le Bon, Le psychologie des foules, *1895*

If Mussolini perceived any contradiction between the all-encompassing internationalism of the socialist movement and his growing sense that power was properly concentrated in an elite class or even in a single strong leader, he did not let on. Nor, apparently, did his war against nationalism prevent his writing (while he was still in Trent, editing *L'Avvenire del Lavoratore*) an admiring review of Giuseppe Prezzolini's 1908 book *Old and New Nationalism*. In harmony with Sorel, Prezzolini put forth a theory of the inevitable domination of one class by another, regardless of particular geographical, ethnic, or historical circumstances. But he also wrote of remodeling the image and identity of Italy, lifting it above its reputation as a country of lazy, easygoing, politically and economically inept people to put it on a par with the most progressive nations of industrialized Europe, a force to be reckoned with in the world.

That Mussolini, by this time a highly visible political editor and journalist, was so blithely capable of very basic intellectual self-contradiction is somewhat less astounding when three things are taken into consideration.

First, he was by all accounts utterly humorless. He almost never smiled and, once his rise to power began in earnest, he aggressively banned all photographs of himself that somehow caught him smiling. He did not customarily joke—unless one counts sarcasm or outright cruelty as joking. For Mussolini could mock others mercilessly as well as tastelessly. Associates recalled that, after the United States entered World War II, Mussolini delighted in making sexually indecent jokes about Franklin Roosevelt's paralysis. Essentially, though, Mussolini was without mirth, a quality that requires, first and foremost, a certain self-irony, an ability to laugh at oneself. This he entirely lacked and, lacking it, may also have been without sufficient consciousness of self to be aware of his self-contradictions.

Second, Mussolini was shameless—and, therefore, quite beyond any concern over self-contradiction. In Switzerland, he had no compunction about begging. He readily lived on the streets. He not only accepted money from his mother, he took from her a month's salary, even though his father had been arrested and was out of work. In 1911, the twenty-eight-year-old Mussolini wrote his first autobiography—*My Life from 29 July 1883 to 23 November 1911*—in which he wrote not only of his political beliefs, but of his history as a juvenile delinquent, a knife-wielding bully boy, and a compulsive womanizer. His list of conquests—Vittorina F., Giulia F., Eleanora H., Luigia P., and so on—brings to mind the comical "catalogue aria" Leporello sings in Mozart's *Don Giovanni*, enumerating his master's innumerable seductions. The sexual litany in Mussolini's autobiography would be mere narcissistic braggadocio were it not for the fact that the author devotes considerable attention to his defeats as well as his triumphs. And could he have imagined that what he frankly depicts as his rape of "Virginia B." made

him look good? The account would be cited frequently by his enemies: how, in 1901, when most of the hamlet of Verano was off listening to an itinerant preacher, he entered Virginia's house, found
her alone, pushed her into a corner, and forced himself on her.
Afterward, she burst into tears, crying that he had robbed her of
her honor. "Perhaps I had," Mussolini wrote, "but what honor was
she talking about?"

There was a third factor that made self-contradiction practically
irrelevant for Mussolini, at least at this stage of his career—his
almost total absorption in revolution as destruction rather than
positive reform. Building a new society requires some semblance of
an orderly progression of doctrines and principles, but, for the work
of social destruction, Mussolini was willing to seize whatever ideas
came to hand. For him, it was the emotional effect of an idea—
could it drive destruction?—that mattered far more than its intellectual content.

Only after he had become absolute dictator of Italy and
believed that no dictator could remain in power if he looked in any
way less than infallible, let alone ridiculous or shameful, did
Mussolini attempt to suppress his early self-confessions and political self-contradictions.

Even when we take into consideration Mussolini's personality
and his destructive approach to politics, the twists and turns in his
thinking during this period can still bewilder. The Italo-Turkish
War—in Italy, known as the Libyan War—that broke out in 1911
sharply divided the Italian Socialist Party. The war was deeply
rooted in Italian imperialism. Italy had begun almost casually col-
onizing the Turkish-held provinces of Tripolitana and Cyrenaica—
encompassing modern Libya—by sending merchants and
immigrants into the region beginning in 1880. By 1911, Libya contained a large population of Italian nationals, and on September
28, 1911, the Italian government of Prime Minister Giovanni
Giolitti, claiming that its people were being abused, presented the
Sublime Porte, the government of Ottoman Turkey, with a twenty-
four-hour ultimatum, threatening immediate invasion. The Turks
did not deign to reply, which gave the Giolitti government an

excuse to invade North Africa the next day with fifty thousand troops.

As this crisis developed, the party line of the Italian socialist majority was stated clearly. The party officially condemned war against the Turks as the product of bourgeois imperialism. Yet a sizable minority quickly grew within the party that cited various statements by socialist luminaries, including Engels and his disciple Eduard Bernstein, to the effect that the conquest of a "less civilized" nation by a manifestly "more civilized" one was "historically progressive" and, therefore, justified. Turkish Libya was obviously less civilized than Italy, so, departing from the party line, the minority supported the action of the Giolitti government.

Mussolini, who was attracted to Sorel's idea of domination by an elite and also to Prezzolini's desire to reinvigorate and promote Italian civilization, might have been expected to join the minority in its support of the Libyan War. Certainly, he had an excuse and the backing to do just that. Yet even though of late he had grown increasingly impatient with mainstream socialism's ongoing efforts to work within the parliamentary system, Mussolini did not break with the majority. Instead, he used *La Lotta di Classe* to broadcast the official party condemnation of the Giolitti government's "imperialist adventure."

But he also wanted to take protest against the war much further than his colleagues were willing to go. Whereas the party called for a general strike against the war—with the railways targeted in particular, to stop troop movement—Mussolini called for a bomb attack on the railroad right-of-way. Blow up the tracks! When a party meeting rejected this proposal, Mussolini took his case directly to the people. On September 24, he spoke out at a town meeting convened on Forlì's central square. He called on his listeners to blow up the tracks.

Although greeted by applause, the call to destruction was not answered. Mussolini probably never expected anything more. As for the war, it went forward, and the Ottoman Turks were quickly overrun. The Sublime Porte concluded the Treaty of Ouchy, on

October 17, 1912, by which Turkey ceded to Italy Libya, Rhodes, and the Dodecanese Islands. In the meantime, three weeks after his speech at the Forlì town square, the police arrested Mussolini on a charge of inciting violence. Tried on November 18 with two other agitators, Mussolini declared to the judge before the verdict was handed down, "If you find me not guilty, I will be pleased; if you find me guilty, I will be honored." Guilty he was pronounced, and he was sentenced to a year's imprisonment, reduced on appeal to five and a half months. Mussolini used the time to write his youthful autobiography.

King Vittore Emmanuelle III, early in the twentieth century.

(Image from the author's collection)

Just two days after Mussolini's release from prison on March 12, 1912, an anarchist attempted to assassinate King Vittore Emmanuelle III. A delegation of socialist members of the Chamber of Deputies joined deputies from other political parties in officially congratulating the king on his escape from death. To this gesture, the freshly released Mussolini responded in *La Lotta di Classe* with a condemnation and a call to expel from the party those who had congratulated the king. At the socialist party congress held in July 1912, Mussolini moved for this expulsion and made a short, stirring speech supporting his motion, which carried by a large majority. Leonida Bissolati, Angelo Cabrini, and Ivanhoe Bonomi, prominent leaders of the party, were ousted. The congress elected a new National Executive Committee, which included Mussolini and Angelica Balabanoff, who had settled in Italy and whose affair with Mussolini continued sporadically, even now that he was living with Rachele.

Mussolini's speech against Bissolati, Cabrini, and Bonomi, and his subsequent election to the National Executive Committee, gained him national as well as international prominence. No less a figure than Lenin, living in Vienna at the time, published praise for him in the newly launched Communist Party newspaper *Pravda*, and Mussolini's Paris-based namesake, Amilcare Cipriani, said of him in *L'Humanité*, the French socialist daily, "I like that man very much. His revolutionary doctrines are the same as mine."

Mussolini, the self-proclaimed perennial outsider, had succeeded in forcing out the most prominent party insiders. Bissolati, Cabrini, and Bonomi set up their own breakaway socialist party, which favored peaceful reform over violent revolution. This implied that the mainstream party was now the party of violent opposition to the government. As for Mussolini, the party not only voted him into its top executive body, it offered him the editorship of its long-established national daily newspaper, *Avanti!* Benito Mussolini was now the voice of Italian socialism.

Chapter 6

Avanti!

Whatever else drove Benito Mussolini—hunger for conquest, political and sexual, an urge to defy and destroy established government, the egomania of a superman—money never much interested him. Even after fascism had become firmly established and corrupt party fat cats grew wealthy at the expense of the people, Mussolini's own needs remained modest. The editorship of *Avanti!* carried a very modest monthly salary of one thousand lire. It was a well-established journal, having been founded in 1896.

In November 1912, when he replaced the current editor, a politically moderate attorney named Claudio Treves, Mussolini insisted that the salary be cut in half. He didn't need one thousand lire a month and he would accept no more than five hundred. The day before he assumed the editorship of *Avanti!* Mussolini got out the last number of *La Lotta di Classe*.

The *Avanti!* offices were in Milan, and so, leaving Rachele and their two-year-old daughter, Edda, in Forlì, Mussolini moved to the big city and immediately hired Angelica Balabanoff as his assistant editor. In the past, he had boasted of his affair with her, and he did so again—although at least one of his modern biographers, Denis Mack Smith, doubts that she was at this time his mistress, if she had ever truly been. The fact is that Mussolini leaned on Balabanoff intellectually, not romantically or sexually. For all the reading that Mussolini did, he was constitutionally incapable of tolerating a great deal of political theory, and Balabanoff made up for this deficiency, which mollified the intellectual wing of the Socialist Party.

Whether or not he was erotically involved with Balabanoff at this time, another woman from his recent past soon joined him in Milan. Ida Dalser moved from Trent to open a beauty parlor in Milan and, evidently, to be with Mussolini. One of Mussolini's recent biographers reports that she and Mussolini effectively lived together in that city, while another biographer writes that the two did not cohabit, but that Mussolini did frequently visit her. Whatever the precise nature of their living arrangement, Dalser attached herself to Mussolini, who, for his part, did nothing to free himself from her grip. At times, she claimed that Mussolini had promised to marry her, and she also said that he often lived off her money. For an interval during 1913–14, Dalser left Milan for Paris, where she opened up another beauty salon. Later in 1915, when Mussolini was at the Isonzo front, serving as a corporal in the Italian army during World War I, he received a letter from Dalser telling him that she had given birth to his son at a Milan hospital on November 11. She named him Benito Albino—and, to Mussolini's great consternation, he would hear much, much more from Ida Dalser over the years.

Yet another woman came to figure in Mussolini's life in Milan. Leda Rafanelli, thirty-three years old when she met Mussolini in 1913, had been born in Alexandria, Egypt, the daughter of a trader who lived in the city's Italian enclave. Like Mussolini, Rafanelli was innately rebellious, but, as with Balabanoff, it was against her father and family that she most immediately rebelled. In Egypt, she converted to Islam, probably to spite her father but also, perhaps, as a genuine protest against European imperialism, and then she added insult to injury by declaring herself an anarchist. Egyptian authorities had little tolerance for anarchists, and, at age twenty, she was deported to Italy, where she delighted in making a spectacle of herself by appearing exclusively in Arab costume and by flaunting her religion. She joined the Italian Socialist Party and earned her bread by writing a series of racy novels, the most infamous of which was called *The Prince's Bastard Daughter*. Her 1921 novel *Enchantments* drew extensively on her relationship with Mussolini.

> *Leda Rafanelli adopted the Islamic religion and Arabic dress. Politically an anarchist, she nevertheless hungered for faith. "The Moslem people," she wrote, "still know how to believe, pray, and meditate. It was exactly for this reason that they will never be animated by the vulgar desires and low ambitions of European people who, in general, are without ... sincere faith." Rafanelli was also a popular clairvoyant, who read Mussolini's palm and told him he would one day "kill and imprison almost everyone in my milieu."*

Mussolini liked to believe—and certainly wanted others to believe—that women were irresistibly attracted to him. The worldly and exotic Leda Rafanelli was clearly interested in him as a personality, but she never yielded to his entreaties that she become his mistress. If Mussolini failed to entice her into romance, it was not for lack of trying. Rafanelli saved some forty-one love letters he wrote to her in the space of a few months, and she published them in the 1940s. Mussolini never found it difficult to lie, and he not only failed to tell Rafanelli that he had a wife and child in Forlì, but, when confronted, made a barefaced denial of the fact. When she told him that she knew he was lying, Mussolini calmly changed tack and explained to her that Rachele was thoroughly accustomed to his infidelities and thoroughly reconciled to them. He went on to tell her that, after all, any prominent newspaper editor required a beautiful and clever mistress, that it was practically an official position. Rafanelli bought none of this, and although she and Mussolini remained close friends for about a year and a half, she concluded that he was not, at bottom, very serious about socialism and, more significantly, that he was mentally unbalanced. (He once told her that he was going to be a "man of destiny." "Like Napoleon?" she teased. Without humor, Mussolini replied, "No, greater than Napoleon.")

In parrying Mussolini's entreaties, Rafanelli told Mussolini that surely he had no real need for her. After all, Benito Mussolini must have plenty of women. Although he was a natural liar, Mussolini could also be disarmingly blunt. He responded, by letter, that he had only two mistresses, one of whom was ugly, he said, but of a generous and noble nature (presumably this was Angelica Balabanoff, not Ida Dalser) and the other was beautiful, but also a mean-spirited schemer—and a Jew. Rafanelli did not comment on Mussolini's assessment of his women, except to chide him for his unsocialist slur on Judaism.

The Jewish woman was Margherita Sarfatti. She was a wealthy resident of Milan whom Mussolini recruited for the staff of *Avanti!* as the paper's art critic. To Mussolini, she imparted some polish in matters of aesthetics and culture, much as Balabanoff had tutored him in political theory. She also authored the first official biography of Mussolini, titled simply *Dux,* published in English in 1925 and in Italian the following year, and she edited the magazine he started in 1921, *Gerarchia.* Indeed, unlike Angelica Balabanoff and Leda Rafanelli, her relationship with Mussolini did not end when he broke with the socialists at the start of World War I. While Balabanoff and Rafanelli remained loyal leftists, Sarfatti made the leap with Mussolini into fascism. She remained his mistress into the early 1930s. She was a woman whose loyalty to the Duce was equaled only by that of Mussolini's wife, until she was definitively displaced in his affections by a new mistress, Claretta Petacci, who had the twin advantages of being much younger than she was and not Jewish. For, in 1938, yielding to pressure from his ally Adolf Hitler, Mussolini authorized passage of anti-Semitic race laws for Italy.

As his fellow socialists saw him, Benito Mussolini was a remarkable success as an editor. When he took over *Avanti!* its circulation was a paltry thirty-four thousand. A bit more than a year later, under Mussolini, it rose to sixty thousand daily, and special editions circulated as many as one hundred thousand copies. His success encouraged him to launch a political magazine of his own, *Utopia,* which was both more intellectual than the populist *Avanti!* and, unlike the daily paper, did not always cleave to the party line. That *Utopia* was never a success may suggest that Italian socialists were not particularly interested in heavy philosophy and reviews of weighty political tomes. Or it may also have been just another indication that Mussolini was far less effective when he approached politics constructively and intellectually than when he focused on the emotion-charged rhetoric of destruction. In a brief book he wrote during this time, *Jan Hus the Truthful,* a didactic biography of the Czech religious and political reformer who was burned at the stake as a heretic in 1415, Mussolini fell back on what he did best, venting rage, outrage, and hatred of the Catholic Church.

If the Italian Socialist Party had reason to be pleased with the new editor of its official daily, Leda Rafanelli was far less impressed. She saw through his pose as the proletarian leader, the man of the people, a speaker who always appeared on the platform unshaven and shabbily attired. In Switzerland, such a uniform had been dictated by financial necessity. But now, even at the half salary he had asked for, Mussolini, editor of two political periodicals, could afford better, and, Rafanelli noted, he wore in private not the bohemian's tatters, but the costume of the bourgeois dandy: a frock coat with silk-faced lapels and patent-leather shoes. He confessed to her that he did not believe he really knew himself, and, as she saw him, Mussolini did seem like nothing so much as an actor. As for his opinions and convictions, these, Rafanelli observed, blew with the wind, shifting with each new conversation. Mussolini, she said, usually agreed with the last person he spoke to.

Doubtless there was more than a glimmer of insight in Rafanelli's observations. But even if Mussolini was not quite so hollow as she suggests, he was always far more effective at reacting to some event or outrage than he was at initiating, formulating, and advocating a positive doctrine or program of action. Just a month after Mussolini began editing *Avanti!,* in January 1913, riots broke out among farm workers at Roccagorge in central Italy. At issue was the government's failure to provide, as promised, a sanitation system for the area. Troops were dispatched, and in the melée that developed, seven farmers were shot dead and another dozen wounded. This incident touched off additional riots, not only in central Italy, but in Sicily as well. In the pages of *Avanti!,* Mussolini did his best to keep the pot boiling. He labeled the deaths of the rioters "state assassination ... at the orders of Savoy (that is, the royal family of Italy)." Mussolini exhorted the people to respond with "defensive" violence, a stopgap pending the advent of true revolution.

Both Mussolini and *Avanti!* were hauled into court on charges of sedition and incitement to violence, but both were quickly acquitted. In the meantime, an anarchist laborer, Augusto Massetti, took matters into his own hands. He shot an army officer. Although his action came in protest of the army's response to the riots, his target had been chosen at random. His victim had had nothing to do with the killing and wounding of the farmers. Arrested and tried for murder, Massetti was found not guilty by reason of insanity and was duly thrown into an asylum. On June 7, 1914, trade unions throughout Italy called for a general strike in support of Massetti. The Socialist Party and Mussolini's *Avanti!* called on all Italian workers to support the labor action.

In part due to Mussolini's rabble-rousing in *Avanti!*, Italy was gripped nationwide by a strike of almost all of its labor force on June 7, the Constitution Day holiday. To what must have been Mussolini's disappointment, however, the strikes were almost universally peaceful. But in Ancona, the army was called in to separate the strikers from conservatives who were commemorating Constitution Day. Apparently with little provocation, the strikers attacked the soldiers, who opened fire in self-defense. Three strikers died, and ten were wounded. This provoked a general strike of indefinite duration in Ancona as well as Milan.

On the first day of the action in Milan, Mussolini was struck by a policeman's club. He was proud of the wound, incurred at the very start of what came to be called "Red Week."

Stirred—in part—by *Avanti!*, Red Week appeared to have the potential to ignite a general socialist revolution not only in Italy, but elsewhere in Europe. Mussolini was not alone in thinking this. The entire European establishment was alarmed by what was happening in Italy and by the labor actions Italy's Red Week was igniting elsewhere. All of Italy's major cities, save Venice, were paralyzed by an almost one hundred percent work stoppage. In Milan and Genoa, the trams still ran—but nothing else moved, and no other work was done. Ancona, where it had all begun, was in a state of outright civil insurrection, and the town was put under martial law.

As Mussolini and extremists such as Italy's leading anarchist, Errico Malatesta, saw it, the golden moment was now. The Liberal government of Antonio Salandra, who had recently replaced Giolitti as Prime Minister, was at a loss for a meaningful response. Enforce order, local officials were told by the government, but also exercise restraint. These ambiguous instructions were intended to avoid further inflaming the left wing, but, instead, the orders mobilized the right wing to action against the strikers. Mobs of conservatives staged counter-demonstrations in Parma and Milan, and they often clashed with the strikers, sometimes deliberately targeting small groups of demonstrators for vicious assault. Such ferment was the essence of the "class struggle" Mussolini promoted, and, managed properly, it could be fanned into full-scale rebellion.

But, to Mussolini's consternation, far from fanning the flames, the Socialist Party declined to give its official sanction to the general strike. In the face of this, Mussolini must have been tempted to ignore his socialist colleagues and answer instead Malatesta's call to revolution. But he did no such thing. Instead, Mussolini swallowed hard and published the party line—even after the party's General Confederation of Labor, on June 10, called for an end to the strike. On June 11, Mussolini exhorted workers at a rally in the Milan arena to return to their jobs. The strike, he assured them, had been a success, and he repeated this message in *Avanti!* on June 12.

Inwardly, however, Mussolini was profoundly shaken by Red Week. A *success?* What had succeeded? The truth was that events had raced ahead of the Socialist Party, which, when confronted with the reality of revolution, temporized briefly and then launched into full retreat. Mussolini had ascended through the ranks to the top echelon of the Socialist Party. He had allowed himself to believe that he was, therefore, one of the elite Georges Sorel had written of or, perhaps, one of Nietzsche's supermen.

But into what had he risen? A body of men and women who mouthed revolutionary slogans and cliches, but who never took truly decisive action. Riots and strikes there were in plenty, but they never produced any lasting or real reform. Red Week might have moved the country to revolution, but, in the end, it was not the conservatives or the bankers, the bourgeoisie, the Chamber of Deputies, or King Vittore Emmanuelle III who blocked rebellion. It was the Italian Socialist Party.

What prevented Benito Amilcare Andrea Mussolini from breaking with Italian socialism right then and there? Could it have been the shadow of his father, the violence-loving but ever-faithful socialist who had raised him? It is intriguing that two of the rebellious women who most attracted Mussolini, Angelica Balabanoff and Leda Rafanelli, rebelled first and foremost against their fathers, while about the only person young Mussolini was *not* prepared to rebel against was his.

Or did Mussolini's lingering loyalty to socialism, even after the Red Week revelation, spring from his own essentially bourgeois desire for status? After a life of itinerant poverty and rejection, acclaim from the party and a modest degree of financial well-being that allowed him to wear a silk-trimmed frock coat and patent-leather shoes must have felt rather good.

Red Week began on June 7, 1914, and fizzled out by June 12. Two weeks after this, an event occurred that changed the world and, in the process, propelled the reluctant Mussolini out of Italian socialism and into a brand-new arena of political action.

Sometimes the greatest of cataclysms begin in the most obscure places. Back in the late nineteenth century, the mighty architect of the modern German State, Otto Von Bismarck, predicted that one day a world war would erupt because of "some damn foolish thing in the Balkans." On June 28, 1914, Franz Ferdinand, arch-duke of Austria-Hungary and heir apparent to the imperial throne, made a state visit to Sarajevo, the obscure capital city of the obscure Balkan province of Bosnia-Herzegovina. With him was his wife, the Duchess Sophie.

Franz Ferdinand had chosen the day of his visit with great delib-eration. June 28 was St. Vitus's Day, celebrated by Serbs as a Vidovan, a great national holiday. Serbia, which had won its inde-pendence from Austria-Hungary, actively encouraged the empire's Balkan provinces, including Bosnia-Herzegovina, annexed in

1908, to declare their independence as well. In making his visit on Vidovan, therefore, the archduke thumbed his nose at Balkan nationalism. But waiting for the archduke and his wife on the streets of Sarajevo was a band of assassins, who had been coached and supported by a secret Serbian society known as the Black Hand. One of these young men, a tubercular student named Gavrilo Princip, was number two in the line of assassins deployed along the route of the archduke's motorcade. Princip never expected the first assassin to fail, so when the archduke's car passed him in the street—with Franz Ferdinand and Sophie very much alive—Princip was so stunned that he forgot even to take his pistol out of his pocket. Dejected by his failure, he walked to Moritz Schiller's delicatessen and outdoor café to console himself with a cup of coffee.

At 11:15 A.M., a chauffeur's wrong turn suddenly put the archduke's car no more than five feet from where Princip was sitting. At pointblank range, the young man fired three times. The duchess died first, and the archduke a few moments afterward. "Are you suffering, your highness?" a courtier asked him. "It is nothing, it is nothing, it is nothing." They were his last words—and among the last for a long time that anyone would speak in a world at peace.

In *Avanti!* Mussolini called the assassination at Sarajevo a "tragic event," but he also hailed it as a blow against the corrupt imperialism of the Hapsburg monarchy. It was, however, clear to Mussolini that Austria-Hungary intended to use the assassination as a pretext for starting a war with Serbia, which it believed it could quickly defeat and then annex to the empire. What Mussolini did not immediately realize—and he was hardly alone in this—was that Austria-Hungary's declaration of war on Serbia would activate a network of alliances and counteralliances that would draw almost all of Europe into the most terrible war the world had ever seen.

During July, as the crisis triggered at Sarajevo developed and as general war increasingly appeared inevitable, Mussolini, the faithful socialist, churned out a stream of antiwar propaganda in the pages of *Avanti!* He iterated and reiterated the familiar socialist slogan, "Not one man, not one penny for imperialist war!"

On July 28, after presenting it with an impossible ultimatum, Austria-Hungary declared war on Serbia. Within two days, Serbia's ally and avowed protector, Russia, mobilized. In response to the mobilization, Germany, on August 1, declared war on Russia and also decided to act preemptively against Russia's ally, France. When the German army marched through neutral Belgium on its way into France, England, bound by treaty to defend Belgian neutrality, entered the war on August 3.

Thus the Great War began with the inevitability and indifference of a massive machine, one gear meshing with another. In the meantime, on July 29, Angelica Balabanoff rushed to Brussels to represent the Italian Socialist Party at an emergency meeting of the Executive Committee of the Socialist International. International socialism's standing position on war was clear: absolute opposition. Its course of action was also prescribed: a general strike in every belligerent country designed to bring the gears of combat to a grinding halt.

At the July 29 meeting, however, the Austrian socialists announced that they would support not the International, but their country. They favored the war. French and Belgian socialists announced the same. There was opposition, even within these delegations, but it was overwhelmingly outnumbered, and when the French socialist Jean Jaurès was perceived (mistakenly, as it turned out) as a pacifist holdout, he was assassinated on July 31.

By August 4, when Mussolini addressed a meeting in Milan to honor Jaurès as a martyr to true socialist internationalism, the German socialists had already announced their support for Germany in the war. The massive opening phase of combat, the so-called Battle of the Frontiers, was in full swing as the German army launched its lightning offensive in the west and set up a stout defense along the Eastern Front.

Italy was a signatory to the Triple Alliance, ostensibly pledged to enter the war on the side of Austria and Germany, but the Italian government now scrambled to find reasons to abrogate the alliance. Officials pointed out that Italy was not obliged to support Austria and Germany in a "war of aggression," which is what Italy deemed the present war to be. Moreover, the original Triple Alliance, as concluded in 1881, expressly specified that the alliance was not directed against England. Italy's ministers did not reveal that they had also, much more recently, concluded a secret agreement with France, agreeing to remain neutral if Germany attacked France or if France, to protect its "national honor," attacked Germany.

For once, then, the traditional antiwar position of socialism, in Italy at least, coincided with government policy, and it therefore looked to be easy enough for the Italian Socialist Party to maintain its opposition to the war.

There was, however, growing pressure on the government to enter the war, not on the side of Germany and Austria, but on the side of the Allies. Although during August and into September Mussolini continued vigorously to publish and promote the antiwar party line in *Avanti!* he, too, felt the pressure to declare for the Allies. The family of the national hero under whose portrait Mussolini had been raised in his parents' house in Predappio, Giuseppe Garibaldi, not only voiced its support for the Allies, but Garibaldi's grandson Peppino raised and led a band of Italian volunteers, including five of his brothers, to fight in the service of France.

Still, Mussolini kept the socialist faith as he understood it. On September 9, he addressed a rally in Milan's Teatro del Popolo demanding that Italy maintain neutrality and speaking out against the interventionist campaign afoot throughout Italy. Three days later, in *Avanti!*, he published a pro-interventionist argument by Sergio Panunzio, a dissident Italian Socialist, then followed this the next day with an article he himself had written rebutting Panunzio. Although he wrote a letter to Leda Rafanelli expressing his confidence that he had "crushed" Panunzio, his arguments in opposition to him were actually half-hearted and, by all accounts, not very persuasive. To Rafanelli he bemoaned the fact that so many socialists were yielding to the clamor for war, but he pledged to her that, come what may, he would continue to "hold the rampart" in opposition to it.

*The grandsons of Giuseppe Garibaldi, left to right: Ricciotti,
Peppino, and Sante. All were passionate interventionists in
World War I.*

(*Image from ArtToday*)

What came the next month, October 1914, was a new organization, formed by Italian socialists who had decided that intervention on the side of the Allies was the only proper course for Italy.
This breakaway group called itself the Fasci d'Azione Rivoluzionaria Intervenista. To translate this, one must know that the

fasci was an emblem of office carried by the lictors of ancient Rome. It was nothing more than a bundle of sticks bound tightly together into a mace or club. The point of the emblem was that, while an individual stick is easily broken, a bundle of sticks fastened together is unbreakable. Thus these renegade socialists were a band—*fasci*—for "revolutionary interventionist action." They were, at least in a linguistic sense, Italy's first *fascists*.

Massimo Rocca, who edited a nationalistic Bologna newspaper, *Il Resto del Carlino,* and who was a vocal interventionist, reported to Leda Rafanelli his knowledge that Mussolini was about to come out for intervention on the Allied side. When Rafanelli incredulously denied that this was possible, Rocca told her that, on the contrary, it was a certainty. How he knew this to be so, he did not reveal. We can only speculate that groups such as the Fasci d'Azione had begun to sway Mussolini and that his change of heart was becoming evident to astute observers.

In any case, Rocca resolved to smoke Mussolini out. Writing under his pen name, Libero Tancredi, Rocca published in *Il Resto del Carlino* an "Open Letter to Benito Mussolini" headed "The Editor of *Avanti!* Is a Man of Straw." He claimed that Mussolini published in his paper one position while secretly holding another. In effect, Rocca accused him of being a closet interventionist. He now challenged him to come out of the closet, to act in good faith, and to act for the good of Italy by finally declaring what he truly believed—that Italy should abandon neutrality and enter the war on the side of the Allies.

Just before she left Milan for the winter, Rafanelli spoke to Mussolini, insisting that he must, of course, respond to Rocca. Mussolini assured her that he would, and, with that, the two strolled out into the street. Bidding one another good-bye, they separated at a corner. Leda Rafanelli would never speak to Mussolini again.

He published his reply to Rocca the next day. The reply reasserted his stand for international socialism and Italian neutrality, but Mussolini cryptically added "all those who, instead of making history, are only observing it, are men of straw. ... We will see who is the man of straw, I or Libero Tancredi, or rather Massimo Rocca."

Just a few days later, on October 18, Mussolini published an article in *Avanti!* advocating something new, a swing from "absolute neutrality" to "working neutrality" or "active neutrality." This linguistic sleight of hand was actually nothing more or less than a leap from neutrality to interventionism. The very next day, fourteen members of the National Executive of the Italian Socialist Party, including Angelica Balabanoff and Mussolini himself, met for a heated debate that lasted into the night. On the morning of October 20, 1914, Mussolini introduced a motion that the National Executive resolve to affirm the party's opposition in principle to war, but that it further acknowledge the dogmatism of "absolute neutrality" and, therefore, introduce a new policy of *flexible* neutrality. In other words, Mussolini was calling for an end to neutrality. His motion was defeated, thirteen to one. In its place, the majority resolved to support nothing less than absolute neutrality and to be faithful to one flag and one flag alone, the flag on which is written, "Proletarians of all the world, unite!"

In the face of rejection, Mussolini demanded that the National Executive convene an emergency congress of the entire Italian Socialist Party to reconsider the party's position on the war. When this request was denied, Mussolini resigned as editor of *Avanti!* The next month, on November 15, he would start his own paper—*The People of Italy, Il Popolo d'Italia*—and, nine days later, on November 24, the Socialist Party would vote to expel him from their number.

Chapter 7

Il Popolo d'Italia

Minds change, and, as a socialist, Mussolini was hardly alone in declaring himself in favor of the war. After all, the socialist parties in Austria-Hungary, France, and Germany had rapidly fallen in line behind their governments. Even a minority of Italy's own socialists supported the war. But what stunned the Italian socialist mainstream, including Mussolini's closest associates, such as Angelica Balabanoff and Leda Rafanelli, was the completeness of the reversal and the suddenness of the betrayal.

They can hardly be blamed for feeling shocked. After all, the editor of *Avanti!* had argued passionately for neutrality, and, before this, had been highly critical of any apparent cooperation between the Italian Socialist Party and the government. However, looked at in the context of Mussolini's career up to this point—and, for that matter, beyond—his reversal on the war issue appears more comprehensible and less astounding. Like most political thinkers, Mussolini's colleagues saw power and influence as the means of implementing ideology. For Mussolini, in contrast, it was ideology that was the means of achieving power and influence. It was the power and influence that counted, not the ideology; so, unlike most of those around him, Mussolini was really very little concerned about the content and consistency of his ideology. He used whatever worked at the moment, and he had a remarkable gift for expressing whatever worked at the moment as if it were an ideology for all time, the sovereign answer to the problems of the Italian nation and even the world.

What he saw now was that the way of war was a more effective route to power and influence than the way of peace. This may be understood as nothing more than a return to the mode of thought most natural to Mussolini. Although he had once argued for the disbanding of the army and a refusal to fight in any war for nationalism, the role of pacifist was ultimately a strange one for him. Violence and war, not consensus and peace, lay at the core of his politics. For him, coming to support the world war was, intellectually and emotionally, a coming home.

And there were also more immediately pragmatic motives for Mussolini's change of position. Italian socialist leaders accused him of nothing short of treason. It was generally known that Mussolini had long wanted to *own*—not just edit—his own major paper. *Il Popolo d'Italia,* which he started on November 15, 1914, was that paper. It belonged to him. But where had the financing come from? The socialist leaders he had betrayed claimed that it had been launched with funds provided by the French intelligence service in return for his propagandizing on behalf of Italian entry into the war. Confronted with this accusation, Mussolini denied that the French had, in effect, bribed him. He was lying. Indeed, throughout the war, other Allied nations, including Belgium, Britain, and, very likely, Russia and the United States, also contributed money to *Il Popolo d'Italia.*

Money for the new daily came from other compromising sources as well. The paper of the "People of Italy"—by which was clearly meant the Italian proletariat, the working class—was heavily financed by major Italian industrialists, big business concerns that stood to profit mightily from Italy's entry into the war. Even more significantly, elements of the Italian government funneled funds to a paper that would help pave the road leading an overwhelmingly reluctant nation out of neutrality.

Surely, Mussolini's erstwhile colleagues were amply justified in labeling him a sellout. But it is a key feature of his perverse political genius that he could reverse himself 180 degrees, accept funding from the belligerents, the capitalist oppressors, and the Italian government itself, publish a newspaper that satisfied *their* immediate needs, yet still promote *himself* as an advocate of social revolution. In *Il Popolo*, he presented the Great War to a neutral Italy much as President Woodrow Wilson would present it in 1917 to a recently neutral United States. Mussolini called it a war to liberate the oppressed, whereas Wilson would dub it a war to make the world safe for democracy. Very early in his advocacy of entry into the war, Mussolini even wrote against fighting for motives of territorial aggrandizement. He wrote against fighting for the annexation of Dalmatia, because the Yugoslavs were allies in this war of liberation, and against lusting after Fiume and Trieste, long targets of Italian expansionism. Finally, he advised Italians to renounce, once and for all, any dream they had of an Alpine frontier. When the Italian Socialist Party, buying none of these demurrers, voted on November 24, 1914, to expel him, Mussolini replied in the pages of *Il Popolo d'Italia* that he was more of a socialist than they. Later, after his expulsion from the Italian Socialist Party, he would remind his readers of something he had written in October 1914: "It is necessary to assassinate the Party in order to save Socialism."

Call himself what he would, declare, as he did, the need to destroy the Socialist Party for the sake of socialism's salvation, Mussolini was in fact rapidly moving away from socialism and anything ideologically associated with it. In the 1920s, after the Fascist Party had assumed power, Mussolini would lay claim to having created "the *Fascisti*" in December 1914 as a group dedicated to pressuring the government into intervention. From the beginning, Mussolini was at pains not only to assume full credit for the creation of fascism, but also to present it as something entirely new in the world.

The fact is that the Fasci d'Azione Rivoluzionaria Interventista, mentioned in Chapter 6, "*Avanti!*" had been organized as a pro-war socialist splinter group in October 1914, and not by Mussolini. In December, he *joined* this ongoing group of socialists who had preceded him in making their break with the party. No sooner had he joined the Fasci, than he began to dominate the party, making it his own. He drew up a manifesto that no longer had anything to do with the Karl Marx of socialism but instead had everything to do with the Giuseppe Mazzini of nineteenth-century Italian nationalism. In this leap from one ideological hero to another, Mussolini also abandoned his socialist position of a few months earlier. He now called for Italy's war objectives to include expansion, not only the acquisition of Trieste and Fiume, but expansion into the Balkans and colonization in the Middle East. Echoing Mazzini, he also called for the nation of Italy to be pushed to its "natural frontier," the Alps.

Fascism would not emerge as a significant political force until after World War I, but the moment of its conception came in October 1914, and the time of its birth was when Mussolini took it over in December.

Although elements of the Italian government were pleased with the direction in which Mussolini and his newspaper were moving *Il Popolo*'s readership—which grew rapidly, to encompass not only disaffected elements of Italian socialism, but also Italian republicans and nationalists—the parliamentary majority was still opposed to the war at the end of 1914. The opposition was based less on moral grounds than on general approval of Prime Minister Salandra's policy of remaining neutral while bargaining with both the Allies and the Central Powers, the object being to put Italy in a position to gain as much territory as possible from the war. This meant, at the very least, delaying entry until the right moment and circumstances presented themselves. With real luck, Italy might not even have to fight at all. A mere guarantee of neutrality could bring the promise of profit from the war. As for popular opinion, beyond the walls of the Chamber of Deputies, most Italians were not even concerned with what they, let alone their country, could get from the war; they just wanted to stay out of it altogether.

In *Il Popolo d'Italia*, Mussolini approached the task of stirring the nation to war from two directions. First, he fell back on his old standby: the threat of violence. He declared that if the government failed to end Italian neutrality, he would create a civil war and a coup d'etat. How he would do this, he did not say. Second, he assuaged the fears of the people by assuring them that the war would be short, probably lasting only a few weeks, because the Italian army was prepared to attack. Sacrifices to the sons of Italy would be slight, and the impact on the home front virtually nonexistent. These lies were, at least in part, founded on Mussolini's lack of information about the poor state of Italy's military preparedness. In tone and content, however, they were no different from what Austrian leaders had told their people, and Kaiser Wilhelm II had told German troops marching off to the invasion of France in August 1914: "You will be home before the leaves fall," he assured them.

By the spring of 1915, Mussolini—and others—had succeeded in diverting the interventionist movement from a course of parliamentary change to exclusive reliance on intimidation and violence. Nor did the editor of *Il Popolo d'Italia* remain behind his desk. On April 11, 1915, he went to Rome to address a mob of interventionist rioters ("demonstrators" is too mild a term), only to be overpowered by police before he could speak. Felled by a blow from an officer's baton, he was arrested, though held only a few hours before being released. In the meantime, Rome, Milan, and just about every other major city in Italy witnessed riots.

Still, the interventionist faction was relatively small—loud and violent, but decidedly a minority. On May 5, they found a way to make their extreme point of view suddenly appear to be the irresistible will of the people. On the occasion of the fifty-fifth anniversary of the Expedition of Garibaldi's Thousand, a volunteer force that had sailed from Quarto, near Genoa, to free Sicily from Bourbon rule, a new Garibaldi monument was being dedicated at Quarto. The main speaker at the unveiling was Gabriele D'Annunzio, a highly popular poet and novelist celebrated for his theatrical sensuality and violent patriotism. He let the interventionists know that he was quite willing to transform the dedication of the Garibaldi monument into a call to arms. Among government officials, this heightened the perception of war fever, if not its actual temperature. A few days later, on May 11, Mussolini pressed the point home. Whereas D'Annunzio had appealed to patriotism and Italy's destiny among nations, Mussolini, speaking to a crowd of demonstrators from the window of his newspaper offices, again resorted to threat. If Italy failed to wage war on the Austrians, he declared, civil war would come to Italy. A few days later, D'Annunzio spoke again, inciting a mob to storm the

Chamber of Deputies. Police forced them back, but the message of impending rebellion was clear.

Gabriele D'Annunzio: Mussolini sought his support, basked in his glory, but feared his fame.

(*Image from ArtToday*)

It was even clearer, perhaps, than it needed to be. For while Mussolini and D'Annunzio were stirring rebellion in the name of nationalism, the Salandra government had been courting both the Central Powers and the Allies, looking for an alliance that would yield the greatest territorial dividends. Although Austria-Hungary finally agreed to cede the Trentino to Italy in exchange for an alliance or even nothing more than a pledge of continued neutrality, Britain and France, in exchange for Italy's active entry into the war, offered the Trentino, Trieste, Fiume (and environs), Rhodes, the Dodecanese Islands, and, in Africa, Jubaland (part of present-day Kenya, at the time British East Africa), which would be annexed to Italian Somaliland. Pleased with this deal, on April 26, Italy concluded with France and Britain the secret Treaty of London. The Salandra government's pragmatism in negotiating the secret treaty was more than matched by the cynicism of the other two signatories, who kept the treaty most secret from none other than the "gallant Serbians." To discourage hard-pressed Serbia from surrendering to Austria and the Germans, the Allies had already promised the Serbs those provinces of the Austro-Hungarian Empire with predominantly Slavic populations, including Fiume and the surrounding region. The exigencies of war moved many "honorable" statesmen to tell convenient lies. This lesson was not lost on Mussolini, who, however, came to regard government as a *perpetual* state of war, a permanent exigency that warranted any number of lies any time.

On May 23, 1915, a little less than a month after the Treaty of London was signed, Italy ordered a general mobilization. On May 24, it declared war on Austria-Hungary, which entailed war with the other Central Powers: Germany, Turkey, and Bulgaria. Unaware of the secret Treaty of London, Mussolini claimed credit for having pointed Italy in the direction of its destiny. The son of a violent, often confused, but always committed international socialist, Mussolini had, up until a few months earlier, denounced patriotism and exulted internationalism. On the day mobilization was ordered, he wiped that all away in the pages of *Il Popolo d'Italia:* "From today there are only Italians ... united in a bloc of steel."

In *Mein Kampf,* published in 1924, Adolf Hitler reflected on his emotions the moment he heard that the Great War had commenced. He felt it as a birth of his political spirit: "To me those hours seemed like a release from the painful feelings of my youth. ... I fell down on my knees and thanked Heaven from an overflowing heart for granting me the good fortune of being permitted to live at this time." Similarly, in the 1930s, at the height of his power, Mussolini looked back at the riots that had preceded Italy's declaration of war as the birth of the spirit of fascism, the very beginning of what he liked to call the fascist revolution.

When Italy entered the war, Mussolini was a far more prominent figure than Hitler—at the time nothing more than a failed art
student and all-around misfit—had been when his country
marched against the Allies. Yet, for both men, as they saw it in retrospect, the great cataclysm of the Great War forged their personal
destinies and—again, as they saw it—the collective destiny of the
world. In truth, the impact of Corporal Adolf Hitler on the origin
and course of World War I was negligble, and, his illusions to
the contrary notwithstanding, so was that of Benito Mussolini.
Nevertheless, Mussolini concluded that he, more perhaps than any
other individual, had moved Italy to war and—most important—
had done so not through parliamentary, legal, and constitutional
means, but through the exercise of raw power in the form of riot,
intimidation, and the threat of civil war.

Mussolini's eagerness to thrust Italy into war was informed by
no knowledge of the sorry state of the nation's military, which was
undermanned, ill-trained, poorly equipped, and led by Gen. Luigi
Cadorna, a marginally competent martinet who had never seen
combat. Salandra and his ministers should have known better. But
even after Italy had sacrificed the flower of its young manhood and
had suffered crippling economic loss, only to be cheated by the
Treaty of Versailles of most of the territorial gains the Allies had
promised, Mussolini would continue to celebrate the Great War as
a national and personal triumph. In a way, he was right to do so.
For Italy's entry into the war had persuaded him of his power to use
extralegal means to gain the ends he desired. It gave him, too, a
glimpse of what fascism—whatever that would turn out to be—
could achieve. Finally, by soaking the Italian land in blood, the
very hardship, heartbreak, and ruin of war created a soil abun-
dantly fertile for what Mussolini called the "garden of fascism."

Part Three

"The Garden of Fascism"

Chapter 8

Steel Meets Steel

With the announcement of Italian mobilization on May 23, 1915, Mussolini declared, in *Il Popolo d'Italia*, an end to all factionalism: "From today there are only Italians ... united in a bloc of steel." What he hadn't considered is that Italians would face the soldiers of other nations, each believing they, too, were united in their own "bloc of steel." Italy's general in chief, Luigi Cadorna, proposed a simple two-pronged strategy: to hold a defensive position against the Austrians in the Trentino while launching an immediate offensive along the Isonzo River north of Trieste.

Cadorna's stated plan was to advance eastward from Venetia across the lower Isonzo valley to create an Italian salient—a bulge—into Austro-Hungarian territory. From this salient, he would take the town of Gorizia on the east bank of the Isonzo. Such was the *stated* objective of Cadorna's strategy. But this general, who had hitherto commanded nothing more than a desk, had a much bigger dream, which he dared not make public. He envisioned the Italian army as a latter-day Roman legion, which would march through Trieste and, ultimately, into Vienna itself, capital of Austria-Hungary, the hated Dual Monarchy.

It was a dream worthy of the later Mussolini himself. But between it and reality yawned a wide gulf, first of mud and then of blood.

Focused narrowly on his vision of conquest, Cadorna paid no attention to the weather. He began his advance eastward in May, only to find his armies blocked by seasonal flooding of the Isonzo. Whatever Cadorna's strategic aspirations, the Allies—France and Britain—greeted the entry of Italy into the war with great hope and enthusiasm. They were locked in static slaughter along the trench line of the Western Front. With Italy opening up a new front against the enemy, the deadlock might well be broken. At the very least, it was believed that Italy would make real progress against the Austro-Hungarians. But the flooding, by halting Cadorna's advance, put an end to hope and enthusiasm; for when the Italian army stopped moving, both it and the Austro-Hungarian forces dug in. Before combat had even begun, the Isonzo front became just another line of trenches, murderous and unmoving.

Fantasy, especially in the mind of a general placed high above the level of his competence, does not die easily. Unwilling to accept the permanence of trench warfare, Cadorna resolved to resume his advance—at any cost. After all, he enjoyed significant superiority of numbers over the enemy. He attacked.

Numerically superior though they were, the Italians met nothing but death in their assault against the well-developed enemy defenses in the First Battle of Isonzo, June 23 to July 7, 1915. Not to be deterred, Cadorna launched another offensive during July 18 to August 3. When his artillery ammunition ran out, he broke off the Second Battle of the Isonzo. Together, the two battles cost the Italians sixty thousand casualties versus forty-five thousand for the Austro-Hungarian army. By this ghastly bloodletting, Cadorna had gained nothing.

None of this seemed to discourage Mussolini's fellow advocates of intervention from rushing to enlist. Mussolini himself held back. Although he later claimed that he had *tried* to volunteer but that the army told him to wait until he was drafted, there is no evidence that he did any such thing, even when his patriotism and courage were called into question. Instead, he continued to flog the war from behind his editorial desk, until August 31, 1915, when he was, at last, drafted.

Leaving the paper in the hands of subordinates, he went off to join the 11th Regiment of the Bersaglieri. On September 2, he shipped out for an encampment at Brescia and was on the front lines, at Udine, by September 17. At various times in Mussolini's life, detractors and outright enemies accused him of cowardice. Angelica Balabanoff, who had remained faithful to the antiwar position of Italian Socialism, turned viciously against Mussolini as soon as he trumpeted intervention. Over the years, her hatred of him would intensify, and, by way of personal and political revenge, she freely published any number of accounts of his craven and cowardly ways. She claimed, for example, that he was always afraid to address hostile crowds at political meetings, that he had a phobic aversion to dogs, that he was fearful of visiting the doctor, that he would under no circumstances go near a cemetery, and that he would not venture out into the city streets after dark. When violence broke out at a May Day rally in 1913, Balabanoff said, Mussolini allowed her to speak, but would not mount the podium himself. When a shot was fired in the direction of the coach that was taking her and Mussolini to the railroad station after the rally, Balabanoff reported that Mussolini "shrank down in his seat, trembling and cursing. Long after we were clear of the crowd he was still shaking." Now that the war was raging and Mussolini hadn't scrambled to enlist, accusations of cowardice came from other quarters as well.

Yet Balabanoff was hardly impartial where Mussolini was concerned, and while Mussolini would show himself to be capable of many very bad things, there seems little basis to accusations of physical cowardice. When his captain, an avid reader of *Il Popolo d'Italia*, offered to make Mussolini editor of the regimental newspaper, a safe desk job at headquarters in Udine, the draftee declined and asked instead to be sent immediately to the trenches so that he could fight Austrians.

As with his earlier period of service, during 1905–07, army life agreed with Mussolini. He was popular with other enlisted men and was quite pleasing to his commanders, who almost instantly promoted him to corporal—the very rank held by Adolf Hitler, enlisted with the enemy, in a Bavarian infantry regiment. Although he volunteered for combat duty, Mussolini did not abandon journalism. At irregular intervals, he continued to write articles for *Il Popolo d'Italia,* and he kept a war diary, subsequently published, which avoided politics but was graphic in its representation of the hardships willingly shouldered by the troops.

Through the fall and into the winter, Gen. Cadorna launched additional offensives, resulting in the third and fourth Isonzo battles. Cadorna broke off the failed Fourth Battle of the Isonzo on December 10. The two latest Isonzo offensives cost the Italians one hundred seventeen thousand dead and wounded. On the Austro-Hungarian side, almost seventy-two thousand men had become casualties, and the front had not budged an inch.

Corporal Benito Mussolini, 11th Regiment of the Bersaglieri, in 1916.

It was at the start of the Fourth Battle of the Isonzo that Cpl. Mussolini received Ida Dalser's letter informing him of the birth of their son (Chapter 6, "*Avanti!*"). He had little time to digest this news, however, because on November 24 he became desperately ill with what was called at the time paratyphoid and is now recognized as salmonella poisoning. He was transferred to a military hospital, and, while there, met for the first time King Vittore Emmanuelle III, who toured the facility. When Mussolini had recovered sufficiently, he was sent to a suburb of Milan for convalescence, then given thirty days' leave. He rushed to Forlì, where, on December 16, 1915, he and Rachele were married in a civil ceremony. (Exactly nine months later, on September 21, 1916, their second child, Vittorio, was born.) Shortly after the wedding ceremony, he returned to Milan to visit Ida Dalser and their son—with whom he was thoroughly delighted. He put Dalser and the child up at the Hotel Gran Bretagna, recording in the hotel's register that she was his wife. After delivering a few articles to the *Popolo* offices in Milan—pieces intended to combat the nation's growing war weariness and sentiment of defeatism engendered by the static horrors of the Isonzo—he returned to his unit at the front.

In May 1916, Austrian field marshal Conrad von Hötzendorf launched the so-called Asiago Offensive to counter Cadorna's many Isonzo offensives. Ultimately, the Italians would lose another one hundred forty-seven thousand men, including forty thousand taken prisoner, in beating back the Asiago Offensive. (Austro-Hungarian losses numbered eighty-one thousand, of which twenty-six thousand were POWs.) During this action, Mussolini volunteered for hazardous reconnaissance duty and on July 17 was slightly wounded by shrapnel.

At this time, of far more consequence than his superficial wounds was the news that Ida Dalser had started legal proceedings against him in Milan. Although Mussolini acknowledged Benito Albino as his son and arranged it so that Dalser would be paid a stipend for her support and that of the baby, she was not satisfied. Now she demanded alimony in addition to other support, and she backed up her claim that she was Mussolini's wife by presenting in court the register of the Hotel Gran Bretagna. The court declined to rule on the legitimacy of her marriage claim, but it did order Mussolini to increase his payments to her. Mussolini complied, but he bitterly broke off the relationship with Dalser—and, as a consequence, any relationship he might have established with his son as well. For her part, Dalser paid a call on Rachele in Forlì, where she started a row, loudly proclaiming that she, and not Rachele, was Mussolini's wife.

Had Rachele been aware of the affair with Dalser? Did she know about Mussolini's child? Or was this all news to her? And if it was news, did she—knowing her husband as she did—find it shocking or even surprising? We don't know. Perhaps it was just as well for Mussolini that he was away, fighting a desperate war, when all of this took place.

After the Sixth Battle of the Isonzo, Mussolini was promoted to *caporalmaggiore*, a rank above corporal but below sergeant. Early in 1917, with the onset of cold weather, an eerie but welcome lull set in on the front. On February 22, Mussolini was assigned to participate in a test of a new artillery piece. At about one in the afternoon, after the gun had been fired a number of times, Mussolini warned the lieutenant in charge that the weapon was becoming overheated. The lieutenant replied that only one more round remained to be fired and that there would be no harm in firing one more round.

The round was loaded and fired, and the gun exploded, killing (according to Mussolini's *War Diary*) two men and wounding five—although his later account in the 1928 My *Autobiography* puts the death toll at four. Other biographers report at least five killed and many wounded. This is not the only discrepancy relating to the incident. Whereas Mussolini's most authoritative biographers say the accident took place not in combat, but during the test firing of a gun, My *Autobiography* portrayed it as a battle event, "during a bombardment of the enemy trenches in Sector 144." What exploded, Mussolini says, was not a gun, but "one of our own grenades," which "burst in our trench among about twenty of us soldiers." Mussolini's version records the event as an accident, but an anonymous accident of combat, not the result of a lieutenant's bad judgment during a period of idleness.

All sources do agree that Mussolini was seriously and painfully wounded by metal splinters. He was taken by armored car to Camp Hospital 46 at Ronchi, not far behind the front lines. "The patience and ability of the physicians succeeded in taking out of my body forty-four pieces of the grenade," Mussolini recorded in the *Autobiography*. "Flesh was torn, bones broken"—actually, only his thighbone was broken. "I faced atrocious pain; my suffering was indescribable. ... I had twenty-seven operations in one month; all except two were without anaesthetics."

> *Mussolini's biographers neither corroborate nor dispute the number of operations that followed his wounding, and only one of his early biographers, Emil Ludwig, thought to ask him why he refused anesthesia. He replied that he wanted to keep an eye on the doctors. One of his more recent biographers, Jasper Ridley, believes that Mussolini's real motive in toughing it out was to "demonstrate his heroism to himself and to those who watched him." It is, of course, also possible that Mussolini simply fabricated the detail about his refusal of anesthesia.*

Rachele was brave enough to visit her husband in Ronchi, and, in *My Autobiography*, Mussolini reported that the king visited the hospital as well. He elaborated on this in a later newspaper story, reporting that Vittore Emmanuelle III paused to ask him "How are you?" Mussolini, who had once all but openly urged the assassination of the king, replied politely: "Not too well, Your Majesty."

As if his wounds were not misery enough, Mussolini wrote that his "infernal life of pain lasted until a furious bombardment burst into pieces one wing and part of the central building of my hospital at Ronchi. All the wounded were rushed to a far-away refuge, but my condition would not permit my removal. Unable to move, I remained for days under the intermittent fire of the enemy guns among the dirty, jagged ruins of the building. I was absolutely defenseless." Other sources corroborate that the hospital was indeed shelled on March 18.

Mussolini's wounds were severe enough to warrant his discharge from the army in June. He made his way into the offices of *Il Popolo d'Italia* on the fifteenth, hobbling on crutches. "I took my place as a fighter in my newspaper office," he wrote later.

Chapter 9

Man of Destiny

Mussolini's wound took him out of the fighting at a time when the war, which had never gone well for the Italians, was going especially badly. Gen. Cadorna persisted obsessively in feeding his men into the slaughter mill of the Isonzo. Italy's allies on the Western Front seemed to be buckling under a series of all-out offensives thrown against them by German generalissimo Erich Ludendorff. The make-or-break offensives had been instigated by the entry of the United States into the war in April 1917. Ludendorff knew that it would be months before fresh troops from this new enemy would arrive at the front, so he was determined to defeat the Allies before the Americans could mobilize in earnest.

And he had reason to believe that he now had the men to do it. From the beginning of the war, the one ally that France and Britain, as well as Italy, counted on most heavily was Russia. True, its army was not the most modern and its generals not the most brilliant, but the nation had a vast population to draw on, and its available manpower was so great that the Western powers took to calling it the "Russian steamroller." Who could stop it? Yet from the beginning, the Russian army—inadequately equipped, poorly trained, miserably led, unwieldy because of its very size—withered under attack from generally smaller German forces. Even the Austro-Hungarian army, also ill-equipped and poorly led, often triumphed over the Russians.

The litany of Russian defeats weighed down the already faltering government of Czar Nicholas II, until, it seemed, the slightest breeze might blow it down. In March 1917 came the first of the year's Russian revolutions. The czar was pushed from the throne, and while the provisional government that replaced him vowed to continue the war, the people were agitating for peace, and mutinies within the army ranks became increasingly commonplace. In the winter, soon after Vladimir Illyich Lenin led the Bolshevik Revolution, his new communist government took Russia out of the war with the Treaty of Brest-Litovsk, an ignominious surrender to Germany. No longer having to fight on two fronts, Ludendorff could throw everything he had against the West.

The Russian army was not the only Allied force swept by defeatism, rebellion, and mutiny. In April and May, much of the French army turned mutinous after the bloody failure of its senseless "Nivelle Offensive," and, after suffering pointlessly through one Isonzo offensive after another, mutiny and desertion in the Italian ranks had also become epidemic. The worst crisis for the Italians began at 2 A.M. on October 24, 1917. The Twelfth Battle of the Isonzo—better known as the Battle of Caporetto—began with a massive Austro-German artillery barrage of high-explosive shells and poison gas. After six hours of this, a fierce infantry assault began, which penetrated the Italian line at several points. Subsequent infantry waves exploited the breaches and rolled up one Italian position after another with the heavy use of hand grenades and flame-throwers.

The violence of the Austro-German assault was utterly devastating on the already demoralized Italian troops. Men in the front lines either surrendered or fled. Cadorna made a bad situation worse by having positioned his reserves too far to the south to be brought into place rapidly, and, by nightfall, the attackers had penetrated a dozen miles, routing, killing, or capturing the defenders. Cadorna could do nothing but order a retreat to the Tagliamento River, yielding to the enemy a wide swath of Italian territory. Ten thousand Italian soldiers were killed in action at Caporetto, thirty thousand wounded, two hundred ninety-three thousand taken prisoner—and, most telling of all, four hundred thousand fled, deserting the ranks.

Count Luigi Cadorna, inept, brutal, and heartless commander in chief of the Italian forces during most of World War I.

(Image from the author's collection)

How was Mussolini, who claimed credit for having pushed Italy into the war, to respond to the current situation? Two things he did not do. He did not blame himself or other like-minded war-mongers. And he did not now use the pages of *Il Popolo d'Italia* to counsel anything resembling peace. War, even if it was going badly, was violence, and violence, for Mussolini, was always valuable, an opportunity never to be thrown away.

He considered interpreting the military crisis as an occasion to rally the masses to outright revolution against the civilian government. His first impulse was to incite a popular rebellion against parliament and parliamentary government. And in this he was not alone. Some other politicians—as well as Gen. Cadorna, unwilling to accept the blame for Caporetto and the lesser disasters that had led up to it—contemplated a coup d'etat, but Cadorna backed down and, ultimately, so did Mussolini.

Instead of using Caporetto as an occasion to overthrow the government, Mussolini, with his characteristic genius for inverting reality, decided to exploit this abject defeat—he dubbed it "the greatest military defeat in the history of the world"—as a call to victory.

Mussolini criticized Cadorna and other commanders for blaming Caporetto on the cowardice of the troops, thousands of whom they executed by firing squad. Instead, Mussolini wrote, army command should examine itself—not, however, for an absence of skill in the art of war or for having failed to provide equipment and training, but for a lack of zeal. The Italian army, he wrote, was defeated because the generals were secretly against the war. Rid the nation and the army of defeatists and defeatism, and Italians could not fail to be victorious. What Italy needed now, Mussolini declared, was discipline, universal and complete. What was needed in this crisis was a dictator who would, in a single stroke, do away with the pettifogging defeatism of parliament and militarize the entire nation.

But there was more. Italian discipline was to be energized and driven by hate. In August, before Caporetto, Mussolini had begun writing about the necessity of destroying Austria-Hungary. The ancient Roman writer and statesman Cato had proclaimed the famous battle cry, "Delenda est Cartago," Carthage must be destroyed. Mussolini echoed this in the headline of an article in *Il Popolo d'Italia:* "Delenda Austria." In August, this meant nothing more than ensuring the break-up of the Austro-Hungarian Empire—something, in fact, the Treaty of Versailles would later do. But, in October, after Caporetto, "Delenda Austria" became something more visceral. It now meant the utter destruction of Austria-Hungary, not in the name of granting independence to the peoples of Bohemia, Transylvania, Bosnia, and Italy, but as an expression of sheer, unbridled hatred.

Out of the blood and shame of Caporetto, four key elements of fascism were born. First, the myth of Italian invincibility and an irresistible will to power; second, the necessity of steel discipline; third, the necessity of absolute dictatorship to create and enforce steel discipline; and fourth, raw hatred to propel it all. The great enemy was not Austria and Germany, but defeatism—defeatism in parliament, defeatism among the socialists, defeatism among weak-kneed army officers.

Nor was Mussolini alone in the formulation of his new doctrine. In the wake of Caporetto, Gen. Cadorna was dismissed and replaced as general-in-chief by Gen. Armando Diaz, a much more competent commander who, with the help of French and British reinforcements sent to stem the tide of the Austro-German advance, managed to block the enemy at the Piave River. Among the contingent of Brits sent to Italy at this time was an intelligence officer, Lt. Col. Samuel Hoare, who decided that the bellicose fanaticism of Benito Mussolini was just the ticket to counter defeatism on the Italian front. Through an intermediary, Hoare contacted Mussolini about not only subsidizing *Il Popolo d'Italia* but also financing additional action against pacifists. According to Hoare's 1954 autobiography, Mussolini replied—again, through a third party—"Leave it to me. I will mobilize the *mutilati* in Milan, and they will break the heads of any pacifists who try to hold anti-war meetings in the streets."

This wasn't an idle boast. Hoare noted in his autobiography that Mussolini "was true to his word, the Fasci ... made short work of the Milanese pacifists." This may well have been the first time Mussolini mobilized the Fasci d'Azione Rivoluzionaria Inter-venista (Chapter 6, "*Avanti!*") to use the strong-arm tactics that would later become the stock in trade of the fascist *squadristi*.

This period also saw the birth of the association of anti-Semitism with fascism. Anti-Semitism would be a part of Hitler's Nazi philosophy from the beginning; *Mein Kampf* (*My Struggle*), published in 1924, was, among other things, a virulently anti-Semitic book. But Italy had no ingrained tradition of anti-Semitism—nor of ethnic or racial persecution generally—and, until late in his career, Mussolini was never a very enthusiastic Jew hater. He had to work himself up to it, deliberately, and he did so by identifying the Jews with the German enemy and, after the Treaty of Brest-Litovsk, with the Bolsheviks as well.

The European allies and the United States feared Bolshevism beyond all rationality, equating it with anarchy and seeing in it a threat not only to religion and capitalism, but to virtually any form of government, whether democracy or monarchy. Mussolini was by no means the first political journalist to notice that many Bolsheviks were Jews, but he boarded that bandwagon quickly and loudly trumpeted, in *Il Popolo d'Italia*, the phrase "Bolshevik Jews." The Bolshevik Jews, he wrote, were not only responsible for Russia's separate peace with Germany, but were actually agents of the Kaiser. Thus Mussolini began to write of "Jewish-German Bolshevism." The Treaty of Brest-Litovsk was not the desperate agreement of a beaten and infinitely war-weary nation, but a deliberate conspiracy for which Jews were ultimately responsible. At this point, Mussolini did not carry anti-Semitism any further—he did not incite beatings or persecution—but he had laid the foundation for these, giving Italians one more group to hate and, therefore, one more reason to continue fighting.

Concluded on March 3, 1918, Soviet Russia's "separate peace" with the Central Powers, the Treaty of Brest-Litovsk, not only took the Soviets out of the war, but delivered to Germany Poland, Lithuania, the Baltic Provinces, Finland, and the Ukraine, either by occupation or through the creation of puppet governments. The Bolsheviks signed away thirty-four percent of the Soviet population, thirty-two percent of the Soviet farmland, fifty-four percent of the Soviet industrial base, eighty-nine percent of Soviet coal mines, and almost all Soviet cotton and oil. Fortunately for the Soviet Union, the treaty was nullified by the terms of the 1918 armistice and the 1919 Treaty of Versailles.

It is a measure of the blithe ease with which Mussolini could espouse contradictory values that during this period, when he launched his first anti-Semitic campaign, his ongoing affair with Margherita Sarfatti, a Jew, became increasingly intense. Not only was she Mussolini's lover, but she was also his employee, a writer for *Il Popolo d'Italia,* now, in part, a vehicle of anti-Semitism. Did the paper's new message disturb her? There is no evidence that it did. As for Mussolini, he had no difficulty praising the heroism of Roberto Sarfatti, Margherita's son (as Mussolini was a married man, she was a married woman), who was killed in action in February 1918. Perhaps sharing his bed or dying on the Isonzo front were, for Mussolini, sufficient expiation for the sin of Judaism. Or perhaps he just failed to recognize the contradiction between what he wrote and how he lived.

Awareness of intellectual and moral contradiction, let alone being disturbed by such contradiction, requires commitment to ideology. Mussolini had started *Il Popolo d'Italia* as a breakaway socialist newspaper. That was his ideology. But, in short course, the war had torn away whatever ideological shreds still clung to Mussolini's journalism. As 1917 gave way to 1918, the paper was not only increasingly financed by the Allies and by the Italian war industry, it openly carried lucrative advertisements for big arms manufacturers. At the very least, socialism had fraternal links to Bolshevism and a common ideological foundation in Karl Marx. Mussolini, however, now wrote of Marxism as a "heap of ruins." He changed the original subtitle of the paper from "A Socialist Newspaper" to "The Newspaper of Combatants and Producers." Most dramatic of all was his new belief, voiced on the editorial page of his paper, that Karl Marx had been wrong to pronounce the death of capitalism. Far from being moribund, Mussolini declared, capitalism was just now in its early stages of development.

No wonder those great capitalist powers, Britain and France, had little trouble accepting Mussolini and his paper as an ally against pacifism. After the war, as fascism rose in the 1920s, some of Mussolini's greatest admirers would also include citizens of the greatest capitalist power of all, the United States. Among them Richard Washburn Child, the U.S. ambassador to Italy, who called Mussolini a great man and encouraged him to write *My Autobiography.* This despite the fact that Mussolini made no secret of his disdain for democracy—at least during wartime. He praised Premier Clemenceau of France, Prime Minister David Lloyd

George of England, and President Woodrow Wilson of the United States as "democratic dictators." In 1918 Mussolini declared that dictatorship was the very means required to achieve democracy.

Oxymorons such as "democratic dictators"—the more outrageous the better—were rhetorically indispensable to Mussolini, as was the crisis of war, which made such oxymorons possible, plausible, and even palatable. No British, French, or American statesman argued against Mussolini's advocacy of dictatorship. There was a war on, and Mussolini and his paper were proving themselves useful. The true scope of the insidious genius of Mussolini would become apparent only after the war, when he would successfully carry on the wartime atmosphere of crisis to enable him to continue equating dictatorship with choice, coercion with liberty, and state-enforced discipline with freedom. He could do this because the war had given totalitarianism and democracy a common enemy: first German militarism and then Russian Bolshevism, which Mussolini, remarkably enough, managed to identify not only with Lenin and the Jews, but with the German Kaiser as well. During the closing months of World War I and afterward, the fear of Bolshevism was so great as to make even Mussolini's most dictatorial, totalitarian, and hateful pronouncements seem preferable to the language of Lenin.

For now, though, Mussolini had more than competing ideologies to energize his journalism. Following Caporetto, he had the specter of defeat to fight against. After the new Italian commander, Diaz, held the line at Piave against an Austro-Hungarian offensive, then, on October 24, 1918, launched a counteroffensive that captured the town of Vittorio Veneto and sent the Austro-Hungarians into a panic-stricken rout, Mussolini had a glorious victory to celebrate. On November 3, Austria-Hungary asked for an armistice, and on November 11—at the eleventh hour or the eleventh day or the eleventh month—the Great War itself, on all fronts, came to an end.

Italy had lost in the war more than six hundred thousand men killed and well over a million severely wounded. For Italy, most of the war had been a losing proposition, a tragic slaughter. But, as Mussolini saw it, Vittorio Veneto made up for it all. As he had called Caporetto the worst military defeat in the history of the world, he now claimed, in *Il Popolo d'Italia,* that Vittorio Veneto was the greatest of all the victories of all the armies that had fought in the Great War. It made the war worth all the sacrifice. Surely, Italy would now take its place as the greatest of the great powers that had defeated the Germans and the Austro-Hungarians. This Mussolini felt and believed with every fiber of his being. And Mussolini, who had taken his place "as a fighter in my newspaper office," also believed that he would begin to become *the* man of destiny in this new and newly powerful Italy. In November 1918, he was not quite sure how the march to this destiny would begin, but he knew that its direction would be away from socialism, from Bolshevism, and, yes, away from political liberty, individual freedom, and democracy—outmoded concepts all.

Chapter 10

The Fasci di Combattimento

Six hundred thousand dead, more than a million wounded, almost a quarter-million disabled for life. As Mussolini (or his brother, for him) observed in *My Autobiography,* "There is not in our country one single family which during the forty-one months of the war had not placed in the holocaust, on the altar of the country, a part of itself."

At the end of 1918, Mussolini was well aware of the part he had played in egging on to war a reluctant and unenthusiastic Italy. If anything, he had an inflated view of his role in bringing about Italy's involvement in the war. Did he now regret it? Did he now feel guilt? There is no evidence for either, but he was concerned that the readers of *Il Popolo d'Italia* and the people of Italy in general would hold him and those like him responsible for the losses the nation had suffered. Accordingly—and understandably—he used his newspaper to trumpet the glorious victory of Vittorio Veneto, as if this single entry in the ledger book of war outbalanced bloodstained volumes of recorded losses.

Today, the world remembers Mussolini as Il Duce, a politician and a dictator, the inventor of fascism, but he was, first, foremost, and always, a journalist—and never a highly principled one at that. Although Mussolini always portrayed himself as a man of action, for him words more than deeds—more, even, than the results of deeds—were reality. If he proclaimed often enough and loudly enough that Vittorio Veneto was the greatest victory of all the victories of all the armies in the Great War, a victory that amply justified Italian sacrifices, then, he reasoned, this would be the truth. Vittorio Veneto, Mussolini wrote, was a triumph in what President Woodrow Wilson himself called a "war to end all wars." It brought to a victorious conclusion a struggle to liberate the oppressed and to emancipate the working classes, who could now look forward to "centuries of celestial felicity." Mussolini had advocated the methods of dictatorship to achieve victory, telling his readers that dictatorship was the road to democracy. Now that the war was won, he proclaimed it a victory *for* democracy in that it ended the reign of monarchs in Austria-Hungary and Germany.

None of this was all that different from what politicians and other apologists for the war were telling the masses in Britain, France, and America. The difference was that, in these countries, most of the people had more enthusiastically supported the war. Another difference between Italy and the other Allies became increasingly apparent in the course of hammering out the Treaty of Versailles in 1919.

In an extraordinary departure from diplomatic precedence and the law of nations, the Allies high-handedly informed Germany that it was to be excluded from the peace conference that commenced in January 1919. Germany would have no choice but to accept, without reservation and without negotiation, whatever terms the Allies dictated. Although twenty-seven Allied powers participated in the peace conference, proceedings were dominated by the so-called Big Four: Britain, France, the United States, and Italy. The truth of the matter was that the conference was dictated by a "Big Three"—Britain, France, and the United States—with Italy very much a junior member and expected to rubber stamp whatever Prime Minister Lloyd George, Premier Clemenceau, and President Wilson finally agreed to.

What they agreed to was the most momentously tragic document of the twentieth century. It was so punitive and humiliating to Germany and the other Central Powers that it ensured more than enough national misery to create a *second* world war. Germany was obliged to make great territorial cessions and to admit guilt for having started the war. It was compelled to disarm and to render to the Allies monetary reparations of impossibly staggering propor-tions. The empire of Germany was dismantled, and the reign of the house of Hohenzollern ended; Kaiser Wilhelm II was branded a war criminal. The object of the Treaty of Versailles was to destroy Germany once and for all as a threat to world peace. As for Austria-Hungary, it, too, was taken apart, and the centuries-old Hapsburg monarchy was torn down.

Mussolini and other pro-interventionists had no objection to the destruction and humiliation of Germany and Austria-Hungary, but they were shocked at the mean rump portion of the spoils of war the "Big Three" apportioned to Italy. The Treaty of Versailles gave Italy the Trentino and Trieste, but not—as promised in 1915—Fiume, the rest of Istria, Dalmatia, and the Dodecanese Islands. Nor was there to be the promised international recogni-tion of an Italian "zone of influence" in Albania. As for Jubaland in Africa, which Britain had pledged to cede in the secret Treaty of London, no action was taken. All those Italian dead, wounded, and mutilated had purchased nothing more than Austria-Hungary had promised Italy in exchange merely for neutrality. On balance, Italy had lost much and gained nothing by the war.

When the terms of the Treaty of Versailles were announced, Mussolini, with his customary effortlessness, turned one hundred eighty degrees from celebrating the glorious Italian victory to bemoaning the betrayal of what he called a "mutilated peace." During the war, Mussolini had gotten behind the government; now he denounced Prime Minister Orlando as a traitor. Although he still claimed to be a socialist—a *true* socialist—Mussolini denounced the Italian Socialist Party for its continued policy of internationalism, and when the party invited hungry children from Vienna to come to Italy, Mussolini fulminated. Italian children were also hungry, he cried. Why not raise money to feed *them?*

But it wasn't just the Orlando government and the Italian Socialist Party that Mussolini now attacked. He saw the other Allies—indeed, practically the entire world—as turning against Italy. Earlier, Mussolini had been an enthusiastic supporter of a league of nations. Now that the creation of the League of Nations was attached to the Treaty of Versailles, he saw it as an international plot to check Italian imperialism. This interpretation had an ethnic slant; for he called the League an instrument the Anglo-Saxon "race" had developed specifically to rob Italy of its "great imperial destiny."

In originally supporting the war, Mussolini had taken pains to demonstrate nonimperialism: Italy should be proud to realize no territorial gains from fighting this war to liberate the oppressed. Very soon, however, he altered this position: Italy should acquire new territories in order to liberate the oppressed people living in them. Now even that poor counterfeit of a nonimperialist war aim was dropped. Mussolini simply demanded that Italy annex Fiume and Dalmatia, with or without international consent. He also wanted to send military aid to the peoples of India, Egypt, and Ireland who were rebelling against the English—those perfidious Anglo-Saxons.

The fish market in Fiume, the Croatian city coveted by Italy after World War I.

(Image from ArtToday)

Sometimes Mussolini denied that his plea for conquest was in itself extravagantly imperialistic. It had nothing to do with imperialism, he argued. Taking Fiume, Dalmatia, and possessions in Africa was nothing more or less than an exercise of Italy's rights. For Mussolini, it was as if redefining imperialism as a nation's right changed the nature of imperialism. But sometimes he didn't even attempt this linguistic sleight of hand. Sometimes he didn't even bother to deny that he was urging Italy to pursue an imperialist course. The ideological contradictions simply didn't bother him.

What Mussolini learned early in his journalistic career was that even the boldest reversals and self-contradictions could be made palatable if they were sufficiently extreme and stated with sufficient vehemence. Extremism—especially as Mussolini wielded it—appealed to people. It excited them enough to outweigh any inconsistencies of position. Adolf Hitler would state a similar discovery in his *Mein Kampf* of 1924: "In view of the primitive simplicity of their minds, (the masses) more easily fall a victim to a big lie than to a little one." Mussolini found out the secret of the "big lie" much earlier than Hitler did.

As Mussolini did not apologize or express regret at the end of 1918 for having helped pull Italy into war, arguing instead that Italy had gained great things from its sacrifices, so now he did not apologize, even after adopting the position that Italy's sacrifices seemed to be coming to nothing. The war, he insisted, had been right—whatever the cost—but socialists, internationalists, the English, maybe most of the world were conspiring to rob Italy of what was right. Mussolini realized that, in depriving Italy of its "rights," Versailles had given him a great gift: an occasion for popular discontent and outrage, the most fertile soil in which to grow a new political party.

He decided to graft the new party on the sapling trunk of the Fasci d'Azione Rivoluzionaria Interventista, the political organization he had not founded but had come to dominate in 1915. He liked the idea of "fascism," which, at this point, was chiefly the concept of lowly, disenfranchised people, individually powerless, banding together like the bundle of sticks bound in the ancient

Roman *fasces*, the mighty cudgel that served as the emblem of the Roman Senate. Once tightly tied, those sticks, fragile in their individuality, became unbreakable. Mussolini changed the wartime name of the party that met for the first time on March 23, 1919, in the offices of the Circolo dell'Alleanza Industriale e Commerciale in the Piazza San Sepolcro, Milan. He called it the Fasci di Combattimento, which may best be translated as the "Bundles of Combat."

In later years, after fascism was a well-established fact of Italian life, this meeting at the Piazza San Sepolcro would be spoken of in reverent tones, and those who had attended it were referred to collectively as the *Sansepolcristi*. At the height of fascist corruption and cronyism, being a *Sansepolcrista* landed one a high party or government position, a better salary, and many other perks. Hundreds laid claim to the title, although Mussolini remembered that only about fifty people were present at the March 23 meeting. He was, in fact, profoundly disappointed by the poor turnout, and he was even more discouraged by the scant attention the national press and established politicians paid to the meeting of his new party.

It is little wonder that the Fasci di Combattimento at first drew little notice. Times were turbulent, the nation was reeling from the war, factions and fanatics were everywhere. What was this new so-called "party" but a miscellaneous gathering of anarchists, communists, syndicalists, republicans, nationalists, Catholics, and liberals? The only truly distinctive faction among the Fasci were the "Futurists," led by the artist Filippo Tommaso Marinetti. He had coined the word "Futurism" in his 1909 "manifesto" (it was really a tract on modern art) written and titled in French *Le Futurisme*. He intended the manifesto as a wake-up call to his countrymen, whom he scolded (in his borrowed French) for having worn "second-hand clothes for too long." It was time for Italians to create a new art, an art that embodied the beauty of speed and that glorified the violence of war.

Marinetti, in fact, defined art as the essence of violence, cruelty, and injustice. He soon attracted a following of other artists, who wrote manifestos not only on a wide range of aesthetic subjects, but on all aspects of everyday life, including clothing, food, odors, war, and sex. By the time he and some of his followers joined the Fasci di Combattimento, Marinetti aimed not merely to reinvent art, but life itself. In the population of the modern, technological world, he saw the opportunity to create a new race of human beings, machine-extended, technological creatures.

If the voice of the Futurists was the most prominent and most provocatively extreme heard in the initial meetings of the Fasci, it hardly resulted in a political philosophy that reinvented humankind. Instead, early fascist ideas, while progressive, were not terribly bold or even unconventional. The Fasci shared an anticlerical point of view, they opposed the Church, and they wanted the government to nationalize and confiscate Church property not used directly in worship. They wanted to see an end to the monarchy, but they did not favor a dictatorship or any other form of arbitrary, absolute, central power. The judiciary was to be independent of any other branch of government. The Fasci further demanded an end to any sort of censorship, whether on moral, religious, or political grounds. Mussolini summed up the fascist credo as "above all … libertarian."

The first meeting resolved to demand suffrage for all Italians over the age of eighteen, without regard to property ownership. Women were to be given the vote as well as men. The first meeting also called for reform of the Chamber of Deputies, the lower house of the Italian parliament. A system of proportional representation was to be demanded, and the qualifying age for election as a deputy was to be lowered from thirty-one to twenty-five. The upper house of parliament, the Senate, was to be abolished, and newly elected deputies were to form a National Assembly to draw up a new constitution for Italy. For the present, it was agreed that the constitution would guarantee an eight-hour workday. The meeting also resolved that Fiume and Dalmatia had to be given to Italy.

Once in power, and despite earlier promises, Mussolini did not give women the vote. In a 1932 interview with biographer Emil Ludwig, he observed that people would "laugh at him" if he introduced woman suffrage into Italian life. Indeed, Mussolini's continual concern with his nation's declining birthrate prompted him to urge a rollback of female emancipation. A woman's place was in the home—and as a breeder. In 1926, he specified twelve children as the ideal for a fascist mother; Italy needed soldiers. Abortion and birth control were severely punished, a tax was levied on "unjustified celibacy," and infection with syphilis was made a criminal offense. Mussolini also encouraged women to give up such "masculine sports" as riding, skiing, and cycling, which, he believed, had an adverse effect on fertility and would lure women away from "their natural and fundamental mission in life," bearing children. As for suffrage, Italian women would not get the vote until 1945.

In subsequent meetings, the platform of the Fasci di Combattimento would come to include some changes that were more sweeping and more radical, including the redistribution of land (a "land-to-the-peasants" movement) and the inclusion of worker representatives on the boards of industrial management. In due course, the Fasci called for a progressive tax on capital, an increase in the rate of taxes on inheritances, government confiscation of excessive war profits, nationalization of certain lands, industries, and factories, a fixed minimum wage, and a general decentralization of government. At first, the Fasci even supported the League of Nations—although this was mainly out of respect for Woodrow Wilson, who was extraordinarily popular among Italians.

These were all proposals any good socialist would be pleased to sponsor, and Mussolini found himself wondering how the public would ever distinguish the fascist platform from that of Italian socialism. The answer came to him on April 15, 1919.

Among the disparate groups whose members gravitated to the Fasci di Combattimento were loosely constituted bands—gangs, really—of discharged soldiers known as the *arditi*, the "intrepid ones." The *arditi* of postwar Italy were roughly similar to the *Freikorps* of postwar Germany, although not nearly as well organized. The *Freikorps* was a collection of private armies recruited by former senior officers in the demobilized German army originally for the purpose of defending Germany's borders against what was believed to be an impending invasion by the Soviet Red Army. After this menace seemed to have passed, the *Freikorps* took it upon itself to oppose homegrown attempts at revolution in Germany by beating up—or killing—left-wing radicals and demonstrators. Ferruccio Vecchi, a member of the Fasci di Combattimento, was an *arditi* leader. On April 15, with Marinetti, he led the *arditi* in an attack on the offices of the socialist newspaper—and Mussolini's former employer—*Avanti!* They destroyed a printing press, a linotype machine, and the paper's subscription list. Then the violence spread to the street, and a riot erupted.

Mussolini did not participate in the April 15 operation, but he subsequently proclaimed it the commencement of the "fascist revolution." In truth, it was little more than an act of vandalism followed by a street brawl—although it did teach Mussolini two important lessons. First, he observed that the police favored the *arditi* at the expense of the socialists. Officers' batons found their mark far more frequently on socialist skulls than on those of the militant war veterans. Second, although many socialists spoke of violent revolution, almost all were, at heart, pacifists. Mussolini realized that he did not have to out-argue the socialists, nor even create a political platform radically different from theirs. All that was necessary to take their place as the dominant opposition party in Italy was to beat them—not with ideas, nor even with rhetoric, but with fists, clubs, knives, and guns. After the April 15 riot, Mussolini began recruiting his own force of *arditi*, and, using funds from *Il Popolo d'Italia*, he purchased military-surplus arms and ammunition on the cheap. His editorial offices were soon transformed into a small arsenal and armory.

Assuming the Fasci could displace the Italian Socialists as the chief opposition party in Italy, how would they then manage to compete with the mainstream parties, the Conservatives, the Liberals, and the Catholic People's Party? Although the events of April 15 were encouraging, branches of the Fasci disappeared almost as soon as they sprung up. By the end of August 1919, there were sixty-seven local Fasci throughout Italy, but by the end of the year, this number had been reduced by more than half, to thirty-one local Fasci cells. The total membership of the Fasci di Combattimento as of December 1919 was eight hundred seventy individuals. Based on the rise and sudden decline in numbers, the party seemed a sure bet to disappear.

Italians are individualists. Only with the greatest of difficulty and in the direst circumstances, Mussolini concluded, could they be brought together in unified action. The world war had furnished at least the semblance of a common enemy against which Italy mobilized, however reluctantly. In 1919, with the war over, Mussolini's Fasci di Combattimento needed for their survival a new common enemy to unite the people against. Versailles had produced discontent and outrage, which was very good indeed, but now that energy needed the focus of a very specific menace.

It wasn't hard to find. In 1919 the entire world was swept by two epidemics. One was the so-called Spanish flu, which threatened to become a modern Black Death and which did, in fact, kill almost twenty-two million people worldwide. The other "epidemic" struck many as no less terrifying. It was called international Bolshevism—not a Black Death, but a Red Menace. Vladimir Lenin and his associates were bent on ensuring that Russia's communist revolution would explode on an international scale. Italy, like every Western government, groped frantically for an effective way to oppose the *Comintern*, the international communist movement. Few, however, had faith that the Italian government could mount an effective defense against the communists any more than it could fight off the flu. Thus Mussolini had found the common enemy, and, for his purposes, enemies were always far more valuable than friends.

Chapter 11

An Enemy for Everyone

Socialism and communism have more in common than they
have significant differences. The socialism of Mussolini's father
and of young Mussolini himself was not vastly different from what
Lenin preached. Karl Marx lay at the core of socialism and communism, the same Marx whose image was stamped on the medal
Mussolini faithfully carried in his otherwise empty pocket during
his "wander-life" as a young radical (Chapter 3, "Wander-Life").

Up to, into, and through the Great War, Mussolini strongly differed with the Italian Socialist Party, but, even after he was
expelled from the party, he continued to call himself a socialist.
Now, however, in the discontented aftermath of the war, when
the Treaty of Versailles denied Italy what Mussolini and many
others believed the nation had paid for in blood, he saw less and
less advantage in calling himself a socialist. Communism—
Bolshevism—was widely seen as a threat, and socialists were
increasingly identified as agents of that threat.

Mussolini now wanted to distance his fascists from socialists and
socialism. Was this the result of an intellectual and philosophical
evolution in his thinking? Maybe. More likely, though, it was a
product of his recognition that the socialists were becoming
increasingly identified with the "common enemy," Bolshevism,
and, because of this, he now had an opportunity to elevate fascism
at the expense of socialism. It mattered little that the fascist ideas
and political platform, at least as articulated so far, were not

dramatically different from socialist ideology. What mattered was that people were starting to see socialists as Bolsheviks and, therefore, bad; whereas they were prepared to see any force that opposed Bolshevism as good. The details of political philosophy were unimportant. It was the broad, brute concepts of *bad, good, opposition,* and *force* that counted.

The socialists looked at the disappointing results of the Great War and told the legions of Italian veterans—many burdened by unemployment and poverty in the economic depression of postwar Italy—that they had been duped to fight and die in a war for the bourgeoisie. They were, according to the socialists, not heroes, but victims.

If this message had been intended to rouse the masses of unemployed and underemployed ex-servicemen to angry rebellion against the government and to rally them to the cause of international socialism, the party was dreadfully misguided. Veterans felt insulted, and they voiced their hatred of the socialists, melding this hatred with fear of Bolshevism. For their part, the socialists began acting in ways that truly merited the hatred of the veterans. Vilified by the veterans, socialist activists responded in kind, denouncing the ex-soldiers with increasing volume and vehemence. Socialist workers even physically attacked veterans. There were murders.

Strikes, the favorite socialist weapon, became rampant. Socialist railroad engineers and train crews often refused to operate trains that carried military men or even ex-military men as passengers. (Priests, too, were sometimes asked to leave trains.) Labor actions were not confined to the railways. Strikes hit all industries and services, crippling an already beleaguered economy.

The veterans and their supporters did not take socialist abuse lying down. Spontaneously, they formed themselves into gangs of *arditi,* sometimes called *squadristi.* Mussolini observed that these groups were true paramilitary forces, fiercer and more effective fighters than the socialists. For every blow the veterans received, the *arditi* and *squadristi* dealt back a dozen.

All of this came as a great gift to Benito Mussolini. He could set aside the niceties of ideology and simply declare fascism's opposition to socialism. On the strength of this, he could then recruit members from among the *arditi* and *squadristi*. Much as he had done in 1915 with the Fasci d'Azione Rivoluzionaria Intervenista, Mussolini leaped into an already operational movement—the *arditi* and *sqaudristi*—and came to dominate it.

As mentioned in the previous chapter, the editor of *Il Popolo d'Italia* stockpiled weapons and munitions in his office. At first, he took the precaution of hiding in bookcases and the like such items as grenades and bombs, but soon the stockpile outgrew the available hiding places, and Mussolini simply heaped material on tables in the room reserved for his copy editors and editorial assistants. As a youth and young man, Mussolini drank and smoked heavily. As he became increasingly serious about politics, he drank less— eventually becoming a teetotaler—and smoked little. In 1919, however, he still used cigarettes, and Margherita Sarfatti recalled one occasion when Mussolini, intent on other matters in the office, absent-mindedly set his lighted cigarette atop a grenade or bomb. Sarfatti, presumably in some excitement, pointed this out— and the two had a good laugh.

A cavalier attitude toward weapons and explosives was not the only macho affectation Mussolini cultivated during this period. He took up fencing, practicing for hours in the courtyard of the *Popolo* offices. His purpose was to prepare himself for the duels to which he planned to challenge politicians and others who insulted Fascism. (Indeed, such duels would come.) He practiced with firearms as well, and, perhaps under the influence of the speed- and technology-loving Futurists in the party, Mussolini took flying lessons.

The stockpiling of weapons, the smoking around bombs, the preparation for duels, and then the flying lessons—one wonders whether Mussolini was merely cultivating a hyper-virile image as a "man of danger" or whether he had a genuine death wish. His interest in flying developed *after* the crash of a large plane in Verona had caused the deaths of sixteen, had (according to

Mussolini) plunged all Italy into mourning, and led Italian authorities to discuss banning most aviation. Mussolini was horrified at
the thought that Italy would bar itself from exploiting the air with
the new, fast machines. He *had* to learn to fly, not to gratify himself, not to exhibit his courage, not to defy (or invite) death, but to
save Italy! Shortly before he obtained his pilot's license, he was
involved in a serious crash, which put him on crutches for several
weeks.

For all his macho posturing, however, Mussolini was upstaged in
September 1919 by Gabriele D'Annunzio. The poet, playwright,
and novelist commanded a loyal following among fans of his literary output as well as admirers of his passionate nationalism. He had
been much more effective than Mussolini in rousing Italy to join
the Allies in the Great War, and he had cut, in that conflict, a far
more dashing figure than Mussolini. He served in several branches
of the Italian military, always seeking out the most dangerous
assignments. Whereas Mussolini had been wounded in the but-
tocks and thigh during what amounted to an artillery exercise,
D'Annunzio gallantly lost an eye in real air-to-air combat. Now,
while Mussolini and others whined about being robbed of Fiume
(today the Croatian town of Rijeka) by the Treaty of Versailles,
D'Annunzio decided to *do* something about it. He mustered some
three hundred men, mostly mutineers from the Italian army, near
Trieste on September 12, then marched on Fiume and occupied it.
D'Annunzio proclaimed himself "commandant" of what he dubbed
the "Reggenza Italiana del Carnaro."

Mussolini found himself in a delicate position. On the one
hand, he wanted a share of the acclaim D'Annunzio was receiving
for his bold act. On the other hand, the Italian government could
certainly end the occupation of Fiume by a mere three hundred
men any time it chose to do so, and, depending on how this was
done, the whole episode might end up appearing a humiliating,
even rather ludicrous, defeat. As he had done before, most notably
in the case of the vandalism of the *Avanti!* offices (Chapter 10,
"The Fasci di Combattimento"), Mussolini hung back and
watched waiting to decide when and how he might claim credit for
some part of the Fiume action. He had earlier discussed with

D'Annunzio the feasibility of raiding Fiume, and now, from Fiume, D'Annunzio wrote him a letter in which he chided Mussolini for his "cowardice" in failing to join him. Mussolini published the letter in *Il Popolo d'Italia*—minus the unflattering reference.

This 1919 political cartoon by O. Gulbransson, titled "Fiume," depicts Gabriele D'Annunzio, seated on his rocking horse, pricking the idealistic bubbles President Woodrow Wilson blows at the Versailles treaty conference.

(Image from ArtToday)

The mere fact that he published correspondence from D'Annunzio, Mussolini hoped, would bathe him and fascism in a heroic nationalist light. The reflected glory of men like D'Annunzio, dashing and histrionic, could be very valuable to the leader of a rising political movement. Yet men like D'Annunzio were always dangerous because they could so easily outshine such an aspiring leader. As early as 1919, D'Annunzio may have raised the topic of a march on Rome. Mussolini temporized, and his hesitation drove some impulsive fascists to line up behind D'Annunzio. Mussolini did not want D'Annunzio to steal his thunder or preempt his fascist revolution, yet he was not ready himself to lead a march on Rome. In this, he certainly showed good judgment. For he lacked the manpower to carry off anything resembling a coup d'etat. For the moment, then, he placated D'Annunzio by assuring him that he had a plan to capture a number of cities and to make D'Annunzio honorary president of an Italian republic. He explained that part of this plan was first to secure the support of Italy's army and navy before marching on Rome, and he further cautioned D'Annunzio against making any radical move now, just before the November elections, in which he expected the fascist candidates to claim many parliamentary seats.

D'Annunzio acquiesced, continued to occupy Fiume, and refrained from agitating further for a march on Rome. In the meantime, Mussolini used *Il Popolo d'Italia* to raise money to support the Fiume occupation, but he also diverted a large amount of the incoming cash to finance his own election campaign.

> Gabriele D'Annunzio (1863–1938) was Italy's most celebrated living poet, novelist, and dramatist. He was renowned for his richly sensuous imagery and innovative use of the Italian language—although detractors pointed out that his works tended to be shallow and histrionic. A heroic flier during World War I, he led an illegal expedition against Fiume after the war and established a minor dictatorship opposed by both the Italian government and the rest of Europe. D'Annunzio cut such a dashing figure that Mussolini simultaneously courted his support and feared him as a rival. But D'Annunzio had little taste for the political life. After the initial glory of a conquest faded, he lost interest in the enterprise, and he was never very active in the Fascist Party nor as a competitor for Mussolini's power. The Duce appointed him president of the Royal Italian Academy in 1937, but he died before taking office.

The fascists put up a substantial slate of candidates for parliament, including Mussolini and the enormously popular opera and symphony conductor Arturo Toscanini. The campaign was marked by violence, which Mussolini enthusiastically encouraged in the pages of his newspaper. Despite all the noise, however, Mussolini was stunned by disappointment when he polled 4,637 votes against the socialist candidate's one hundred sixty thousand. The November 16, 1919, elections made the Socialist Party the biggest in Italy, with one hundred fifty-six seats in the Chamber of Deputies. The Catholic People's Party (also called the Popular Party) came in second with one hundred one seats. Lesser parties claimed a few miscellaneous seats, while the fascists won not a single seat.

That night, socialist demonstrators paraded in front of the Mussolini home, bearing torches and a coffin. They shouted that the coffin contained the body of Mussolini's political career. *Avanti!* reported on the day after the election: "There is a corpse in a state of putrefaction, which has been fished out of the canal. We are talking about Benito Mussolini."

To make matters worse for Mussolini, *arditi* leader Feruccio Vecchi and other fascists were arrested for storing arms intended either to help D'Annunzio in Fiume or to carry out a coup d'etat in Rome. Francesco Nitti, Italy's timid current Prime Minister, warned the prefect of Milan that it was a dangerous step to arrest prominent political figures, and Vecchi was released the next day. The others were held longer, but never formally charged.

Mussolini was disappointed by the dismal showing of the fascists in the elections of 1919, but he did not let this defeat diminish the volume or vehemence of his journalism. He continued to support D'Annunzio's occupation of Fiume, and, in June 1920, he denounced the incoming prime minister, Giovanni Giolitti, for making one of his very first acts an order for Italian troops to evacuate the port of Valona, Albania. In 1916, during the war, an Italian force had occupied Albania to fight Austrian invaders. With the end of the war, and in violation of the Treaty of Versailles, the troops stayed on. By and by, under international pressure, they withdrew from all parts of Albania—except Valona. The Italian troops repulsed an Albanian attempt to retake the port town before Giolitti ordered them to leave. The Socialist Party applauded the evacuation.

Shortly after the evacuation of Valona, violence broke out in the Dalmatian town of Split. Croatians attacked Italian settlers and murdered an Italian naval officer. In retaliation, on July 13, Trieste-based fascists burned down that city's Balkan Hotel, the center of Slav cultural activity. In Rome, on the twenty-first, fascists torched the Rome office of *Avanti!* Mussolini extravagantly praised both of these actions in *Il Popolo d'Italia,* and while the Italian government condemned them, the police took little or no action to find, let alone punish, the perpetrators.

The socialists complained of the pro-fascist bias of the government and its police. That the police customarily went easy on fascists did not come as news to Mussolini. Indeed, it heartened him after the miserable election results, for he understood where the bias came from: an ever-growing fear of Bolshevism. On March 21, 1919, the communists had seized power in Hungary, installing a regime that was soon overthrown by Adm. Niklos Horthy, who installed himself as dictator of a right-wing government.

As Mussolini saw it, the experience of Hungary had three lessons for Italian fascism. First, the possibility of a communist coup d'etat was very real, and Hungary wasn't far from Italy. Second, Horthy had shown that strong, violent, right-wing leadership was effective at countering communism. Third, an important element of such leadership was anti-Semitism. Much as Mussolini had done earlier, Horthy identified communism with Judaism. This third lesson gave Mussolini what he needed to link Bolshevism to a group many people distrusted if not hated outright. It also provided an opportunity to connect Bolshevism with an international conspiracy and simultaneously to divorce it from identification with the rights and welfare of the working class.

During the world war, Mussolini had found it effective to identify Bolshevism with German Jews. Now that the war was over, it was far more persuasive to show that Bolshevism was the product not of German Jews, but of an *international* Jewish conspiracy. Not only, then, did Bolshevism have nothing to offer the working man, it was actually a plot by which Jews the world over planned their vengeance against Christianity. Here, it seemed to Mussolini, was the perfect enemy with which to associate socialism and against which to define fascism.

There were just two snags. First, a number of Jewish businessmen found fascism very appealing because it seemed an effective way to oppose socialism as well as communism, both of which fomented strikes and economic instability and, ultimately, threatened the end of capitalism. These Jewish businessmen began contributing to the Fascist Party and to *Il Popolo d'Italia*. Second, Italians were not really inclined to be anti-Semitic. In Germany, Austria, and France, anti-Semitism was well established, a centuries-old institution. This was not the case in Italy, which had a tradition of general toleration. So, after flirting with anti-Semitism, Mussolini, in the October 19, 1920, issue of *Il Popolo d'Italia*, wrote an article repudiating the very proposition he himself had tendered, that Bolshevism was a product of an international Jewish conspiracy.

In any case, events beginning in the summer of 1920 made it less necessary to gild the lily of political threat by adding the notion of Jewish conspiracy to Bolshevism. An epidemic of violent, economy-paralyzing strikes demonstrated that Bolshevism and socialism were enemy enough, with or without the Jews. All over Italy, workers seized factories, and some raised red flags over the plants they struck and occupied. All through the summer and fall, many factories were held by workers, management locked out, production halted. Prime Minister Giolitti refused to send troops to evict the workers and instead summoned factory owners and trade union representatives to meet under his auspices in Rome. Giolitti directed the factory owners to give the workers the higher wages they demanded and to share management responsibility with them. Feeling blackmailed, the owners caved in. Although production began again as 1920 drew to a close, higher wages and other concessions caused profits to slump. The Italian stock exchange crashed, and the value of the lira plummeted. Italy seemed on the verge of a Red revolution.

Most revolutions crystallize around the disenfranchised classes, the peasants, or the proletariat. The crisis in the Italian economy, brought on by action of the working class, spread panic throughout the upper and middle classes. These were people who, a year earlier, would never have dreamed of joining something called the Fasci di Combattimento. But they did now. For the government, the Prime Minister, and the king, Vittore Emmanuelle III, all were failing: All had failed to stem economic collapse, and all would fail to stop a Bolshevik revolution in Italy. More and more, people were prepared to believe that the fascists had the method and the muscle to reverse the decline and stop the socialists and the communists. True, many in the middle and upper classes did not approve of fascist criticism of the king, nor of fascist rants against the Catholic Church, but they were willing to overlook these foibles if the party really was able to take control of the present situation.

Mussolini was eager to give the impression that this was precisely what he would do: take control of the situation. But how, without a single seat in parliament?

Before the war, Mussolini had criticized many of his socialist comrades for insisting on the necessity of working within the parliamentary system. The fascists had lost the election. Very well, but so what? The fascists could work *outside* the parliament. After all, Mussolini had a whole office full of political tools more powerful than votes, than rights, than laws.

Chapter 12

Black Shirts, Beatings, and the Poetry of Terror

By the end of 1919 and beginning of 1920, *arditi* and *squadristi* routinely clashed in the streets with socialists. In Mussolini's later accounts of this period, he gave the impression that this was all part of a "fascist revolution" he personally orchestrated. Actually, at this time, the *arditi* and *squadristi* were independent of the Fascist Party, although increasing numbers of these groups were joining the party. Mussolini repeatedly identified himself with the activities of *arditi* and *squadristi*, but he didn't direct or even instigate most of their actions. Indeed, Mussolini was not even the sole acknowledged leader of the Fasci di Combattimento at this point.

The movement was quite decentralized, consisting of local groups, *fasci* (singular, *fascio*), each run by a local boss—"leader" is too dignified a term—nicknamed a *ras*. The word was borrowed from Italy's hitherto dismal experience of warfare with Ethiopia— then called Abyssinia—whose local chieftains were called *ras*. Some *ras* willingly subordinated themselves to the central authority of Mussolini, but many others acted independently. In some of the more remote *fasci*, the name of Benito Mussolini was hardly known, if at all.

As with leadership and organization, the politics of the Fasci di Combattimento was also a highly fluid matter. The party had put together a platform for the 1919 elections that closely resembled socialism. In fact, even in 1920, when pressed, Mussolini still called himself a socialist, albeit a dissident one, even as he sanctioned the vandalism and beatings meted out against members of the Socialist Party. As one of Mussolini's modern biographers, Denis Mack Smith, points out, some observers of the fascists at this time "were reminded of the magic mirror in which everyone, whether militaristic reactionary or extreme pacifist on the left, could see his heart's desire."

Nevertheless, by 1920, it was becoming clear to Mussolini that the international encroachment of the common enemy, Bolshevism, was shifting the popular center of gravity in Italy from the left to the right. The Socialist Party remained firmly anchored to the left. It was, therefore, advantageous for the fascists—even those, like Mussolini, who still persisted in calling themselves dissident socialists—to move to the right.

In an effort to explain the "prelude" to World War II, general histories of the years between the wars typically speak of the great right-wing ideologies, fascism and Nazism, struggling with great left-wing ideologies, socialism and communism, for control of Europe. But the reality was never so neat. Fascism did not begin as a right-wing ideology, but as a dissident movement overlapping socialism, nationalism, imperialism, and anything else that embodied discontent with the powers that be. In 1919–20, the *fasci* included members on both ends of the political spectrum and everything in between. All that united them was an unshakable commitment to violence.

In Bolshevism, Mussolini found a common enemy on which he could focus the violence of fascism and thereby take greater control of the movement. When we study the careers of some of the other major leaders of the interwar period, Franklin D. Roosevelt, Winston Churchill, even Adolf Hitler, we find distinct, passionately held beliefs. Roosevelt and Churchill opposed the extreme right wing and extreme left wing because they considered such ideologies immoral, dangerous, and destructive. Hitler's various animosities were visceral to the point of madness and beyond. For Mussolini, however, opposition to a particular ideology did not spring from deeply held convictions or gut instincts, but from a sense of how such an opposition might make him more powerful. Many Italians feared Bolshevism and believed it was a great force of unmitigated evil. Mussolini, however, did not seriously believe that Italy was in danger of becoming a Bolshevik country. He did not see in Italy anyone of the caliber of Lenin or Trotsky capable of initiating, let alone sustaining, a communist revolution.

Mussolini neither hated nor feared communism. If anything, the modern politician he most admired was Vladimir Illyich Lenin. Publicly, in the pages of *Il Popolo d'Italia*, Mussolini might have criticized Lenin for his totalitarian tyrannies, for denying Russians freedom of speech, for outlawing strikes, for closing the opposition press; but privately he admired him for doing these things. Lenin was a successful revolutionary—and a successful dictator. Mussolini studied him closely. But even as he did so, he fostered, promoted, and reinforced the fear among Italians that a Bolshevik revolution was imminent. More important, he took every opportunity to show how Italy's present government was powerless to stem the tide of Bolshevism, whereas he and the fascists could and would do just that.

How?

Not by ineffectual laws and decrees, but by swift, efficient, focused violence.

Mussolini saw it happening already. In the major industrial cities of the north, socialists claimed large majorities in the November 1919 elections. In Ferrara, for example, the socialist-dominated city council lowered Italy's tricolor from the city hall flagpole and raised the red flag there instead. Local families were urged to stop naming their children after the traditional Catholic saints, and begin drawing on the heroes of socialism, from Spartaco (Spartacus) to Lenin. The Ferranese city council even changed the official day of rest from the Lord's Sunday to the Worker's Monday. Actions such as these were sufficient to provoke the formation of a *fascio* in Ferrara in October 1920 and to attract to it a youthful, violent membership.

Italo Balbo, a dashing young war veteran who had been a committed Republican and interventionist, became a leader of the local *fascio* and spearheaded actions that included tearing down the red flag at city hall and replacing it with the tricolor and generally meting out gang beatings to communists and socialists. When a band of communists ambushed a group of fascists near the city's favorite fascist hangout, Café Mozzi, killing three, the fledgling *fascio* suddenly had a trinity of martyrs. Fourteen thousand people turned out for the fascists' funeral on December 20, 1920, and membership in the *fascio* exploded from three hundred before the funeral to three thousand by the end of December. Thrust into the local and then national spotlight, Balbo would become one of the most visible of Italy's fascists—both an ally and a threat to Benito Mussolini.

In other cities, similar, if less dramatic, incidents occurred, and not always pitting fascists against socialists. In Lucca, for example, the Catholic People's Party—the "Popular Party"—won a majority and decided to hoist over city hall its party's flag, white instead of red, in place of the national tricolor. Fascists tore it down and raised the tricolor, triggering street violence.

Nor was the violence confined to the cities. Major landowners, especially in the Po Valley, were confronted by socialist activists demanding that the large estates be broken up and the land redistributed for farming by peasant collectives. In the province of Ferrara, many of the smaller landowners as well as tenants of the major landowners had already been intimidated into joining socialist collectives. The major landowners, about twenty rich and powerful men who called themselves the agrarians, appealed to local fascists for help. Count Dino Grandi, a prominent fascist and the leader of a local squad, answered the agrarians' call.

Italo Balbo, in the uniform of marshal of the Italian air force, in the late 1920s.

(*Image from the Library of Congress*)

Grandi explained to them that fascists believed the land should belong to those who farm it. Now, had Grandi been a socialist, this would have been the end of it. The discussion would have gone no further. But while proclaiming allegiance to the working class and peasantry, fascists never scrupled over working with the rich and powerful. Grandi persuaded the agrarians to begin charging their tenant farmers more reasonable rents. This would placate the peasants while avoiding the necessity of breaking up the large estates. Once the agrarians had agreed to this, Grandi led his *squadristi* in vicious assaults on the socialists in the collectives. The beatings readily persuaded the peasants to give up the collectives and accept reduced rents from the agrarians. It wasn't so much that Grandi presented them with a better idea, it was that he made the fascists seem a more intimidating force than the socialists, and by early 1921 the collectives had been dissolved.

Balbo and Grandi led the most active *squadristi*—they were rarely called *arditi* then—and they became both increasingly paramilitary and tribal in character. They developed esprit de corps through singing rousing marching songs, paramountly "Giovinezza" ("Youth"), a traditional tune sung before World War I by youngsters hiking through the Italian countryside, then adopted during the war by the troops (grown into young adulthood), and now by the *squadristi,* most of whom were veterans. By the early 1920s, the lyrics had been modified as the unofficial anthem of fascism.

The emphasis of the fascist lyrics was on freedom—"Fascism is the salvation of our liberty"—and the *squadristi* groups had every reason to feel free. They were free to choose, by informal election or acclamation, their squad leaders, and they were free to raid socialist gatherings, doling out beatings, burning down newspaper offices and meeting halls, and committing the occasional murder—typically without fear of police or other official interference and, often, even with the expectation of aid from these sources.

The emphasis was on arson and speed. During the first quarter of 1921, *squadristi* conducted fifty-seven organized raids and burned down twenty-five buildings. When they were not burning buildings, they sped about on motorcycles, often deliberately veering into individual socialists and groups of socialists, threatening to run them down. Although each fascist squad had a leader—a boss, a *ras*—the real terror derived not from organization, but from the opposite sense, that the violence was only loosely directed, barely controlled, and always threatening to explode.

Bizarrely, there was also a slapstick element to the fascist violence. Added to the *squadristi*'s arsenal of motorized harassment, beatings, arson, and outright murder was the forcible administration of castor oil. Several fascists would pin down a socialist or communist and pour a large quantity of castor oil down his throat. The result, of course, was violent diarrhea—at the very least an excruciating humiliation, but sometimes worse, even fatal, especially when the *squadristi* began mixing diesel fuel with the castor oil. Nevertheless, later apologists for fascism contrasted the relatively "innocent" practice of administering laxatives to political opponents with the far more brutal methods employed by the Bolsheviks and by the Nazis. Anyone who looks back at the terrorist methods of the fascists is struck by their peculiar combination of unbridled brutality and coarse comedy, apparently incompatible elements that were present in fascism from the beginning. One wonders if they were deliberately blended or just a happy accident in the recipe of the movement's appeal, for the simultaneous presence of grim violence and violent comedy allowed Italy and the world to see fascism as a combination of ruthless, irresistible efficiency and earthy joviality. The collocation of these jarring elements is most vividly symbolized in the many profile and partial-profile photographic portraits of Mussolini himself, head up, chin jutting out, arms akimbo, the simultaneous attitude of a potent dictator and a strutting buffoon.

Not that the nature of the violence in 1920–21 was designed by Benito Mussolini. In fact, during this time, he had very little direct control over the *squadristi,* over Grandi, over Balbo, over the violence, or over the image of fascism. But he did recognize that the movement had a life of its own, that it was powerful, and that he needed to nurture it. Most of all, he saw that he had somehow to get himself in front of it.

Mussolini understood that the violence of the *squadristi* was no ordinary thing. Socialists, especially the radical fringe, had been acting violently for years, but to relatively little avail. Fascist violence, in contrast, was all but openly welcomed by the authorities. The lyrics of "Giovinezza" sang of liberty, and, indeed, the police were for the most part quite willing to let the *squadristi* burn and beat and "medicate" freely, at will, and without punishment. In February 1921, the prominent socialist deputy Giacomo Matteotti moved a resolution in the Chamber of Deputies condemning local authorities for doing nothing to curb fascist violence, which, the motion claimed, was leading to civil war. Instead of producing legislative censure of fascism, Matteotti's motion backfired, provoking several deputies to speak out in favor of the fascists as veterans and patriots determined to act against Bolshevism when the government seemed incapable of doing so. The motion was soundly defeated.

The sanction of the Chamber of Deputies gave Mussolini the springboard he needed to leap ahead of the gathering tide of fascism. He wrote articles in *Il Popolo d'Italia* condemning the government, condemning Matteotti, and explaining the fascist application of violence. *Explaining*—never apologizing. Whereas the socialists used violence indiscriminately and dishonorably, Mussolini wrote, massing thousands to attack one or a few, the fascists used violence intelligently, wielding it as a surgeon uses a scalpel, to cut away disease only. Violence, Mussolini wrote, was a fact of life, a necessity; but, in fascist hands, it became the noble weapon of the chivalrous warrior, not the indiscriminate cudgel of the cowardly socialist thug. The *squadristi* were soldiers acting in the defense of Italy.

> I had suddenly understood, that through newspaper propaganda, or by example, we would never attain any great successes. It was necessary to beat the violent adversary on the battlefield of violence.
>
> As if a revelation had come to me, I realized that Italy would be saved by one historic agency—in an imperfect world, sometimes inevitable still—righteous force. ...
>
> In certain contingencies violence has a deep moral significance. ...
>
> It was useless to attempt to blaze a trail by fine words, by sermons from chairs. It was necessary to give timely, genial recognition to chivalrous violence. The only straight road was to beat the violent forces of evil on the very ground they had chosen.
>
> ... It was necessary to make our way by violence, by sacrifice, by blood; it was necessary to establish order and discipline wanted by the masses, but impossible to obtain them through milk-and-water propaganda and through words, words and more words—parliamentary and journalistic sham battles.
>
> —Benito Mussolini, My Autobiography, 1928

And developing events soon gave Mussolini more ammunition for his argument. Anarchists made a number of bomb attacks in

Milan, hitting, among other buildings, the Diana Theater, which produced an explosion that killed eighteen theatergoers and wounded many others. Mussolini waded into the public outrage created by the bombing and stirred it up: "The blood of women and children ... cries out for vengeance ... and we are waiting for popular justice to express itself." *Squadristi* stormed and destroyed the offices of *Umanità Nuova,* the newspaper of the leading Italian anarchist—and early political hero of Mussolini—Errico Malatesta. Mussolini then pointed out the difference between fascist violence and that of the socialists, Bolsheviks, and anarchists (taking care to tar these three groups with the same brush): Fascists targeted only the enemies of Italy, whereas socialists, Bolsheviks, and anarchists blew up Italy, indiscriminately. He reminded his readers that one of the eighteen "innocent dead" in the Diana Theater bombing had been a little girl, only five years old.

Although at this time Mussolini did not by any means exercise authoritative control over the fascists, he did not hesitate to present himself to the public as the undisputed voice of fascism. Similarly, when the pressure on Prime Minister Giovanni Giolitti became greatest in the wake of the Diana and other bombings, Mussolini presented himself to the government as the undisputed leader of the Fascist Party. At this point, the most radical socialists were defecting from the Socialist Party to join the communists. Mussolini recognized that the more moderate socialists who remained loyal to the party might now be persuaded to join the tenuous coalition assembled by Giolitti. This could prove fatal to fascism for the simple reason that such a coalition might create a parliament that actually functioned. A viable government was the last thing fascism needed. To preempt the socialists, Mussolini approached Giolitti with an offer of a fascist coalition.

Studying the history of the years between the world wars makes for profoundly depressing reading; especially, of course, toward the end of the period, when the "appeasement" policy of British prime minister Neville Chamberlain was introduced. Bit by bit, territory by territory, Britain led the democracies of Europe in giving Hitler everything he demanded, and giving it to him all in the name of peace, even as the misguided policy led Europe ineluctably into war. Winston Churchill was one of a small minority of politicians who saw that appeasement was a timid, craven policy that would never stop the likes of Hitler. From our perspective of historical hindsight, we want to shake Western Europe by its shoulders and warn it to listen to Churchill and not to Chamberlain. If only, we say, Europeans had acted with timely courage instead of expedient cowardice in 1938.

But the truth is that the principle of "appeasement" was established long before Chamberlain and the conference at Munich. It began not as an international policy, but as an Italian political maneuver, when Giolitti agreed, in 1921, to a coalition with what he inaccurately thought of as *Mussolini's* fascists. If Giolitti had possessed sufficient self-confidence and spine, he could have ordered his government to respond to Mussolini's arrogant offer by crushing the fascist movement, even now. After all, in December 1920, he had successfully authorized a naval bombardment to end D'Annunzio's occupation of Fiume. However, opposing three hundred extremists operating outside of Italy was not the same as acting against a growing political party within the country. Giolitti deceived himself with the thought that he was not really caving in to Mussolini, but, rather, coopting him. Absorbing the fascists into the coalition would defang them—would it not?

As for Mussolini, the approach to Giolitti was also a calculated risk. He disturbed, even alienated, some fascists by joining forces with what amounted to the Establishment. He also compromised the personal image he had worked so hard to create, of the political extremist in service to no one and no party, but Italy. As usual with Mussolini, however, pragmatism triumphed over principle. By compromising, by appearing more conservative, conventional, and respectable, he believed he would gain parliamentary power.

Mussolini's gamble proved a fourfold winner. First, it did succeed in thrusting him to the forefront of fascism, ahead of Balbo and Grandi, and most fascists were willing to follow Mussolini into the coalition. Second, it prompted Giolitti to ask the king to dissolve parliament and hold a general election in 1921. The fascists put up candidates all over the country, and Mussolini stood for election as deputy from Milan. Third, although Mussolini had donned the mantle of official respectability by agreeing to form a coalition, the violence accompanying the election campaign was extreme, even by contemporary Italian standards. Some one hundred people, fascists, socialists, and others, were killed—and this, Mussolini believed, was all to the good, for in most places, the police and other officials winked at fascist intimidation of voters. In some areas, the socialists were unable even to hold election meetings. In several districts, the police and even the military actively aided the fascists, the police lending the *squadristi* trucks for transport, and the army distributing weapons. In Fiume, D'Annunzio had uniformed his small army of occupation in black shirts, as Garibaldi, in the nineteenth century, had clothed his freedom fighters in red shirts. Taking their cue from D'Annunzio, the *squadristi* also adopted the black shirt. Armed by the military and aided by the police, the now uniformed *squadristi* looked less like a gang of thugs and more like a fascist army—organized, impressive, and unstoppable. Under the prevailing circumstances, no magistrate would dare prosecute. Giolitti expressed his regret at the violence, but he did virtually nothing to upset his partners in the coalition, and thus he connived the rise of fascism into the official precincts of government.

The fourth fold of Mussolini's triumph was the election result: Including his own election as deputy from Milan, the fascists won thirty-five seats in the Italian parliament—a one hundred percent increase over the elections of 1919.

On the face of it, thirty-five seats was not an overwhelming triumph, representing only seven percent of the total. The socialists still held one hundred twenty-two seats, the Catholic People's Party one hundred seven. Yet it was a toehold in parliament, and it conferred on Mussolini and the fascists official respectability— not to mention immunity from arrest. By law, a deputy could not be prosecuted for most crimes, and, immediately, a case pending against Mussolini, a charge of intent to overthrow the government by violence, had to be dropped.

But there was even more. Even though election made fascism legitimate, it had been a victory achieved largely by force, by intimidation, by violence. As Mussolini saw things, this kind of victory was far more powerful than one achieved by the lawful process of a democratic constitution. It proved a point: Force constituted authority. In legitimating fascism, the election victory legitimated violence as a means of government. And no sooner did the new Chamber of Deputies convene on June 15, 1921, than Mussolini instigated a lawless attack on one of its members.

During the election campaign, Mussolini had singled out for scathing criticism a communist deputy, Francesco Misiano, who had deserted the army during the world war on the grounds of not wanting to fight for imperialism. On the stump, Mussolini whipped crowds into a chanting frenzy of "Death to Misiano! Death to Misiano!" When Misiano won the election anyway, as deputy for both Turin and Naples, Mussolini directed fellow fascist deputies to eject him from the Montecitorio, the parliament building. Cesare De Vecchi, one of the original leaders of the *arditi*, grabbed Misiano by his coat collar and dragged him along the hallway, all the while spitting in his face. Another half-dozen fascists took over from De Vecchi, dragged him to the steps at the entrance to the building, and one of them, Francesco Giunta, kicked him down those steps and into the street—as members of the Royal Guard looked on and did nothing. Having instigated the act, Mussolini took no direct role in its execution.

The communist deputies called for the expulsion of the fascist deputies who had manhandled and ejected their duly elected colleague. But the entire moderate and right wing of the Chamber of Deputies stunned the communists and socialists by uniting behind the fascists. The Catholic People's Party, the nationalists, and all the lesser parties—everyone except the communists and the socialists—not only voted down the motion to expel the fascists, but voted officially to exclude Misiano from the Chamber. Having achieved office, in large part through violence, the outnumbered fascists had managed to work their will, to eject a legally elected representative, again through violence. Moreover, this action met not with censure, but validation. It was an episode and a lesson Deputy Mussolini took to heart.

Chapter 13

New Legions

The response of the Chamber of Deputies to the ejection of Francesco Misiano confirmed in the formal political arena what Mussolini had already intuited as a journalist. Italians, whether in the streets or in the parliament, were remarkably willing to accept extreme political actions—the more extreme, it seemed, the better. Mussolini deliberately took a seat in the Chamber amphitheater at the far right, where few deputies wished to sit. His maiden speech before this body was an extreme stand against the collectivization of agriculture and against the nationalization of industry, two key planks in the socialist platform. He went beyond this, however, and called for privatization of postal and rail services. Most astoundingly, he announced that Italy might well have to renounce any pretense to democracy altogether and embrace the absolute rule of a strong dictator.

But such talk, it turned out, was premature. Dictator of Italy? Although he now held the semi-formal party title of *Duce*, party leader, Mussolini did not at this point even hold sway over his own party. As part of his extremist stance, he decided to boycott the king's opening speech to parliament, and he instructed the other fascist deputies to do likewise. To his astonishment, they refused. An enraged Mussolini resorted to threats of physical violence. Such threats made against fascists were so many coals to Newcastle. Having achieved their seats through violence and threats of violence, Mussolini's fellow deputies were hardly intimidated. They voted down Mussolini's "proposal" to boycott the speech.

Mussolini now clearly recognized a crisis in the fascist movement. He wanted to keep it ideologically fluid, so that the fledgling party could appear to offer something to everyone, attracting (as, indeed, it did) people from all across the political and social spectrum. Yet he also recognized that any fluid requires a container of some sort. Without one, it was no more than a formless puddle. That the fascists were a heterogeneous bunch created many problems, but, even worse, some of the key early adherents, the *Sansepolcristi,* the founders, were now leaving the party. The futurist Marinetti, the *arditi* leader Ferruccio Vecchi, and the enormously popular opera conductor, Arturo Toscanini, all were drifting away by the summer of 1921.

And then there was the violence. Mussolini was learning something more about that, too. In the cities, *squadrismo*—as the violent culture of the *squadristi* was called—had taken on a life of its own. Even as Mussolini claimed that fascist violence was surgical in nature, controlled and therapeutically intended, it was increasingly clear to everyone that *squadrismo* was running wild. This in itself was bad enough, but the real danger, Mussolini saw, was that the uncontrolled nature of the violence was beginning to turn the police, hitherto overwhelmingly sympathetic to fascist activity, against the movement. In a riot at Saranza, for example, the police had actually fired on the *squadristi*—and the fascists simply melted away under fire. This was not good.

The issue of violence was also creating an internal rift within fascism. Although Mussolini had been raised in a rural district, his political home was urban Italy. Violent as his brand of street fighting was, it was not conducted on the scale of the operations Grandi led against the agricultural collectives. Mussolini began to fear that "agrarian fascism" would become a rival to "urban fascism." At least two very bad results were possible from such a conflict. The unbridled violence of the agrarian fascists might finally provoke a full-scale response from the police or even the army, turning these forces against fascism once and for all. A second possibility was war between urban and agrarian fascism, resulting either in the overthrow of urban fascism (and the end of Mussolini's leadership) or the disintegration of fascism itself (and the end of Mussolini's leadership).

To head off both possibilities, Mussolini made one of those radical, sudden changes of direction that were already characteristic of his career. In July 1921, following the general election, Prime Minister Giolitti resigned and Ivanhoe Bonomi, a member of the right-wing Reformist Socialist Party, became Prime Minister. Among his first acts was to invite representatives of all the political parties and trade unions to meet with Enrico De Nicola, president of the Chamber of Deputies, to hammer out a permanent truce among them. The communists indignantly rebuffed the invitation. The response of the Catholic People's Party was more polite—an expression of best wishes—but they, too, declined to attend. Mussolini, however, persuaded the fascists to attend, as did the socialists and the socialist confederation of trade unions.

As a result of the talks, the parties concluded on August 3 a grandiosely titled "Treaty of Pacification." It was a remarkable document for Mussolini to have signed. The fascists agreed to end all violence against the Socialist Party and, even in the absence of their representatives, against the Communist Party as well. The emblems of all parties were to be respected, and only the government had the authority to decide what flag to fly over public buildings.

In the pages of *Il Popolo d'Italia*, Mussolini hailed the Treaty of Pacification as a fascist triumph, enabling the party at last to focus on exclusively political ends. Moreover, the treaty would greatly enhance Italy's prestige abroad, since it would allow the nation to present to the world a dignified and united front. These arguments notwithstanding, Count Grandi and many other fascists denounced the treaty. Grandi, in *L'Assalto*, a local fascist newspaper published in Bologna, called it a victory not for the fascists but for the socialists. On August 14, he successfully sponsored a resolution signed by one hundred forty-four representatives of local *fasci* nullifying the Treaty of Pacification and calling for an immediate national congress of all *fascio* branches.

It was a revolt, a revolt against the treaty and against Benito Mussolini, and it soon became more intense. Whereas Grandi rebelled within the structure (such as it was) of the Fascist Party, Italo Balbo, always the firebrand, decided to act on his own and in his own way. He organized a fascist march on Ravenna, ostensibly to pay homage at the tomb of Dante on the six hundredth anniversary of his death. In fact, Ravenna was a socialist stronghold, and Balbo knew that a fascist march into this city would be a provocation impossible for the socialists to ignore. It was superfluous for the local *fasci* to vote the Treaty of Pacification up or down. This march would simply break it.

> The great medieval Tuscan poet Dante Alighieri (1265–1321) may strike us as an unlikely object of a fascist pilgrimage, but, in fact, he was a hero of the fascists and is even mentioned in the fascist anthem, "Giovinezza." Not only did Dante's Divine Comedy help establish his native Tuscan dialect as the literary language of Italy and establish him as one of the great poets of Western literature, his life spanned the turbulent and critically formative years of the late Middle Ages. Although Dante's works have the timeless appeal of great literature, he was also deeply immersed in the issues of his day, and he was a powerful early advocate of Italian nationalism. His vision was of a unified Italy, bordered by the sea and the Alps. It was a vision that inspired a number of Italian nationalist movements, including fascism.

Three thousand fascists began the march on September 9. At Bagnara di Romagna, a sniper shot and killed one of the marchers, provoking his comrades to violent reprisals. In Ravenna, on September 12, the *squadristi* were fired on again, moving the fascists to respond by burning down the local offices of the Socialist Party. And so the Treaty of Pacification was broken—and Mussolini's leadership thereby defied.

Against a background of escalating violence, Italo Balbo approached Gabriele D'Annunzio, returned now from Fiume, to replace Mussolini as party Duce. D'Annunzio, however, fancied himself an international military adventurer, a gallant "filibusterer," not a political boss, and he therefore declined the offer. But the leadership of Benito Mussolini was still in serious trouble. On the face of it, he was in an impossible situation. To survive and grow, Mussolini believed, fascism needed to be sufficiently respectable to reassure Italians as well as the statesmen of the world that it was a responsible, legitimate party, not just a mob of anarchists and criminals. Yet fascism had achieved what legitimacy it had through violence. Moreover, its membership was violent, attracted by violence, and willing and eager to use violence for political ends. To embrace violence risked fascism's being dismissed as a mob movement rather than a political party. To reject violence, however, was to reject fascism itself.

Frustrated, Mussolini's initial response to the revolt of Grandi and Balbo was to claim that fascism was his "child" and that it must obey him, its father, or he would destroy it. But, within days of this outburst, he retreated. Suddenly resigning as party Duce, he agreed to convene a national congress in Rome, to be held beginning on November 7. Preparatory to this congress, he began a campaign of what today's politicians would call damage control. In *Il Popolo d'Italia*, he published the names of fifteen fascists killed by communists between August 5 and September 4, *before* the outbreak at Ravenna. The Fascist Party, in conformity to the treaty, had made no reprisals in response to the fifteen fatal shootings. On the contrary, Mussolini pointed out, it was the socialists who had broken the treaty by firing on the Ravenna marchers. Thus Mussolini sought to demonstrate that his signature on the Treaty of Pacification had been authoritative after all. "His" fascists had not broken it.

Another boost to Mussolini's sagging political stock came at the end of October when Ettore Ciccotti, a Socialist deputy, challenged him to a duel over an insult printed in *Il Popolo d'Italia*. Mussolini had been fencing for years and had already fought a number of minor duels with political foes. Accepting Ciccotti's challenge, he chose sabers as the weapon, and the two met in a Leghorn garden on October 27. When police officers, who had been shadowing Mussolini, attempted to intervene (duels, though common in Italy, were illegal), both Mussolini and Ciccotti withdrew to a house adjacent to the garden and locked the doors. The police abandoned their attempt at intervention, and the rivals fought, indoors, for an hour and a half, until Ciccotti, exhausted to the point of collapse, quit. It was announced that the fight would be resumed the next day, but, apparently, this never happened.

Mussolini, surrounded by political associates, about 1922 or 1923.

(Image from the Library of Congress)

It hardly mattered. Mussolini was seen as the victor, a man who might sign a treaty with the Socialist Party, but who had no fear of fighting a socialist man to man.

If the duel did much to rehabilitate the image of Mussolini on the eve of the fascist congress, the speech he made on the second day of that congress was his apotheosis. In it, he attacked socialist internationalism as the implacable enemy of Italy. To this, he contrasted fascism as the party of patriotism and, even more to the point, as the party not merely of the Italian nation, but of the Italian *race*. Amid the gale of cheers that greeted this speech, no less a figure than Count Dino Grandi mounted the platform to embrace Mussolini warmly. One week later, Mussolini formally notified the president of the Chamber of Deputies that the Fascist Party regarded the Treaty of Pacification as null and void.

In the meantime, throughout the entire national fascist congress, the socialists had staged a general strike in Rome. This provoked an orgy of violence in the streets. Balbo's squads were the most disciplined among the rioters. They were uniformed in black shirts and they had adopted from D'Annunzio's Fiume legion the ancient Roman salute: right arm extended up and out, palm down. Beholding all of this, Mussolini instantly shed his earlier, momentary fear that fascist violence had gone too far. Now he believed it had yet to go far enough. He called on all local *fasci* to form their own squads. His object was to create a national militia, a shadow army, modeled loosely on the example of the great Roman legions. Local squads would be organized into larger cohorts, which, in turn, would be grouped into legions, each legion under the command of a consul, and each group of legions under the command of a zone commander, or inspector general.

> *Adolf Hitler's Nazi Party also adopted the Roman salute in Germany. In Italy, Mussolini, who apparently had a morbid fear of germs, promoted it not only as an appropriately grand official and military courtesy, but also as a general substitute for the "unhygienic handshake" among civilians, party members, and the military alike. After he was installed in power, those in the know never offered the Duce a handshake, but always the salute—which, moreover, was held stiffly aloft until returned by Mussolini. Often, perhaps to assert his personal power or simply to amuse himself, Mussolini pretended to be distracted with other matters and took his sweet time returning the salute. The unfortunate visitor might remain many minutes in a most uncomfortable position.*

Mussolini's Roman organization of the *squadristi* would achieve two things. By creating a shadow army, fascism would possess the muscle necessary to seize the government. And by creating a *disciplined* body of violent men, fascism would offer Italy a strong yet orderly alternative to a weak and anarchic parliament.

The national fascist congress held in Rome at the end of 1921 had begun in crisis, with Benito Mussolini on the brink of being toppled from leadership of the party and with the party itself threatened by rupture into rival agrarian and urban wings. After his speech and his orders for the general arming of the *fasci* and the reorganization of the *squadristi* into a national party militia, the Fasci di Combattimento, already familiarly called the Fascist Party, officially became the National Fascist Party, and Mussolini was reaffirmed as its absolute leader. At the end of 1920, there were little more than twenty thousand fascists in Italy; at the end of 1921, that number had exploded to 249,036.

The year 1922 began with the introduction of the sixth new government and Prime Minister since the end of the world war. Luigi Facta was a journeyman liberal politician who, in one sense at least, elicited more unity than any prime minister of the previous five years: Everyone, of every political stripe, was united in contempt for him. Chosen by liberal forces as the least threatening lowest common denominator, he seemed to Mussolini a godsend— a liberal milquetoast who would never stand up to the fascists and who would amply demonstrate once and for all the impotence of parliamentary government.

Acting on the pronouncements he himself had made at the national congress, Mussolini prepared the *squadristi* to confront and overwhelm the new government. He decided that the best way to use Italo Balbo was to install him as field commander of the squads. For one thing, Balbo had already shown an aptitude for such a command and, for another, it would keep him sufficiently satisfied with power to discourage him from hatching any new plots with D'Annunzio. Balbo did not disappoint Mussolini. He elaborated the black shirt uniform to include a black sash, the liberal use of leather belting, riding breeches, and military-style puttees. Headgear was a black fez, with officers to be distinguished by a Roman eagle insignia.

From ancient Rome as well were borrowed the names of the old legions, and Balbo worked out in detail the Roman-modeled military organization Mussolini had broadly expounded at the congress. The smallest operational unit was the squad, with twenty to fifty men. Every four squads were formed into a *centuria*, every four *centuriae* into a cohort, and every three to nine cohorts a legion. The legions were commanded by consuls, who were accountable to inspector generals. Despite this chain of command, all officers were to be nominated directly by Mussolini, down even to the lowly squad leaders—who formerly had been elected by the squads themselves. Mussolini held the rank of Duce, supreme leader, not only of the National Fascist Party, but also of the *squadristi*. In fact, there was no longer any real distinction to be made between the party and the squads. Mussolini ordered that all party members were ex officio members of their local squads, so that the Fascist Party was, by definition, an army.

By way of confirming the nonexistence of the Facta government's backbone, Mussolini instigated a fresh uprising in Fiume. Fascist squads evicted the city administration at gunpoint and installed a new, fascist administration. As Mussolini had expected, the government did nothing. This emboldened Mussolini to turn Balbo loose on cities all across Italy. The fascist campaign was a simple one. Black-shirted squads marched into one Socialist-governed city or town after another, entered the town hall, confronted the officials they found there, and asked them, please, to resign and get out of town. Facing an organized gang of men armed with guns and clubs, most officials readily complied.

On May 12, 1922, Balbo led a huge force of sixty-three thousand Blackshirts into Ferrara. Without firing a shot, cracking a skull, or torching a single building, the fascist presence succeeded in driving the socialists and Populari out of their offices. The entire process of transforming Ferrara into a fascist city took just forty-eight hours.

Two weeks later, Bologna was similarly assaulted. This time, however, Balbo met resistance from the local prefect, Cesare Mori, who refused to resign when that was demanded of him. Moreover, he mounted a stout defense, barricading city hall against a fascist siege force. Intimidation having failed, Balbo was as yet unwilling to commit an act of outright violence against a government official. Once again, the fascists resorted to coarse slapstick. Balbo ordered his Blackshirts to urinate against the wall directly beneath Mori's office, as if he somehow expected this to drive Mori from his desk.

In the end, it was the ever-fearful Facta who broke the stalemate. He ordered Mori removed from Bologna and appointed him instead prefect of Bari, in southern Italy, where fascist activity was, at this point, minimal. Thus the fascists took over the administration of Bologna.

Balbo's Blackshirts marched against Ravenna, and when a fascist was killed there, they retaliated by burning down the Hotel Byron, venerable headquarters of the socialist cooperative movement in Mussolini's native Romagna. On July 28, Balbo and his men occupied Ravenna and got into a shooting match with the local communists. Nine Blackshirts fell in battle, and Balbo responded by burning the headquarters of all the leftist parties in town, communists, socialists, and anarchists. Having done this, he brazenly approached the local chief of police and demanded trucks, which he promised to use to get his men out of town. He warned the chief that if his men were not provided with transport, they would burn down every communist and socialist house in Ravenna. The chief complied, and the next day Balbo used the vehicles to carry his men throughout the Romagna, where they burned left-wing headquarters in every part of the district, including Mussolini's hometown of Forlì. The Italian army, Balbo recorded in his diary, watched without taking action.

Clearly, this was a revolution. In the Chamber of Deputies, the major parties condemned Prime Minister Facta for failing to act against the Blackshirt army. King Vittore Emmanuelle III recalled Facta—thereby bringing down his short-lived government—and the communists and socialists joined in calling a general strike to protest the government's inability or unwillingness to end the fascist reign of terror.

The strike began at midnight on July 31. Mussolini himself could not have asked for more. In *Il Popolo d'Italia*, he published an ultimatum drafted by National Fascist Party Secretary Michele Bianchi warning that if the government failed to break the strike within forty-eight hours, the fascists would do it themselves and would, furthermore, "supplant the State, which will once again have shown its impotence."

The Blackshirts did not even wait the promised forty-eight hours. In Genoa, La Spezia, and Ancona, fascists assaulted striking tram drivers and conductors, throwing the men off the streetcars and operating them themselves. When a communist gunman fired on a fascist-operated tram, the army intervened with armored cars, from which troops poured machine-gun fire on the communists. The fascists burned socialist clubs and offices even as they cooperated with the police and army in quelling communist and socialist responses to their strikebreaking efforts.

Similar scenes were played out all across Italy, and in less than a single day the general strike was broken, and city and town governments were put under fascist administration. Only in Parma, where the army acted *against* the fascists with a well-defended roadblock, did Balbo's Blackshirts fail. After fourteen of his men had been killed by army machine guns, Balbo withdrew.

On August 11, the Chamber of Deputies debated the strike and its failure. Or, rather, they attempted to debate it. When a communist deputy, a man named Raposti, spoke out in support of the strike, he was shouted down by the fascists. When he spoke louder, Francesco Giunta, the fascist deputy who had kicked Misiano down the stairs of the Montecitorio (Chapter 12, "Black Shirts, Beatings, and the Poetry of Terror"), started to draw a revolver from his hip pocket, but was restrained by others in the nick of time. Facta and his ministers, seeing that the fascists were indeed liable to shoot someone, instantly withdrew from the Chamber, and the president of the Chamber of Deputies hastily announced that the debate would be temporarily adjourned. During the recess, another fascist pointed a revolver at Raposti, but was talked out of squeezing the trigger by one of Facta's ministers—perhaps the only occasion on which an agent of the Facta government intervened effectively.

The session resumed, but the uproar from the fascist deputies was deafening, and Raposti was never able to speak his piece. He had been shouted down. As the summer of 1922 drew to a close, the voice of fascism was by far the loudest in Italy. It would soon be the only voice Italians would hear.

Chapter 14

"Roma! Roma! Roma!"

During World War II, Allied propaganda lumped Mussolini together with Japan's Hideki Tojo and Germany's Adolf Hitler as one of a triumvirate of power-mad despots. By the 1940s, when the war was underway, this description may not have been very enlightening, but neither was it entirely inaccurate.

Mussolini, like his Axis allies, was by this time self-deluded, having lied so often and so loudly about fascist invincibility that he believed it himself. But two decades earlier, whatever else Mussolini may have been, he was in no sense mad with power, drunk with power, or self-deceived. It would have been very easy for Mussolini to fall into this trap. Fascism was on the rise, and Mussolini's position at the head of the party had never been more secure. The beauty of having broken the general strike was that the fascists had not only defeated the socialists and communists in their biggest battle with them ever, but had defeated them in the name of defending Italy. No longer was fascism an outlaw gang. It had, at least so far as handling the strike was concerned, "supplanted the state" in defending the law—just as Mussolini had promised. Many of Mussolini's fascist colleagues now pushed him to seize the government by a coup d'etat. What better time would there be?

In 1923, no less a figure than Adolf Hitler would yield to a similar urge to act, launching his Beer Hall *Putsch* in Munich, only to discover that he lacked the popular support to carry off the coup.

His rise would be put off for a decade. In contrast, Mussolini demurred, even though he, in 1922, had much greater backing than Hitler had a year later. Instead of forging ahead with a revolution, he was balancing on the edge of a sword. On the one hand, he offered the government the prospect of a coalition that would reinvigorate parliament while renouncing republicanism and supporting the king, that would revive the economy, that would reduce taxes, that would balance the budget, and that would annex Dalmatia and other territories to make Italy the major Mediterranean power. On the other hand, he continued to give free rein to the Blackshirts, who were now loosed against the towns of Bolanzo and Trent. Here the city administrations were not socialist, but representative of the mainstream government. Even as he offered to support, bolster, and revive the government, Mussolini authorized action against it.

What he concluded from the success of operations against Bolanzo and Trent was that the government was so weak, divided, and indecisive, it was ready to fall—or, at least, to usher Mussolini into the very highest levels of power, the cabinet itself. But Mussolini was more than a clever politician. He was a *popular* leader. As bewildered, discouraged, and frightened as the government of Italy was, the people, Mussolini noted, were in an even more desperate condition. Everyone, at all economic and social levels, was oppressed by hard times, and the majority were also gripped by fear of anarchy, socialism, and communism—evils, they felt, that would dispossess them of what little they still had. The people would support whatever man or party or force they thought capable of saving them. They didn't have to love fascism, Mussolini concluded; it was enough that they saw fascism as the least of the many evils that beset Italy.

While he continued skillfully to "ride two horses," as Mussolini biographer Jasper Ridley aptly put it, "the respectable conservative horse and the revolutionary Fascist horse," Mussolini patiently weighed the government and the people in the balance. What the people saw was a government in collapse, the nation in a state verging on civil war, the postal system breaking down, the railways the laughingstock of Europe, labor working or not at will, public officials working or not at will. What Mussolini could offer the government was the possibility of functioning again. But why offer the *government* anything? Instead of repairing the ramshackle structure, why not just tear it down? Why shore up the government for the people, when he could give the *people* a new government? This, at last, seemed to Mussolini the greater opportunity: not a role in the government as it was, but an end to that government, and a new one in its place.

Having made this decision, Mussolini, in a campaign of bad faith spectacularly brazen even for him, pushed all the harder on the idea of a coalition. He encouraged liberal elements to believe that a coalition with the fascists would forestall a fascist revolution while bolstering the individual careers of the liberal politicians. He did the same with conservatives. To each contender for the post of Prime Minister, to Francesco Fausto Nitti, to Antonio Salandra, to Giovanni Giolitti, and to Luigi Facta, Mussolini secretly offered support in exchange for a fascist coalition. In this way, he proposed to neutralize all opposition. Then, on October 16, 1922, Mussolini met in private with the fascist inner circle. The purpose of the meeting was to devise a plan for overthrowing the government he was even then proposing to support.

As Mussolini recounted the meeting, it was he who had to push the idea of outright insurrection on the others. When they balked, he threatened to take action with or without them. Italo Balbo recorded the meeting's minutes, however, and recalled that if anyone present was reluctant to trigger a revolution, it was Mussolini. Whoever actually proposed action, once the decision was made, Mussolini resolved that it would begin with a "March on Rome."

During the more than two decades in which Mussolini governed Italy, he cultivated the impression that every idea, every order, every law, every act issued from him and him alone. Remarkably, this was one Mussolini myth that had a firm basis in fact. As Prime Minister and then as national "Duce," Mussolini was a fanatical micromanager. Everything that did not come directly from him had to go through him, down to the most trivial detail. During the early rise of fascism, however, Mussolini maintained a curious distance from most major events. He instigated the ouster of Francesco Misiano from the Chamber of Deputies, but he stood back while others did the job. He assigned Italo Balbo command of the Blackshirts and let him run the campaign to topple socialism and communism in Italy's "red" cities. And when it came time to plan and organize the March on Rome, the most significant action the Fascist Party had ever taken, he delegated the work to what he called a Quadrumvirate: Michele Bianchi, Italo Balbo, Cesare De Vecchi, and Gen. Emilio De Bono. De Bono, a recent addition to the party, was an officer in the Italian army, a war hero, and, like De Vecchi, a friend of Italy's queen mother, Queen Margherita.

The first order of business was to decide when the march would take place. Balbo and Bianchi insisted that it must commence at once, whereas De Vecchi and De Bono counseled a month's delay in order to prepare more fully. Mussolini, as usual, sought to satisfy everyone. He declared that preparations for the march would begin immediately, but that the date would be determined at the party congress, to be held in Naples on October 24.

On October 17, the day after he had appointed the Quadrumvirate to organize the March on Rome, Mussolini announced to a group of journalists that the October 16 meeting had resolved *not* to create a coalition because it would leave fascism in the minority and, therefore, less effective. Having made this announcement to the press, he nevertheless continued to lead politicians to believe that he was preparing to form just such a coalition. He was similarly duplicitous in proclaiming publicly that he had no aspirations to the "burden" of high public office, even as he told a circle of associates that, for him, fascism existed for one purpose and one purpose only: the acquisition of power.

Even Mussolini could not balance for long on a sword he had sharpened to this degree of razor thinness. On October 24, at the fascist congress, he made two speeches. The first, delivered in a forum to which the public was invited, extolled and detailed the advantages of a fascist government and a fascist economy. The second, in a closed session to Blackshirts only, made no attempt to sell the fascist program. Instead, Mussolini declared that fascists would either be "allowed to govern, or we will seize power by marching on Rome." There, Mussolini growled, we will "take by the throat the miserable political class that governs us." The oration was greeted by frenzied shouts of "Roma! Roma! Roma!"

Both the public and private speeches were fully reported in the press. On their way out of town, the Blackshirts destroyed the offices of every opposition newspaper in Naples.

So there it was: an announcement by the leader of the National Fascist Party that he was starting a revolution. Astoundingly, however, the government made no response. There was no expression of alarm. No protest. No declaration of a state of national emergency. And this stunned silence was precisely what Mussolini had expected. For, in 1922, it was not Benito Mussolini who was self-deluded, but the government of Italy. Nitti, Salandra, Giolitti, Facta, and the rest refrained from acting against a man and party each of them still somehow believed would form a coalition to their benefit or even their salvation.

During the evening of October 24, after Mussolini's two speeches, he met with the Quadrumvirate and a few others in the Hotel Vesuvio to hammer out the details of the march. It would step off at the dramatic hour of midnight, October 26/27. The Blackshirt marchers would immediately capture and hold the key cities of northern Italy. On October 28, they would assemble at three rallying points north of Rome: at Santa Marinella near Civitavecchia, at Monterotondo, and at Tivoli. In concert, these three columns would then advance on Rome itself. To counter any attempts the government might make to stop the march, Balbo decided to send a secret squad into the city beforehand to plant bombs that could be set off in an emergency. The momentous meeting concluded with no ceremony other than the exchange of the now-familiar Roman salute.

On October 26, fascist units moved into the cities of the north, occupying strategic strongpoints and taking over all municipal buildings. Simultaneously, Blackshirt squads began assembling at the designated rallying points north of Rome. The Quadrumvirate itself made for Perugia, selected as the headquarters from which the operation would be directed. Mussolini, who remained in Milan, wrote a proclamation for the Quadrumvirate to issue from Perugia. Fascism, the proclamation declared, would wield the sword to cut the "Gordian knots" that were burdening Italian life.

> *Fascism draws its sword to cut the multiple Gordian knots which tie and burden Italian life. We call God and the spirit of our five hundred thousand dead to witness that only one impulse sends us on, that only one passion burns within us—the impulse and the passion to contribute to the safety and greatness of our Country.*
>
> *Fascisti of all Italy!*
>
> *Stretch forth like Romans your spirits and your sinews! We must win. We will.*
>
> *Long live Italy! Long live Fascism!*
>
> *—Conclusion of the manifesto of the Quadrumvirate on the eve of the March on Rome*

At last, on October 27, Luigi Facta, still serving as Prime Minister in the absence of a viable coalition, belatedly announced that the nation was in a state of insurrection and that he was authorizing the army to maintain law and order.

Gen. Emanuele Pugliese, commanding twelve thousand troops in Rome, prepared the city for an invasion. He shut down theaters, took over the trams, and set up barbed wire around government office buildings. He also dispatched soldiers to hold and occupy Fascist Party headquarters. In Milan, Bologna, Turin, and Genoa, the army took control. Mussolini's editorial offices were surrounded by troops. Mussolini was allowed to enter and leave only after passing through a checkpoint.

Although the army obeyed government orders to deploy, most of the troops and their commanders were openly sympathetic to the fascists. In Cremona, there was a violent exchange between the army and the Blackshirts, resulting in the deaths of eight fascists and the wounding of thirteen more. But in most of the other cities, the army did very little to interfere with the fascists. In Pisa and Bologna, troops stopped Blackshirts from taking over the prefect's office, but they did nothing more. In Perugia and Mantua, the army did not interfere when the prefects in these places surrendered to the Blackshirts, and in Spoleto, the army stood by as Blackshirts commandeered nine thousand rifles and ten machine guns. In Foligno, fascists helped themselves to a government cache of seven thousand rifles and thirty machine guns—as the army looked on. Most outrageous of all was the action of the military commander in Siena, who used soldiers to *deliver* guns to the Blackshirts occupying that city. When Facta bypassed the army and ordered the prefect of Milan to arrest Mussolini, the prefect— a government official answerable directly to Facta—refused. Soldiers there were already celebrating with the Blackshirts.

Still, Mussolini remained aloof from the revolution in progress. He spent the evening of October 27 with his wife, Rachele, and his twelve-year-old daughter, Edda, at a performance of a comedy. He was kept informed of the progress of the march by messengers stationed just outside of his box. Midway through the second act of the play, he took his wife and daughter in hand, quietly left the family box, and went home. The telephone rang continually through the night. Mussolini was informed that the three main Blackshirt columns had taken up their positions outside Rome.

While Mussolini did his best to preserve a front of remote calm, Luigi Facta was finally getting excited. He secured an emergency audience with Vittore Emmanuelle III and asked him to proclaim a state of siege. This would allow the government to declare martial law and deal summarily with the fascists. The king told Facta to draw up the decree for his signature. But when Facta returned with the document at 6 o'clock in morning of October 28, Vittore Emmanuelle refused to sign it. The king later explained that he had been told that one hundred thousand fascists were on the march, and, through the night, it occurred to him that the "five thousand to eight thousand" troops available in Rome would be unable to stop the marchers.

This explanation was certainly a lie.

Only twenty-six thousand fascists were poised to march on Rome, although it is certain that the fascists did deliberately inflate reports of their numbers. Perhaps the king really believed one hundred thousand Blackshirts were poised to invade, but he also certainly knew that Gen. Pugliese had twelve thousand—not five thousand or eight thousand—troops available, heavily armed, with machine guns, armored cars, and artillery at hand. Even greatly outnumbered, the army, deployed in strong defensive positions, could easily have crushed the march, and the failure of the march might well have put a period to Mussolini's rise. Doubtless, then, it was not the disproportion in numbers that caused Vittore Emmanuelle to change his mind, but the very real possibility that, when a confrontation came, the army—at least large parts of it—would side with the fascists. When the king asked Gen. Armando Diaz, hero of Vittorio Veneto, if he could count on the army, the general replied none too reassuringly: "The army will do its duty, but it would be better not to put it to the test." That was sufficient to stay the king's hand.

Later in the morning of the twenty-eighth, Vittore Emmanuelle informed Facta of his decision not to declare a state of siege, whereupon Facta summarily resigned. Immediately, the king asked Salandra to form a government and to extend to Mussolini and other key fascists appointments in the cabinet. The king's private secretary phoned Mussolini a few hours later, inviting him and four other fascists to serve in the Salandra government. Mussolini replied that the fascists had not risked everything on a march to Rome for the sake of a handful of places in the government of Antonio Salandra. He declared that he would accept nothing less than the office of Prime Minister.

That was the end of the phone call. On the next day, October 29, the same private secretary made a second call to Mussolini. He conveyed the king's invitation to form a government. Mussolini would indeed be prime minister of Italy.

Vittore Emmanuelle offered to dispatch a special train to Milan to carry Mussolini to Rome. If Mussolini had possessed the slightest trace of self-irony, the offer would have struck him as comical. He had planned a fascist march into Rome, but before the three Blackshirt columns had even left their rallying points north of the city, the government caved in to his demand. He, Mussolini, hadn't even left Milan. In later years, he would weave a mythic picture of the great March on Rome, when three hundred thousand Blackshirts tramped to the capital city in perfect discipline to enforce the ultimatum the Duce had given the king. Some versions of the myth portray Mussolini, on horseback, leading his Blackshirt legions across the same Rubicon Julius Caesar had so momentously crossed. In fact, Mussolini declined the king's offer of a special train, but he did purchase a ticket on the night sleeper to Rome. He arrived at the Civitavecchia station at 8 A.M., where three thousand Blackshirts greeted him. After a short speech to them, he continued his journey, by rail, into Rome itself. He had not marched, not on foot and not on horse.

A popular image of Mussolini, giving the Roman salute. Fascist myth portrayed Mussolini as having led the 1922 March on Rome on horseback. In fact, Mussolini rode into Rome from Milan in the bedroom compartment of a railway coach.

(Image from the Library of Congress)

Another fascist legend Mussolini approved was the image of him, uniformed in his black shirt, declaring to Vittore Emmanuelle, "Majesty, I bring you Italy of Vittorio Veneto, reconsecrated by a new victory." It is doubtful that Mussolini said any such thing, and it is certain that he did not wear the fascist uniform in the presence of the king. After booking a room at the Hotel Savoia, he changed into the formal morning attire—stand-up collar, cutaway coat, striped trousers, dove-gray spats—he had brought with him from Milan, and presented himself at the Quirinal, the royal palace, complete with a list of ministers he wanted for his cabinet. At thirty-nine, Benito Mussolini was the youngest prime minister in Italian history.

Part Four

Il Duce

Chapter 15

Prime Minister

Most of us are familiar with the nightmare that actors call the "actor's dream" and teachers call the "teacher's dream." In it, the actor finds herself thrust onto a stage, in the middle of a play she has not rehearsed and knows nothing of, or the teacher finds himself at the front of a classroom, responsible for delivering a lesson in a subject he has never even studied. From either dream, one wakes in a sweat.

Suddenly prime minister of Italy, Mussolini, with no experience in government, save a short time in the Chamber of Deputies, would have been justified in feeling himself the dreamer of just such a nightmare. He had achieved office not through popular election, not by painstakingly studying Italy's problems, not by serving an apprenticeship in government, and not even through a long and arduous revolution, but by a brief period of bullying and intimidation. There had been violence, yes, but far more important to Mussolini's sudden elevation to the highest office in the land was the *threat* of violence. He must have realized, too, that his mandate was hardly impressive. The fascists were, as yet, a tiny minority in parliament. The popular support he received was, for the most part, not as the savior of Italy, but as the least of the many evils available.

The nightmarish quality of the teacher's dream and the actor's dream derives from the dreamer's conscience: the sense that it is wrong, terribly wrong, to present oneself under false pretenses, to be an imposter, to claim an expertise or competence one does not possess. Mussolini, however, was assailed by no such pangs of conscience. His first order of business was not learning how to run a country or developing a program to save Italy. It was, rather, to maintain the power he had just achieved, and then to expand it. In typical Mussolini fashion, he set about taking this first step through simultaneous but apparently contradictory actions.

Whereas his fascist colleagues believed that they would all be given places in the government, the government Mussolini formed was made up mostly of nonfascists. Ministers were chosen from the Catholic People's Party (the "Populari"), from the Nationalist Party, and from the various liberal parties. Only the socialists and communists were excluded. Mussolini was determined to co-opt the opposition by including them in his administration. To have made the government chiefly or exclusively fascist would not only have provoked opposition, but would have placed, close to the prime minister, any number of rivals for power. There were, however, two ministries Mussolini would entrust to no one other than a fascist—the posts of foreign minister and minister of the interior. The loyal fascist Mussolini chose for these posts was none other than himself.

While Mussolini created a coalition cabinet, he chose members who for the most part were as new to government as he. Thus the new prime minister would be confronted with very few preconceived ideas to challenge or overcome. More important, novices are always easier to intimidate than old hands.

And intimidation was still very much Mussolini's keynote. He had been named prime minister before all the Blackshirts had even reached Rome. Now that he was installed, they were marching in. To dispel the atmosphere of a paramilitary coup, Mussolini ordered the immediate demobilization of the squads that had already assembled in the city. Simultaneously with this nod toward normal civil government, however, he ordered the remaining Blackshirts, those who had not yet reached Rome, to be transported into town via rail and truck. On October 31, the Blackshirts were then formed into a parade and permitted to march past the Quirinal, the royal palace. No sooner was the parade concluded than the Blackshirts were immediately loaded into special trains and transported back to their homes. As for Mussolini, he declined to review the troops personally, and instead (it was reported) passed the day with a "lady friend."

In the way he handled the Blackshirts, Mussolini once again sought simultaneously to please and intimidate everyone. He displayed his *squadristi* as a revolutionary force, as if to portray himself as a conqueror. At the same time, he demonstrated that they were wholly subordinate to him and would come and go as he commanded. Yet by declining to review them personally, he sought to counter the impression that they were nothing more than his personal army. They were, first and last, an impersonal force, which took a strong man to command.

Impersonal force. This phrase describes the image of leadership that was of paramount importance to Mussolini. During the course of his regime and afterward, critics and historians called fascism a "cult of personality," focused on the person of Benito Mussolini, the Duce. As far as this analysis goes, it is correct. Immediately upon becoming prime minister, Mussolini invited interviews with many journalists and others. One who spoke to him was a young British sculptor, Clare Sheridan, who took special note that the many pictures in the hotel suite he used as his residence and office were of him and only of him. Soon, such pictures would also adorn the walls of homes throughout Italy, hung alongside crucifixes, saints' portraits, and the other religious icons typically found in Italian parlors. Nevertheless, "cult of personality" does not tell the whole story of what Mussolini had begun to develop. For his was a deliberately *impersonal* cult of personality. To Clare Sheridan, he explained the success behind his rise: He had kept, he said, "his heart a desert," rejecting all friendships and loyalties as mere impediments to achieving power.

If, then, he offered himself as the savior of Italy, he was careful not to present himself as the warm friend of the Italian people. He was no one's friend. For him, people were so many objects to be *bent* to his will. He had spent many years, he told Sheridan, watching his blacksmith father forge iron, pounding and bending it to his will. In just such a way would he, Benito Mussolini, manipulate the souls of men and women.

Clare Sheridan's conversation with Mussolini took place while she sculpted a bust of him. In later years, she alleged that, during one session, Mussolini attempted to rape her. Sheridan was sculpting her cousin, Winston Churchill, in 1942 and asked the Prime Minister, "Winston, didn't you at one time rather approve of Mussolini?" Churchill responded that he had: "I regard him as a very able man. He should never have come in against us."

Certainly, he approached parliament with all the sinewy force of a blacksmith. He addressed his first parliamentary session, on November 16, with the equivalent of a hammer beating against an anvil—pounding, bending. Just as, to the disappointment of many fascists, he had formed a coalition government, now, too, he shocked his fascist colleagues by announcing to parliament that he would not discard the constitution. He told the deputies and senators that he would not throw away the constitution, even though he might have done so—and, more important, might yet do so, turning this "bleak assembly hall into a bivouac for my platoons."

Mussolini learned—or, perhaps, instinctively knew—that the threat (provided it was credible) was always stronger than the deed. Had he installed nothing but fascists into his government, he would have created not only a government, but also an opposition to that government. Had he used the parliament for a bivouac, he would have made the mistake of all tyrants, who, in creating tyranny, also create the elements of an anti-tyranny. But the *threat* of an exclusively fascist government created a compliant coalition, and the *threat* to dissolve parliament created not outrage and opposition, but a remarkably compliant parliament.

Having thus threatened parliament, he asked it, in the very next breath, to grant him the powers of a dictator, "emergency" powers to institute immediate reforms of finance, of bureaucracy, of the military, and of education. He had already informed his cabinet (his highly compliant coalition cabinet) that he was going to achieve three things right away: pacification of all opposition, discipline among an inherently undisciplined population, and the most rigorous of budgetary economies. Within parliament, only the socialists and communists protested vesting Mussolini with absolute power. From among the conservatives came a dissenting voice or two that dared bring up Mussolini's early days as a radical socialist, a man who counseled desertion and even regicide. These critics Mussolini shouted down, interrupting them until they gave up even trying to raise their objections. In the end, the Chamber of Deputies readily voted Mussolini the emergency powers he asked for (some even begged him to proclaim himself permanent dictator), and the Senate rushed to do the same. It was, according to one foreign journalist, a vote of confidence "without parallel in the annals of modern parliaments."

From our perspective, in the twenty-first century and outside of Italy, we might well ask what on earth the Italian people were thinking of. At the feet of this brutal mob leader, a boss of bosses, really, who had blithely declared that he had little interest in the "concept of liberty," the hitherto disputatious parliament was now prepared to lie quietly down.

What could Mussolini possibly have offered Italy to elicit such surrender?

The purpose of the "Great War," President Woodrow Wilson had said in 1917, was to make the world safe for democracy. But the war hardly left the world a place safe for democracy or anything else. Italians in particular felt cheated by the Versailles peace settlement, the cost of the war in human and economic terms created a profound economic depression, and it was Bolshevism, not democracy, that panted (the people believed) at Italy's gates. Confused, heartbroken, enraged, terrified, Italians looked to the leaders of their government and, to their horror, found there people just like themselves: legislators who were confused, heartbroken, enraged, terrified. Mussolini was different. Confident and strong, he appeared both fearless and certain of his direction. These facts alone were sufficient to win a following.

Nor was Mussolini's triumph confined to Italy and the Italians.

*Prime Minister Mussolini is received by King Vittore
Emmanuelle III. Mussolini almost always dressed in formal
civilian attire for audiences with the king.*

(Image from ArtToday)

On November 16, 1922, he won from parliament the powers of
a dictator. Two days later, he left for Lausanne, Switzerland, to
attend a session of the Conference of Allied Powers, which was
deciding the terms of the peace treaty with Germany's wartime
ally, Turkey. Before Prime Minister Mussolini could be admitted to
Switzerland, however, there was the most embarrassing matter of

the deportation orders issued in 1903 and 1904, which were still in effect against Mussolini in several Swiss cantons. The government scrambled to revoke these before the new Prime Minister's arrival.

But Mussolini had not come to the conference prepared to discuss the treaty with Turkey. He was more interested in simply throwing his weight around by demanding, first, that the conference be moved from Lausanne to Capri. When the other participants balked at this, he suggested Territet, on the Italian border. The others insisted that it was too late to change, but Mussolini claimed a minor victory nevertheless. He left instructions for French and British delegates arriving in Lausanne to come to a preliminary meeting with him—in Territet. Come the delegates did, and they were appalled by a greeting from Mussolini surrounded, at this *diplomatic* meeting, by a personal bodyguard of Blackshirts accompanied by a band pounding out the "Giovinezza." Why had the Duce asked for this highly inconvenient preliminary meeting? It was to do nothing more than warn the delegates that Italy would not participate in *this* conference if it did not receive a guarantee that it would be treated as the equal of the other Allies.

The members of the British and French delegations were greatly put out by the detour to Territet, and many in Mussolini's own group were embarrassed by what they saw as their leader's uncouth behavior and undignified warning about the treatment of Italy. Yet the official irritation and embarrassment mattered less than the fact that newspapers, in Italy and elsewhere, interpreted the exchange in Territet precisely as Mussolini had intended, some even calling it Italy's first diplomatic victory since 1860.

From the two days Mussolini stayed in Lausanne some journalists came away unimpressed, dismissing the new prime minister as an egomaniac. Ernest Hemingway, then a neophyte correspondent for the *Kansas City Star*, already had a genius for piercing pretension. He reported that Mussolini seemed more concerned with the journalists than with the business of the treaty conference. Hemingway noted that, at a press conference, Mussolini played the role of disdainful dictator to the hilt. He frowned over a book, pretending not to notice that the press corps was ready for the conference to begin. When Hemingway tip-toed to the prime minister to discover what it was that he read, he found that it was nothing more profound than a French-English dictionary—held upside down.

Indeed, Hemingway was right about Mussolini's absence of interest in the conference. He said virtually nothing, and he impressed the other delegates as a man profoundly ignorant of world affairs. Yet he claimed to journalists that he had wrung from the British a promise of increased colonial territory for Italy. This was entirely untrue, but it was widely publicized nonetheless. And while some journalists published unflattering reports of Mussolini's conduct at the conference, most accounts were quite favorable.

After returning to Rome, Mussolini addressed the Senate on November 27 and announced that, as promised earlier, he would neither dissolve nor suppress parliament; however, he had now decided that parliament would be "adjourned" while he wielded the emergency powers it had given him. Without parliamentary interference, he and he alone would implement the measures necessary to save Italy. With parliament effectively silenced, he departed, on December 7, for another international conference.

This one was in London, and its purpose was to discuss what the Allies should do to collect delinquent war reparations from Germany. Again, for Mussolini, the first order of business was to make trouble with insistent demands that the meeting be moved closer to Italy. When this failed, he complained loudly that the French delegation (or so he had heard) had been given a more luxurious set of rooms at Claridges Hotel than the Italian delegation. Once again, Mussolini was surrounded by a phalanx of Blackshirts, much to the embarrassment of the staff of his own embassy—which, at the last minute, at least managed to dissuade the Duce from carrying into Buckingham Palace his *manganello* (the weighty wooden cudgel that had become a Blackshirt symbol) when he made his official courtesy call on King George V.

At the London conference, Lord Curzon, the British foreign minister, already put off by Mussolini's behavior at Territet and Lausanne, got his first taste of the Duce's duplicitous approach to international relations. At the conference, French premier Raymond Poincaré advocated immediate military action against

Germany to force it to pay the reparations it owed. Lord Curzon favored conciliation and believed it was in the interests of European peace to assist Germany in its postwar financial crisis. Mussolini took a stand between these extremes. He declined to send Italian troops as part of an Allied occupation of the Ruhr valley, as France wanted, but he was willing to transmit a diplomatic recommendation to Germany to submit to French demands. Secretly—as Curzon discovered—Mussolini then approached France with a proposal that Italy and France form an anti-British bloc.

In the end, Mussolini succeeded in offending French as well as British diplomats, some of whom thought he was a clumsy opportunist, another a "braggart and an actor," some a buffoon (*"César de carnaval,"* in the French phrase), and still others a dangerous "rascal," who was probably also mentally unbalanced.

But the press didn't ask the opinion of the British and French foreign offices. Instead, the British *Daily Mail* reported on the Duce's "powerful" and "hypnotic" eyes, praising him as the leader who had saved Italy—this despite the fact that, at the time, he had been prime minister for less than two months. A London *Times* editorial concluded that Mussolini's fascism was "a healthy reaction against the attempt to spread Bolshevism in Italy." Yes, the *Times* admitted, Mussolini had employed "White Terror" as a means of gaining power, but, surely, now that power had been gained, the violence would cease.

As 1922 came to a close, Mussolini returned from London to Rome and began dealing with those who still opposed him. On December 30, he ordered the arrest of the communist leaders Amadeo Bordiga and Antonio Gramsci, as well as the entire Executive Committee of the Communist Party, except for two who, as Chamber deputies, were constitutionally immune from arrest. For the moment, Mussolini stayed his hand where the socialists were concerned, and, in fact, he took no action against the Socialist Party or any other political party, except for the communists—and even they were allowed to continue to exist as a party, although under much harassment.

Mussolini took steps to rein in the *squadristi* by reorganizing them as the Voluntary Militia for National Security. Despite this, the violence continued. With or without Mussolini's orders, Blackshirts continued to beat up "Reds" and to burn down socialist and communist newspapers and meeting halls. The civil war, Mussolini announced to the nation, was over. Yet 1923 would see more arson, more assaults, and more murders, all committed by fascists against socialists, than in any other year. Mussolini had not founded the fascist movement, but he had gotten in front of it. Mussolini had not marched to Rome, but he had allowed the March on Rome to make him prime minister. Mussolini had not ordered the violence that now engulfed Italy like a wave, but it was a wave he nevertheless decided to ride.

Chapter 16

Bombing Corfu, Killing a Critic

The new prime minister's show of tolerance for dissent during his first months in office was just that: a show. Fascist violence always had a life of its own, independent from the Duce's direction. Had Mussolini seriously tried to curb it, he would have faced an insurrection of the *squadristi*. As it was, his unwillingness—or inability—to regulate the Blackshirts prompted some moderates within the Fascist Party to plot (with socialists, no less) the Duce's overthrow.

The man some British diplomats were calling a "rascal" and some French officials a "*César de carnaval*" was really more of a juggler. As he juggled public opinion with a show of statesmanlike restraint, he juggled the need of fascist extremists to crack left-wing skulls, while he simultaneously kicked at the dissidents from within his own party to keep them from causing him to drop all the balls.

With all this juggling for the benefit of his very mixed audience, what was it that Benito Mussolini *himself* wanted?

Clearly, what he wanted was a reign of terror. This, he realized, was the surest means of maintaining power and exacting obedience from all factions. Terror satisfied most fascists. Everyone else it either intimidated into obedience, beat into obedience, or killed, rendering obedience moot. For the time being, Mussolini's difficult task was to appear to the fascists to be in control of the violence, to appear to the public—within Italy and outside of it—to be opposed to the violence, even as he continued to *use* the violence to control or eliminate internal dissidents as well as opponents in other parties.

The method he employed for accomplishing his task was, for him, tried and true. He lied.

While continuing to state publicly that criminal fascist violence would be stopped, Mussolini enacted an official amnesty for fascists accused of political violence. Magistrates either sympathetic to fascism or fearful of it tended to interpret "political violence" very broadly, and thus out-and-out thugs, people with long criminal records, were pardoned, along with garden-variety fascist bullies. The freed gangsters knew where their liberty had come from, and they were, in consequence, willing to serve Mussolini. Criminals such as Albino Volpi and Amerigo Dumini, among others, became fascist hit men and assassins. It was work that came naturally to them.

Mussolini did even more than grant amnesty. Upon students wounded in what Mussolini variously called the "revolution" or the "civil war," he ordered that academic degrees be conferred without examination. The families of fascists slain in violent exchanges were awarded pensions similar to those granted the dependents of soldiers killed in the world war.

As he had distanced himself from the March on Rome (Chapter 15, "Prime Minister"), so he kept the violent men of fascism at arm's length. But they were there. In 1923, newspapers reported an average of five acts of fascist violence per day. Against this background of mayhem, which Mussolini really did not control, he ordered—privately, if not entirely in secret—certain specific acts against leftist politicians and, even more frequently, against dissident fascists, those moderates who sought a pact with socialism in order to overthrow him. In this way, opponents of fascism and of Mussolini were steadily silenced.

As valuable as violent intimidation was, Mussolini knew that he could not sustain fascism on the basis of negative force alone. He really did need to do something for Italy. Accordingly, he worked to appease and appeal to the trade unions, to persuade workers that the Fascist Party offered them something the socialists could not: rapport with Italian capitalists. Together, Mussolini preached, labor and capital could make Italy great—to the benefit of all. Whereas the socialists strove to pit labor against capital, Mussolini's message was that both labor and capital were, above all else, Italians.

A surprising number of unions and unionists bought this line of propaganda and even joined the Fascist Party—although this seems less surprising when the alternative is considered: persecution as a socialist. Not surprising at all was the support Mussolini received from industrialists and other capitalists. Crippled by years of unreliable labor, plagued by strikes, saddled with Italy's international reputation as a technologically backward and financially dubious nation, factory owners and financiers were thrilled by the prospect of stability and discipline. Even more, they breathed easier to learn that the Duce was steering the country further and further from the socialist ambition to nationalize industry and curb or eliminate free enterprise.

On March 18, 1923, Mussolini addressed the opening session of the second congress of the International Chambers of Commerce, held in Rome. He not only took the opportunity to point out that such a meeting would have been impossible in Rome just a few months earlier, he also pledged that his government would renounce all economic functions it could not fulfill. That is, he promised a free rein to free enterprise. His remarks were met with cheers.

Labor and capital were two great forces in Italian life, of course, but neither was greater than the Catholic Church. As we saw in Chapter 4, "Angelica and Rachele," the young Mussolini was unsparing in his condemnation of the Church. Now he was anxious not only to gain the approval of this powerful influence in Italian life, but also to win the support of 107 deputies representing the Catholic People's Party, the Populari. As for Pope Pius XI, he was willing enough to overlook the Duce's youthful transgressions, and he was enthusiastic about fascism as a powerful antidote to communism, but some in the Vatican, as well as a number of outspoken parish priests, were appalled by *squadristi* violence.

While Mussolini contemplated how best to handle the Church, two Blackshirts from Argenta took matters into their own hands regarding a troublesome local priest named Father Giuseppe Minzoni. Early in August 1923, they fell upon him with clubs, but were frightened off by passersby. Later in the month, on August 23, they attacked him again, when he was walking with a friend. A hat saved the friend, but the bareheaded priest suffered a fatal skull fracture. Although both assailants were arrested and tried, they were acquitted for lack of evidence—and for lack of witnesses willing to testify against them. Italo Balbo, *ras* of the Ferrara area, which included Argenta, was quick to express his sorrow at the death of Father Minzoni. Mussolini saw to it that the fascist papers throughout Italy paid tribute to the good father as a "courageous opponent."

But, unlike Giuseppe Minzoni, the incident would not die. A year later, in August 1924, the republican newspaper *La Voce Republicana* accused Balbo of having influenced and intimidated witnesses and officials to block the conviction of the murderers. Foolishly, Balbo sued the paper for libel—and lost. Balbo stepped down as head of the local Voluntary Militia, and Mussolini, clearly concerned, kept him in a low-profile position for the next two years (he would appoint him Under-Secretary for Air in 1926). The Duce waited for condemnation from the Vatican, but it never came. The unofficial position of the Church was this: However bad Mussolini and fascism were, the godless socialists and, even more, the godless communists were far worse.

Italians were proving astoundingly ready to accept fascist abuses in exchange for the economic improvements and the political security Mussolini offered. Indeed, they seemed quite prepared to relinquish liberty itself, just as Mussolini had predicted they would. Now that he had conquered Italy, Mussolini turned to the world, or, at least, a small part of it.

Like many Italians, he was not content to accept the beggar's portion of war-won spoils accorded Italy by the Treaty of Versailles. England's King George V—who, like many others, saw the Duce as an implacable foe of Bolshevism—paid a state visit to Rome in May 1923 and awarded Mussolini the Order of Bath. During the visit, George's foreign secretary, Lord Curzon, declined to discuss what Mussolini most wanted from England—Jubaland, the African colony promised Italy in 1915 by the secret Treaty of London (Chapter 7, "*Il Popolo d'Italia*"). Jubaland would be one step toward transforming Italy into an empire—and not just an empire, but a new Roman Empire, one worthy of the Blackshirt legions and the Roman salutes. Mussolini also intended to obtain Fiume, which D'Annunzio had failed to hold, as well as the Dodecanese Islands. For these, too, were promised by the secret Treaty of London, only to be withheld by the odious Treaty of Versailles.

To his consternation, Mussolini found himself in what a later generation would call a catch-22. He negotiated with the Yugoslav government over Fiume, to no avail, and he did the same with Greece over the Dodecanese, also fruitlessly. Lord Curzon, on behalf of the British government, replied to Mussolini's demands for the cession of Jubaland that this territory could be ceded only as part of a full settlement of Italy's other territorial claims. By the summer of 1923, therefore, Mussolini ordered the reinforcement of its garrison in the Dodecanese. Taking alarm, the Greek government expressed its fear to Britain (to which post–World War I Greece looked for protection) that Italy was about to annex the islands. The Italian ambassador to the Court of St. James's assured Lord Curzon that Mussolini had no such intentions.

While Mussolini pondered just what his intentions should be, events took over. Albania had won independence from Turkey in 1912, triggering a dispute between the new nation and Greece over just where the border between them lay. World War I temporarily mooted the dispute, but in 1921 the League of Nations turned the matter over to the Conference of the Ambassadors of Britain, France, Italy, and Japan. The Conference appointed Italian general Enrico Tellini to head a Greek-Albanian commission to settle the line of the frontier. On August 27, 1923, the commissioners were driving from Greece to Santi Quartanta in Albania. While still on the Greek side of the border, Gen. Tellini and his staff, in a separate car from the Albanians and Greeks, were ambushed by gunmen. Five Italians, including the general, were killed.

The Italian government summarily concluded that the assassins were Greek bandits and that local Greek government officials had conspired with them. Greek officials replied with evidence that the murderers' footprints were tracked across the Albanian border and that, therefore, the gunmen surely were Albanian, not Greek. Dismissing this, the Mussolini government delivered an ultimatum to the Greek government on the evening of August 29. It demanded that: The Greek High Command must apologize for the murders, all members of the Greek government must attend a funeral service for the slain Italians, the Greek Navy must salute the Italian tricolor, and the murderers must be apprehended within five days, speedily tried, convicted, and executed. Finally, the Greek government must pay to Italy an indemnity of fifty million lire. Italy gave Greece twenty-four hours to reply—and five days to ante up the indemnity.

The Greeks issued their reply twenty-three hours after receiving the ultimatum. All conditions would be met, with two exceptions. Under Greek law, the death penalty was assessed at the discretion of individual trial judges; it could not, therefore, be guaranteed in advance. Moreover, the indemnity demanded was excessive, and the Greek government proposed that a more equitable penalty be determined by the League of Nations.

Corfu, shortly after the Italian occupation.

(Image from ArtToday)

To the Greek reply Mussolini's government made no response other than to send seventeen warships under Vice-Adm. Emilio Solari into the waters off Corfu. On their arrival at 3 P.M. on August 31, Solari composed a note to the Greek prefect of Corfu, informing him that Italian forces were occupying the island—not as an act of war, but to enforce the demands of the ultimatum. He ordered the prefect to lower the Greek flag over the island's citadel within two hours or his fleet would commence shelling the island. By the time the note reached the prefect, however, it was four thirty. Whether he did not have sufficient time to get the flag lowered or whether he had decided to defy Solari's order is not known, but at 5 P.M., the Greek flag still flew over the citadel, and Solari therefore opened fire directly on the building.

The citadel was only nominally a military facility, with 169 Greek soldiers posted there. Other residents included a civilian police training academy, some six thousand refugees from Smyrna (which had been overrun by Turkish forces), a boy's orphanage financed by the Lord Mayor of London's Fund, and an even larger orphanage financed by Save the Children, an American charity. Reports of casualties from the bombardment vary, from four killed and sixteen wounded to sixteen killed and thirty-two wounded. Although Lord Curzon opined that the "terms demanded by Mussolini" were "extravagant—much worse than the ultimatum after Sarajevo" (Austria-Hungary's outrageous demands on Serbia, which triggered World War I), neither England nor the rest of the world expressed anything approaching genuine outrage. Curzon and others did propose to Mussolini that the matter of Corfu be referred to the League of Nations, but, through his diplomatic corps, Mussolini replied that while Italy would be reasonable, it would not defer to the League in this matter. Indeed, at a cabinet meeting on September 4, Mussolini declared that if the League of Nations claimed authority to deal with the Corfu incident, Italy would leave the organization.

Response to Mussolini's intransigence was mixed. In England, most of the press, which had been enthusiastic about the Italy's new prime minister, now turned against him, although rather mildly. The French press, in contrast, enthusiastically applauded the bombardment of Corfu, expressing the attitude of the French government that Mussolini was a bulwark against communism and that any check or humiliation the fascist regime might suffer could transform Italy into a Bolshevik state. As for Britain's official response, H. W. Kennard, the British diplomat in Rome reporting to Lord Curzon, believed that Mussolini was something of a madman, a "mixture of megalomania and extreme patriotism."

Did this mean that Kennard recommended taking a hard line with him? Not at all. Kennard was worried that the Duce was crazy enough to start a European war rather than back down on the issue of Corfu. To be sure, concerted British action would stop Mussolini before such a war could get very far, but this would cause the collapse of fascism and the consequent onslaught of anarchy or communism. Kennard's recommendation was that Mussolini be humored. Some fifteen years later, at Munich, British Prime Minister Neville Chamberlain would take much the same tack with Adolf Hitler in a policy he called appeasement.

There were dissenting voices in the British government and from elsewhere—most notably Yugoslavia and Czechoslovakia— pointing out that "humoring" Mussolini now would only embolden him to create more trouble later. Besides, to allow a member nation to defy the League of Nations would greatly diminish the authority of that body. In the end, however, the fear of communism won out, and the League referred the Corfu issue to the Conference of Ambassadors, just as Mussolini had wanted. The Conference backed Italy, Greece met all the demands, and Mussolini pulled his forces out of Corfu.

It was another triumph for the Duce: international ratification of his authority and effectiveness. At home, it made him more popular than ever, dispelling the doubts of many. It also greased stalled negotiations with Yugoslavia over Fiume. In January 1924, Yugoslavia at long last agreed to cede the town of Fiume to Italy, provided that Yugoslavia be permitted to retain the port of Baros and other areas just outside of the town. As for the Greeks, the Corfu bombardment persuaded them to back down on the Dodecanese. While the Greek government did not formally cede the island group to Italy, it no longer protested or resisted Italian occupation. In 1925, Mussolini decreed that all residents of the islands must adopt Italian nationality.

With all of this accomplished, Mussolini stunned many of his supporters, both inside and outside of Italy, by suddenly negotiating, in January 1924, diplomatic and commercial relations with the Soviet Union. But even this was seen as another example of the wisdom of Mussolini's judgment, which, Italians were beginning to think, was infallible. The Corfu triumph and the acquisition of Fiume and the Dodecanese, together with the recognition of the Soviet Union, added greatly to the Duce's prestige.

Shortly after taking office, Mussolini proposed a dramatic change in Italy's election law, which would replace the system of proportional representation with a system in which the party that obtained a simple majority of seats would be awarded double the number of its elected candidates. Mussolini's diplomatic successes ensured passage of the new law, and on April 6, 1924, the general election resulted in a fascist gain of two hundred twenty-five seats in parliament, for a total of two hundred sixty. Other parties that were in lockstep with the fascist regime held 116 seats, effectively giving Mussolini's government 376 of the 535 seats in the Chamber of Deputies. The socialists and communists lost 72 of the 138 seats they had held between them before the election. The Catholic People's Party held forty seats, down from one hundred seven. Importantly, the Vatican had directed priests to make no attempt to influence their parishioners.

Mussolini now had the best of all political worlds. He had the power to dissolve parliament, but he had arranged matters so that he didn't have to exercise that power. What could possibly stop him?

Not everyone in the opposition had given up. On May 30, 1924, at the opening session of the newly elected parliament, a prominent socialist deputy named Giacomo Matteotti unleashed an attack on the conduct of the election. His booming voice rising above the voices of the fascist deputies who tried to shout him down, Matteotti reeled off example after example of the violence, mayhem, and intimidation that had been used to ensure a massive fascist victory. Matteotti stated in public what a number of Italians had quietly come to believe: that Mussolini kept close to him a kind of cross between a palace guard and a secret police force, a body that planned and often executed campaigns of beating and intimidation and, when necessary, assassination. Secretly, people referred to this group as the Cheka, after the notorious secret police of the Soviets. Matteotti dared to utter the name out loud and in public. He demanded that the results of the election be annulled. He proposed that the socialist deputies withdraw from the parliament in protest, just as the plebs, in 500 B.C.E., had withdrawn to Rome's Aventine Hill to protest patrician rule and compel the patricians to give them a voice in government affairs.

In speaking out this way, Matteotti made a heroic stand—indeed, as he himself saw it, a suicidal stand. "You may kill me, but you will never kill my ideas," he declared.

Mussolini, as usual, was duplicitous. In the June 1 *Il Popolo d'Italia*, he condemned Matteotti in terms that constituted something more than a veiled threat, but on June 7, he made a speech in parliament that called for national reconciliation. Yet, on that very day, a British journal carried an article by Matteotti claiming that Italian government officials had taken bribes from the Sinclair Exploration Company, a U.S. oil concern, in exchange for facilities to search for oil in Emilia and Sicily. In the past, opponents of the government had argued chiefly on ideological grounds. Clearly, however, Matteotti was mounting a campaign to demonstrate that the trouble with Mussolini's government was not ideological, but moral, that the fascist regime had not only compromised the election, but was thoroughly corrupt.

On June 10, three days after the publication of Matteotti's article, the deputy left his apartment on his way to the parliament. Just outside of his building, Matteotti was set upon by five men, beaten, and bundled into a car. When he failed to return home the next morning, his wife notified the police. Remarkably, the caretaker of Matteotti's building had spotted the car earlier, before the abduction. It was driving around and around the building at low speed. Suspicious, she jotted down its license number. Signora Matteotti now gave the police the license number, but they did nothing with it. When the Matteotti's family lawyer threatened to go to the press, a police official revealed the identity of the car's owner, Filippo Filippelli, editor of *Corriere Italiano,* a fascist newspaper. Then the official continued: The car had been found, abandoned, stained with blood both inside and out.

On June 12, Mussolini announced to the Chamber of Deputies that he had assigned Gen. De Bono to direct the police investigation of the Matteotti case, but that, so far, neither the police nor the government had any clue to the deputy's whereabouts. This was apparently too much for one republican member, who shouted that Mussolini was an accessory to murder. The remark triggered a fusillade of accusations from the socialists and communists. Mussolini, typically a study in stoic posturing, was badly shaken. Those close to him noted that he was trembling.

Days passed without any sign of Matteotti. At last, on June 27, as Matteotti had threatened they would, the socialists walked out of the Chamber of Deputies, withdrawing, figuratively, to the Aventine Hill, and they were known from that day on as the Aventines. Then, on August 16, 1924, the body of Giacomo Matteotti was located in a desolate area several miles outside Rome. He had been clubbed to death.

To the Chamber of Deputies, Mussolini delivered expressions of profound horror, and to Matteotti's family—his wife and two sons, aged six and four—he promised a pension. (It was a promise he rigorously kept.) He also pledged to find the murderers—but he denied that the Fascist Party was responsible, and he made another pledge: to punish anyone who accused the party or the government of the murder. This threat notwithstanding, the police discovered that Matteotti had been slain by five fascists, two of whom, Amerigo Dumini and Albino Volpi, were close associates of Mussolini and had been beneficiaries of the Duce's 1922 amnesty decree. The five were arrested, as was Filippelli, owner of the kidnap car, and Filippo Naldi, another fascist editor, both accused as accessories to the murder.

> ... *the discovery of the corpse in a hedge near Rome, called the Quartarella, unstopped an orgiastic research into the details which is remembered by us under the ignominious name of "Quartarellismo."*
>
> *Fortunes were built on the Matteotti tragedy; they speculated on portraits, on medals, on commemorative dates, on electric signs; a subscription was opened by subversive newspapers and even now the accounts are still open.*
>
> —Benito Mussolini, My Autobiography, 1928

Dumini quickly cracked under the pressure of police interrogation. He said that he and the others had abducted and killed Matteotti on orders of members of the Fascist Grand Council, the party inner circle Mussolini himself had created. Two Council members, Cesare Rossi and Giovanni Marinelli, were arrested. They confessed to having ordered Matteotti's abduction because they had understood this to be the wish of Mussolini. "What is the Cheka doing?" Rossi reported Mussolini as having said. "What is Dumini doing? That man (Matteotti), after that speech (of May 30, 1924), should no longer be in circulation."

From our perspective in history, it is natural to assume that Benito Mussolini ordered the murder of this voice that refused to be silenced. But there is no hard evidence of his direct involvement. Even if Rossi's testimony was truthful, what, really, did Mussolini mean by that "man ... should no longer be in circulation"? Was it really an order of execution?

At the time, various political observers predicted that the Matteotti affair would bring down the fascist regime. But it did not. Mussolini still figured in the popular mind, not only in Italy but throughout Europe and even in America, as the most credible alternative to communism in Italy. One thinks of Franklin Delano Roosevelt's remark about the United States' distasteful support of Nicaragua's right-wing dictator Anastasio Somoza Garcia: "Somoza may be a son of a bitch, but he's *our* son of a bitch." And so fear of the left, combined with political pragmatism, insulated Mussolini—even as fascist violence continued unabated after the murder of Matteotti. Opposition printing presses were wrecked, the houses of lawyers who had defended anti-fascists were ransacked, and more prominent socialists were beaten. At least one, Piero Gobetti, editor of *Rivoluzione Liberale*, was beaten so badly that he never recovered, but died seventeen months after being assaulted. He was twenty-four years old.

In a brilliant act of bravado, Mussolini addressed the Chamber of Deputies on January 3, 1925. Now, instead of parrying accusations of fascist thuggery, he embraced them: "I, and I alone, assume the political, moral and historical responsibility for all that has happened. ... If fascism has been a criminal association ... the responsibility for this is mine." Then he went on to put his "confession" in perspective. The real criminals, he said, were "the Aventines," whose desertion of the Chamber of Deputies was a direct assault on the king.

And the people, most of them, agreed.

Amid the beatings, the killings, the tyranny, and the terror, the fascists had brought Italy the promise (as yet unfulfilled) of internal order and a place of pride within the international community. Over the horizon loomed national greatness, and that was the horizon toward which Mussolini was leading the fascist march. To stop marching now would doubtless mean being overtaken by the communists. This, then, was no time to stop.

As for the murderers of Matteotti, four: Marinelli, Rossi, Filippelli, and Naldi, were acquitted. (Rossi fled Italy and joined a band of anti-fascist refugees in Paris. From there, for the rest of his life, he denounced Mussolini as Matteotti's murderer. Few listened.) Of the five men who had actually abducted Matteotti, two, Giuseppe Viola and Augusto Malacria, were acquitted, and three, Dumini, Volpi, and Amieto Poveromo, were found guilty of murder, albeit unpremeditated and committed "under provocation" (namely, Matteotti's violent resistance to being abducted!). They were sentenced to six years' imprisonment, four years of which were subtracted as a result of a special amnesty. While awaiting trial and in the course of trial, the murderers had already been in jail for twenty-one months. They were, therefore, released after eighty more days, and the case of Deputy Matteotti was officially closed.

Chapter 17

Making the Trains Run on Time

Apologists for Mussolini and fascism, both in the Duce's day and even in our own, point out that while some of the regime's methods were undoubtedly violent, crude, and brutal, Mussolini never went as far as Hitler or Stalin. In terms of the scale of horrors committed, this is true—although the fact that Mussolini was neither as accomplished nor as prolific a murderer as the dictators of Germany and Soviet Russia is hardly a ringing endorsement of his leadership. At that, in the aftermath of Matteotti's murder, Mussolini seems to have contemplated becoming very much more ruthless than he had so far been.

As some contemporaries of Mussolini saw it—and some historians see it today—the "Matteotti crisis" came close to bringing down the Mussolini regime. From the most extreme factions of the Fascist Party, the fear that the murder had shaken support for the regime prompted calls for an intensified reign of terror. Roberto Farinacci, who acted as defense counsel in the murder trial of Amerigo Dumini, called for a widespread massacre of anti-fascists and even nonfascists. "By shooting a few thousand people, we can put everything to rights," he said.

Did Mussolini seriously consider such a policy? We don't know, but it is a fact that he neither said nor did anything to condemn Farinacci's proposal. Instead, he asserted that his regime was "above the law," that it "could not be prosecuted except at the bar of history." He also interpreted his popular mandate not as a plea for liberty, but for strong government, for order. Civilization,

Mussolini explained, was incompatible with liberty; rather, it *required* the diminution and sacrifice of individual freedom. In the promotion and defense of civilization, therefore, cruelty was necessary. Sometimes Mussolini spoke of applying violence and cruelty "surgically" as opposed to wantonly, but at other times his pronouncements on the topic were incredibly unguarded and certainly alarming. For example, he told an American journalist that he planned ultimately to abolish parliament and replace it with a dictatorship that would thrust Italy into the forefront of the world's nations. Preparatory to this, he intended to turn his Blackshirt squads against all internal opponents. These would be blown away, like so much dust. The journalist reported that the Duce finished his sentence by blowing on his outstretched palm: *poof*.

Gen. Emilio De Bono was suspended as commandant of the Voluntary Militia—the Blackshirts—because of his connection to the Matteotti murder. He was replaced by Italo Balbo—who had stepped down as leader of the Ferrara Blackshirts because of his implication in the murder of Father Minzoni (Chapter 16, "Bombing Corfu, Killing a Critic"). Amid a renewed public outcry, Balbo resigned, even though Mussolini gave him a ringing endorsement, which he refused to retract.

The murder of Matteotti presented a golden opportunity for those who opposed Mussolini—or, rather, for those who *should* have opposed him. But the remarkable fact is that a majority of politicians actually rallied behind Mussolini and the fascists at this time. The so-called "Aventines"—the socialists and some others who withdrew from parliament in protest of lawless fascist tyranny—were condemned, not just by Mussolini, but by most mainstream politicians.

Mussolini quickly learned that he had rather little to fear from the liberal and conservative parties, and although some deputies belonging to the Catholic People's Party had joined the Aventines, the Vatican distanced itself from their protest. More threatening was the opposition that came from within the Fascist Party. The *ras*—the local Blackshirt bosses—feared that Mussolini would, sooner or later, yield to popular and political pressure to impose on them some semblance of law and order. Assuming that a day of reckoning was at hand, the extremist *ras* criticized Mussolini for taking half measures, for deceiving himself into thinking that a revolution could be accomplished by a few blows of a bludgeon, that it did not require large-scale bloodshed. They threatened to overthrow the Duce. And as if this threat from the party's right wing weren't bad enough, there were also threats from the other extreme of the party. The moderates, those who wanted to see fascism "normalized" in a return to constitutional government, also spoke of rebellion against Mussolini.

Both the *ras* and the moderates made the same reasonable, but quite mistaken, assumption: that the Italian public and mainstream politicians could never forgive Mussolini for Matteotti's murder, nor would they tolerate much longer fascist violence and lawlessness. They assumed that the Matteotti murder had created a crisis that Mussolini could never survive.

The funeral procession of Giacomo Matteotti, Mussolini's most outspoken socialist critic, abducted and beaten to death by members of the Fascist Grand Council.

(Image from ArtToday)

The murder had indeed created a crisis, but it was a crisis chiefly among the fascists themselves, not those outside the party. Mussolini was at first puzzled as to how to resolve the internal dissension, and he listened seriously to some who advised him to resign. What both steadied and moved his hand, however, was an unannounced visit from some fifty Blackshirts—all militia officers—who delivered an ultimatum: either act forcefully now or be deposed. According to some sources, Mussolini's initial response to this intrusion was a stern admonition about who was boss. According to other accounts, Mussolini broke down and wept.

Whatever his initial response, the Blackshirts' visit launched the Duce into action. As violent as 1923 and 1924 were, the year 1925 began with a nationwide Blackshirt sweep of unprecedented scope and intensity. Socialist offices were ransacked, opposition papers were attacked, and socialist activists were beaten and/or arrested wherever they were encountered. Farinacci, at the time engaged in the legal defense of Dumini, was appointed Secretary of the Fascist Party. This was a strong message to fascists and non-fascists alike: Mussolini had elevated to the very top one of the most extreme and extremely violent members of the party.

By February it was becoming clear that Mussolini would weather the storm Matteotti's murder had stirred. At the very least, the Duce was getting away with murder. Yet the turmoil surrounding the Matteotti affair had taken its toll on him. On February 15, the very day he appointed Farinacci secretary of the party, Mussolini collapsed in pain with excruciating stomach cramps. The diagnosis was bleeding peptic ulcers. Most of his associates attributed the ulcers to the stress of office, although others pointed out that his Spartan diet—mostly vegetables and fruit washed down with milk in meals that never lasted more than ten minutes—may have brought on his gastric problems. Another possibility is that the debilitating attack was psychosomatic. Hoping both to recover and to hide his illness from the public, Mussolini lay low for five weeks—during which time he relinquished to Farinacci sole command of the Blackshirt militia. Thus it was Farinacci who unleashed the most ruthless campaigns of violence, this one against Florentine socialists and another suspect group, the Freemasons.

> Today, in the United States, the Freemasons—or Masons—function mainly as a business-oriented social and service club, a lodge organization neither more or less consequential than such bodies as the Elk and the Moose. In early twentieth-century Italy, however, the Freemasons were a political secret society, mysterious to outsiders, and they were regarded by fascists (as well as by communists, for that matter) as a dangerous rival. The Catholic Church also condemned Freemasonry as anti-Christian.

When he returned to his desk from his sickbed on March 23, 1925, Mussolini made no effort to call a halt to Farinacci's Blackshirt terror. Indeed, shortly after the Duce returned to work, he stood by as Farinacci indirectly but unmistakably ordered the beating of the liberal-conservative leader Giovanni Amendola. The beating, duly administered, proved fatal—and thus Mussolini was rid of a political enemy second only to Matteotti in his outspoken courage. That Farinacci had done Mussolini's dirty work, both in the Duce's absence and presence, did not earn Mussolini's gratitude. In 1926, he used Farinacci's "excesses" as an excuse to remove him as party secretary. Mussolini had allowed Farinacci to dispose of certain enemies, and Farinacci had done so in a way that ensured Farinacci's own self-destruction and consequent removal from the party's inner circle. One stone, two birds: Down went a rival from outside the party as well as one from within.

If Italians were proving themselves remarkably tolerant of fascist lawlessness, they were not alone in the world. Through three years of mayhem, Mussolini's foreign press remained quite positive. In today's terms, his "approval rating" was consistently high.

As we saw in Chapter 16, his relations with the British foreign office had been strained throughout much of 1924, but when the liberal government of Prime Minister Ramsay MacDonald folded and was replaced by a conservative government under Stanley Baldwin, Mussolini was thrilled. He had at long last managed to wrest Jubaland from the MacDonald government, but that hardly made him grateful to the former Prime Minister. Mussolini inwardly boiled at the liberal disdain of MacDonald and his foreign secretary, Lord Curzon. With the new foreign secretary, Austen Chamberlain (half-brother of future Prime Minister Neville Chamberlain), Mussolini got on very well. Chamberlain called him "a wonderful man ... working for the greatness of the country."

Chamberlain was not alone in what seems from our perspective a singularly bizarre assessment. In 1928, the American ambassador to Italy, Richard Washburn Child, called Mussolini "both wise and humane" and ("whether one approves or detests him") "the greatest figure of this sphere and time." Child so admired Mussolini that he persuaded him to write his best-known autobiography, which appeared in 1928, in English before Italian. "I knew him," Child wrote in his introduction to *My Autobiography*, "before the world at large, outside of Italy, had ever heard of him. I knew him before and after the moment he leaped into the saddle and in the days when he, almost single-handed, was clearing away chaos' own junk pile from Italy."

Child continued: "He has not only been able to secure and hold an almost universal following; he has built a new state upon a new concept of a state. He has not only been able to change the lives of human beings but he has changed their minds, their hearts, their spirits. He has not merely ruled a house; he has built a new house. ... Mussolini has made a state. That is super-statesmanship."

As much of the Red-fearing world saw it, Mussolini could do no wrong, no matter how much wrong he actually did. For even though he suppressed rival newspapers, the news of the violence, the beatings, the arson, the bullying, and the murders did not merely leak out, but gushed, reported in great detail by many Italian as well as foreign journalists. There was no secret about any of it. Yet most of the world was prepared to deny it—and would keep on denying it through the 1920s and 1930s, even after Mussolini leagued with Adolf Hitler in a lockstep toward a new world war.

Mussolini biographer Jasper Ridley details an episode in which an Italian company made a bid for an oil concession in Albania.

When the Albanian government awarded the concession to a British company instead, Mussolini, through his ambassador to London, accused the British government of underhandedly forcing Albania to grant the concession to a British firm. This affront tried even the admiring Chamberlain's patience: "If Mussolini proceeds upon the assumption that we can be addressed and bullied like a third rate power he makes a fatal mistake." But this, after all, was Mussolini, the "wonderful man," and Chamberlain soon thought the better of his own outrage. He ascribed the harsh words to Mussolini's recent bout with ulcers, and he settled the matter by personally requesting that the Albanian government cut Italy in for a thirty-three percent interest in the available oil concession. France, another bidder and longtime British ally, was entirely shut out. Even when personally confronted with the Duce's offensive arrogance, many statesmen, like Austen Chamberlain, found him impossible to resist.

His attraction was not entirely personal. Western politicians of the 1920s and 1930s had a need to feel that they were engaged in a common struggle against Bolshevism. At the time, a resolutely anti-Soviet policy was the only prerequisite for membership in the old boys' club of Western leaders. Even Germany was admitted to membership, by virtue of the Treaty of Locarno, signed by Britain, France, Belgium, Italy, *and* Germany in October 1925. It pledged nonaggression and defensive alliance: No signatory party would attack another, and all would come to the aid of any signatory that was the victim of aggression. In a statesmanlike manner, Mussolini himself proposed that the treaty be duly registered with the secretary general of the League of Nations and made subject to the Covenant of the League.

Mussolini was in especially good repute with the international community when, on November 4, 1925, a Socialist deputy, Tito Zaniboni, was arrested just as he had assumed a sniper's perch at a hotel window and was preparing to assassinate the Duce. The incident made the Socialists look as evil to the West as the Bolsheviks—What was the difference between them, anyway?— and it made the nation as well many capitalist statesmen very grateful that Mussolini had survived. Congratulatory telegrams poured in from the various embassies.

As 1925 gave way to 1926, Mussolini was regarded by many Italians as their savior and, if anything, was even more universally admired abroad. British, American, and, to a lesser extent, French diplomats condescendingly marveled at how the Duce was bringing discipline to an inherently undisciplined nation. Mussolini habitually took time out from attending to the great issues facing Italy to focus on the most minute and mundane details of everyday Italian life. He saw to it, for example, that laws were passed to regulate motor and pedestrian traffic in Rome, even to the extent of making certain busy sidewalk traffic one way. Pedestrians were permitted to move in one direction on one side of the street and they had to walk to the other side if they wanted to change direction. In any other national leader, such micromanaging would have been scoffed at and even deemed a sign of mental instability. In Mussolini's case, however, it was admired. Here, after all, was a dictator who could resurrect a dead economy, fight communism, dodge an assassin's bullet, *and* direct traffic.

Soon—especially after the fascist regime outlawed labor strikes of all kinds—the catch phrase most often heard about Mussolini was, "He made the trains run on time." It was uttered as a response to any complaint about the Duce's brutality or tyranny. For in chronically inefficient, strike-afflicted Italy, adherence to a railroad timetable seemed a miracle. People—otherwise rational people—weighed the sacrifice of liberty and personal security against the efficiency represented by trains running on time, and they praised this devil's bargain as a great achievement. (Had anyone actually taken the trouble to evaluate the timeliness of the Italian railways during the Duce's two decades, it would have been found that the trains still did not run on time. At least not very often. It was true, however, that, without strikes, the trains did at least run.)

Among the many people great and small who admired Mussolini, one of the smallest (at the time) was Adolf Hitler. Like many other Austrians and Germans, Hitler was profoundly restless after World War I. In 1920, he founded the National Socialist German Workers' Party, with a charter membership of seven, counting himself. Hitler had been captivated by the 1922 March on Rome and envisioned himself at the head of a similar March on Berlin.

As a result of the world war, Italy had "liberated" the northern Trentino and the Alto Adige from Austria. When he came to power, Mussolini imposed a ban on the public use of the German language in these predominantly German-speaking regions. This provoked outrage among many Austrian and German nationalists. But Hitler, whose German nationalism extended to support of German minorities in many countries, was silent on the region the Germans and Austrians called the *Süd-Tirol*. He admired Mussolini too much to criticize him.

In 1926, Hitler, having served a brief period in prison after his abortive 1923 Beer Hall Putsch in Munich, having written *Mein Kampf,* and having built up a small but growing following, was emboldened to request through the Italian embassy in Berlin a signed photograph of Mussolini. At the time, the Duce was talking tough about the *Süd-Tirol* controversy, boasting that the Italian army could, unilaterally and at will, move the Austro-Italian border much, *much* farther north than the Southern Tyrol. Mussolini's Foreign Office instructed the Italian embassy in Berlin to be polite in declining Herr Hitler's request for a signed photograph.

Chapter 18

Assassins, Workers, Mafia, Pope

History is shaped by great social forces, the actions of which are more or less gradual and evolutionary, and also by sudden cataclysms: wars, natural disasters, plagues, or an assassin's bullet. Many of the "what if" games historians and others play turn upon questions of assassination. What if someone had stopped John Wilkes Booth, and Lincoln had lived to oversee Reconstruction? What if the bullet of would-be assassin Giuseppe "Joe" Zangara had hit Franklin Roosevelt in 1933 instead of Chicago mayor Anton Cermak? What if any of the eighteen attempts against Adolf Hitler's life between 1938 and 1944 had succeeded?

And what of Mussolini? He had been seriously wounded in World War I. He had survived a serious auto wreck in 1919 and an airplane crash the same year. He was the target of an assassination attempt on November 4, 1925 (Chapter 17, "Making the Trains Run on Time"), and again, on April 7, 1926. In this second incident, his assailant was a woman, which is surprising not only because female assassins are rare, but also because Mussolini prided himself on his ability to seduce the women he wanted to sleep with and to charm all the rest. Clementine Churchill wrote to her husband, Winston, that she found Mussolini "most impressive," especially his "beautiful golden brown piercing eyes that you can see but can't look at." When Mussolini gave Mrs. Churchill his photograph, she dutifully reported to her husband that "All the Embassy ladies are dying of jealousy."

The April 7 attempt on the Duce's life came very close to succeeding, as the woman was positioned just a few yards from Mussolini, and the bullet grazed his nose, drawing blood. Mussolini was targeted again on September 11, 1926, by an anarchist, Gino Lucetti, who threw a bomb at his car. The device hit the automobile's front wheel, bounced off, and exploded in the street without hurting Mussolini, although it wounded a number of bystanders.

> *After he learned that his female assailant of April 7, 1926, one Violet Gibson, was mentally ill, Mussolini ordered her deported to her native England without additional judicial action being brought against her. Gino Lucetti, the September 11 attacker, was tried for his attempt and sentenced to thirty years' imprisonment. He was released after the coup of July 25, 1943, toppled Mussolini from power, but, shortly after his release, the unfortunate Lucetti was killed in an Allied air raid.*

On October 31, another anarchist, Anteo Zamboni, aged sixteen, fired on Mussolini's car. Zamboni had clearly contemplated the assassination for a long time and had even infiltrated the fascist youth movement, the uniformed *Avanguardisti*, in order to get close to the Duce. His bullet also missed Mussolini, however, although it tore a hole in the coat of Bologna's mayor. Rough justice was immediately executed against the boy gunman. He was set upon by the crowd, who beat, shot, stabbed, and finally tore him literally limb from limb. His dismembered arms and legs were paraded through the streets of Bologna as trophies of fascist indestructibility.

Mussolini and the fascists made very little of the first three attempts on the Duce's life, but this fourth incident unleashed a new wave of violence. Blackshirts burned the offices of the Socialist Party—and every other opposition party—in Milan, while in Rome, Naples, Cagliari, and Genoa, fascist mobs broke into the homes of prominent socialists and liberals and menaced them and their families. Mammolo Zamboni, the youthful assassin's father, was arrested, as was the boy's aunt, Virginia Tabarroni. They were charged as accessories to attempted murder on the grounds that they had spent their lives indoctrinating Anteo

Zamboni. Found guilty, they were each sentenced to thirty years' imprisonment, but Mussolini personally intervened, pardoned, and released them.

Mussolini was not interested in punishing those associated with Anteo Zamboni. After all, his act had served a valuable purpose. For one thing, it released a torrent of congratulatory messages from prominent Italians and from statesmen and admirers all over the world. Even more important, it provided a rationale for Mussolini, through his Council of Ministers—his cabinet—to issue decrees giving him virtually limitless power to stamp out anti-fascist activity. As of November 5, 1926, the socialist press and other socialist organizations as well as other opposition presses and organizations were wholly suppressed. Up to this time, the socialists and other opponents had been beaten, bullied, murdered, terrorized, and generally harassed, but, until now, they had not been legally throttled. Using the new law, Mussolini expelled Socialist and opposition party deputies from the Chamber of Deputies, and from November 5 on, he could imprison, indefinitely and without trial, anyone suspected of anti-fascist activity. Although capital punishment had been abolished in Italy, the November decree reinstated the death penalty for attempts against the life of the king, the queen, the royal heir—or the head of the government.

If we wish to pinpoint the moment at which Italy became, irreversibly, a fascist dictatorship, the date November 5, 1926, is as good as any. From that day forward, the Italian parliament and constitution were as good as dead.

There was, however, another kind of assassination, a type that Mussolini could not deal with legislatively: the assassination of character. Ida Dalser, who had borne Mussolini's illegitimate son, Benito Albino, in 1915 (Chapter 6, "Avanti!"), never quite left Mussolini's life. She reemerged periodically, and she peppered him, his wife Rachele, and even the Pope with letters professing her love and denouncing his betrayal. Much of this was easy enough to sweep under the carpet. But when Dalser appeared in public during the summer of 1926 and threw a fit—the result either of hysteria or epilepsy—Mussolini's officials saw to it that she was quickly whisked off to a mental hospital in Pergine. Presumably she was treated in much the same way as any inmate—physicians had diagnosed her as a paranoiac—but she was held incommunicado. Even her family was not permitted to visit her, although Dalser was allowed to receive letters from them and to write in return. She escaped briefly in 1935, but was recaptured and confined to a Venetian hospital, where she died two years later.

As for Benito Albino, he seems to have been a good son to his illustrious father—"good" in that he had the sense to maintain a very low profile. Except for a visit during the boy's first days of life, Mussolini never saw Benito Albino again, and, as far as can be determined, the boy never attempted to see his father. He did join the fascist youth movement, but this was expected from *any* child growing up in the Duce's Italy. It is also known that he was engaged to be married and that, shortly before the wedding date, he took a cruise to China.

But at this point, an impenetrable fog closes over his life. All that is known for certain is that he did not marry. Family tradition holds that no sooner did Benito Albino return from China than he was forcibly confined to a mental hospital at Mombello, where he died in 1942, aged twenty-six. The family believes that both he and his mother were locked away on fascist orders and that Benito Albino may well have been murdered during his incarceration. That no record of Benito Albino Dalser's confinement exists does not prove the family's theory wrong, of course. Others who knew the young man say that he was never sent to any hospital, but enlisted in the Italian navy at the outbreak of World War II in 1940, served aboard a destroyer, and was killed in action sometime during the war.

Whatever happened to Benito Albino and whatever the real reason for locking Ida Dalser away, Mussolini neatly avoided character assassination just as he handily dodged the bullets of his other would-be assassins. Having escaped unscathed, he marched on to confront other enemies.

Although there are no recorded references to the Mafia before 1865, most scholars believe that it may have originated in Sicily as early as the later Middle Ages in the form of a loose collection of bands of what may be described as "enforcers" in the service of local landowners. Over many years, these bands coalesced into larger groups that began to hold sway over rural areas of Sicily in the absence of effective government. As official Sicilian governments became more active—if not more efficient—the Mafia evolved into a frankly criminal organization, a violent alliance of many small local groups. During the nineteenth and early twentieth centuries, the Mafia operated by forcing farmers to sell their produce to the organization, which, in turn, resold it to shopkeepers at inflated prices. Farmers or shopkeepers who tried to cut out the Mafia by dealing directly with one another were dealt with violently—often by murder. This led to a proliferation of vendettas: The murders produced vengeance killings, which, in turn, produced additional vengeance killings, and so on, often from one generation to another. In this way, some smaller Sicilian villages all but lost their male populations.

The Mafia was so profitable that members went to extravagant lengths to protect the integrity of the organization. Each Mafia group or "family" was based on either a natural kinship relationship or on an artificial kinship relationship conferred when a man became a member. The chief code of membership was the *omerta*, a rule of silence with regard to Mafia activities, combined with a pledge of absolute obedience to hierarchical authority. By the 1920s, in western Sicily, where the Mafia was most active, there were more than seven hundred murders each year, making the Mafia a far more violent terrorist organization than the Fascist Party.

Mussolini realized that the Mafia was the only force in Italy as feared as the fascists. Italy wasn't big enough for the Mafia *and* fascism. That was reason enough to crush it. Equally important was the fact that no previous government had been able to stamp out the Mafia, and if fascism could slay this dragon, it would indeed prove itself the most potent force Italy had ever known.

When Mussolini recognized that the local fascist leader in Sicily, Alfredo Cucco, had been consistently ineffectual in his efforts against the Mafia, he appointed in his stead Cesare Mori, first as prefect of Trappani and then, in October 1925, as prefect of Palermo. Mori was something of a daring choice. In 1922, as prefect of Bologna, he had resisted Italo Balbo's efforts to take over the city (Chapter 13, "New Legions"), for he had been determined to maintain law and order. Most fascists resented and even hated Mori for his resistance, but Mussolini respected him and believed that fighting the Mafia required a man with a stubborn sense of justice.

Turned loose against the Mafia, Mori began mass arrests of known Mafiosi, anyone with a criminal record, and even those guilty of nothing more than possessing morals less straitlaced than Mori's own (he routinely arrested patrons of "sinful" nightclubs). Mori published a proclamation directed at the large numbers of Mafiosi who had fled to the mountains to avoid arrest. He warned them that if they did not return to Palermo within twelve hours, he would round up their wives and children and put *them* in jail. By the end of the year, large numbers of Mafiosi and banditti of all kinds had been arrested or had surrendered. Mussolini was delighted and, on January 6, 1926, sent Mori a fulsome congratulatory telegram.

During 1926 and 1927, in a series of mass show trials, a long line of suspected Mafiosi were prosecuted. At Termini Imerese, on October 4, 1927, a trial of 154 defendants began. It ended on January 10, 1928, with the conviction of the majority. Seven defendants received life sentences and the others were put away for terms ranging from five to thirty years. Only eight were acquitted. More trials followed, including one that heard the cases of 161 defendants, took the testimony of five hundred witnesses, and stretched over some eight months. Mussolini's only complaint to Mori was that the process of justice in an eight-month trial moved too slowly. He wanted a "rhythm more in keeping with the times, in other words, more fascist." Fascist justice had to be swift as well as terrible.

Thanks largely to Cesare Mori, Mafia activity was almost completely suppressed in Sicily until 1943, when the invading army of the United States secretly collaborated with American leaders of organized crime to revive the organization as a means of undermining fascism's hold on the island. As for Mori, the experience of rounding up and trying the Mafia had been a heady one. It transformed him into an ardent fascist intensely loyal to the Duce, who rewarded him with an appointment as senator. Mussolini admired Mori's efficiency, which was a quality fascism touted but rarely, in fact, achieved. When Mussolini ordered a plebiscite in 1929 to affirm the electorate's approval of fascism and himself, Mori vowed to bring in a strong showing from Palermo. In the past, voter apathy had run high in Sicily, and nowhere more than in Palermo, where elected government had always lagged a distant second to de facto home rule and the sway of the Mafia. About three quarters of the eligible voters generally avoided the polls. But Mori saw to it that an unprecedented ninety-two percent turned out for the plebiscite to voice their overwhelming approval of the Duce: 190,797 voting thumbs up and only 320 expressing disapproval.

Mori had done great things for Benito Mussolini. But the Duce's loyalty never extended very far. Caving in to pressure from other fascists, who never forgave Mori for interfering with Balbo, Mussolini, in June 1929, dismissed Mori as prefect of Palermo, irrelevantly citing his age—fifty-seven—and thanking him for his noble services.

The triumph over the Mafia was hailed by all classes of Italian society as a great achievement. But if Mussolini still risked popular disapproval, it was with the laboring classes, for, knowing who buttered his bread, he came down hard against the trade unions and threw the support of the government entirely behind the capitalists. Not that Mussolini made the mistake of simply outlawing trade unions. Instead, he suppressed the socialist unions and replaced them with fascist ones. The emphasis of these unions was not to pit workers' demands against the vicious parsimony of greedy capitalists, but to forge working relationships between workers and owners that would result in a greater Italy for both groups. In theory, this was a bold and beneficial step for the beleaguered Italian economy. In practice, it meant that Mussolini inevitably supported the owners in any conflict with the workers.

On April 3, 1926, his government passed a law forbidding almost all strikes, at least those intended to "coerce or influence" the conduct of the state. Two months later, a law was passed extending the eight-hour workday to nine hours. Mussolini justified this on the grounds that labor was a "social duty." As for Italian workers, they swallowed hard and peacefully accepted the new laws.

Having disposed of the Mafia and asserted fascism's dominance over labor, Mussolini next turned his attention to the Catholic Church. The mere fact of fascism's opposition to atheistic communism had moved the Church to voice limited support for fascism and to overlook many fascist abuses. Now Mussolini, the former scourge of Catholicism, the radical orator who had built his earliest reputation on impassioned speeches about the martyrdom of Giordano Bruno at the hands of an oppressive and ignorant Church, sought more from the Pope than mild approval. He wanted an outright endorsement and alliance.

In 1871 the unity of Italy was finalized by the restriction of papal sovereignty to a few buildings in the Vatican, in compensation for which the papacy was awarded an annual indemnity for the lost Papal States. The Roman Catholic Church never accepted this arrangement, however, and, year after year, declined the indemnity. Each pope after Pius IX deemed himself a prisoner of the Vatican. In August 1926, Mussolini began secret negotiations with Cardinal Pietro Gaspari, the Papal Secretary of State, to resolve the so-called "Roman question." To demonstrate his goodwill, Mussolini had, late the year before, solemnized his own civil marriage with a Catholic ceremony.

The negotiations with the superannuated Gaspari dragged on and on, but by early 1929, a concordat had been formulated, and on February 11, 1929, Mussolini and an entourage from the Foreign Office went to the Lateran Palace in Rome to meet with Gaspari, the Vatican lawyer Francesco Pacelli (brother of the future Pope Pius XII), and other Church officials to sign the Lateran Treaty.

The signing of the Lateran Treaty. Mussolini is seated at the right, Cardinal Gaspari at the left.

(*Image from ArtToday*)

By the treaty, the papacy recognized, for the first time, the kingdom of Italy, as well as its sovereignty over all Rome, save Vatican City. The Church further agreed that all Roman Catholic organizations would abstain from politics. On its part, the Italian government declared Roman Catholicism the only state religion of Italy and further declared its recognition of Vatican City—a state created by the treaty—as sovereign and independent. Nevertheless, Italy guaranteed Vatican City public services and protection. The delicate matter of canon (Church) law versus civil law was resolved, at least in the case of matrimony. Civil law now recognized marriage as a sacrament and required that banns be published. While divorce was left as a question for the Church, legal separations were to be adjudicated by the state. Italian law pursuant to the treaty now also mandated religious instruction in primary and secondary schools. With the conclusion of the Lateran Treaty, Pope Pius XI pronounced Mussolini "the man of Providence."

It was this moment, with the fascist movement and the Catholic Church locked in fond embrace, that Mussolini chose to abolish free election of deputies to the Chamber. Having already expelled the communists, the socialists, and the republicans, it was not difficult to persuade parliament to enact a law turning over to the Fascist Grand Council the nomination of deputies. The resulting slate of candidates would be presented to the electorate, who would vote it up or down as a whole.

And it was at this moment, too, that Mussolini offered to Italy the plebiscite Mori would manage so well in Sicily. A single question was posed to Italians: Did they support the government, fascism, and Benito Mussolini? A single answer was required: yes or no. On March 24, 1929, 8,519,559 Italian voters said yes, and 155,761 said no.

Part Five

Damnation

Chapter 19

Enter Hitler

An especially important member of Mussolini's cabinet was Professor Giovanni Gentile, minister of education. His main job was to mold a generation of fascist youth. Like most Italians, Mussolini appreciated the Jesuit philosophy of education—*give me the child, and I will have the man*—and he expected Gentile to design a system to produce a generation that would follow and obey him, Benito Mussolini, without question. Yet, while fascism would be built on the robotic obedience of the masses, Mussolini was not anti-intellectual and was, in fact, anxious to explain and justify fascism as an ideology. Another of education minister Gentile's tasks was to oversee production of the *Enciclopedia Italiana*, an Italian encyclopedia with a distinctly fascist slant. The first volume was published in 1929, and by 1932 volume "F" was nearing completion. Gentile asked Mussolini to write the article on fascism—or, to be more precise, to affix his name to the article he, Gentile, had largely written. It was the only signed article in the entire encyclopedia.

The crux of the article was this: Fascism means supremacy of the state. In this it was different from liberal systems of government, which put the rights of individuals above the state. Fascism rejected this error on simple mathematical grounds: Because the state consisted of many individuals and because the whole is self-evidently greater than any part, it stands to reason that the individual, the part, must be subordinated to the state, the whole.

Socialism was also incompatible with fascism, because it placed allegiance to class above loyalty to the state. Fascism was opposed to democracy as well, because democracy was wishful thinking, an illusion, and an outright lie. Fascism opposed pacifism, which was really nothing more than another word for cowardice. Instead, fascism celebrated war, which requires the maximum human energy and effort and ennobles those who have the courage to fight.

Since fascism demanded absolute loyalty and subordination to the state, strict adherence to logical consistency should have squeezed religion out of the picture. But as a practical consideration, Mussolini needed the Catholic Church with which his government had just signed a key treaty. Therefore, the *Enciclopedia Italiana* article noted that fascism supported religion in general and Roman Catholicism in particular. For fascism, unlike Bolshevism, did not pretend to create its own god. Yet the article made menacingly clear that fascism did serve a certain irresistible force: the vitality of the Italian nation, which would find its ultimate and unavoidable expression in a mighty drive to dominate territories and peoples.

Mussolini's concern with fascist education and with defining fascism in all its cultural dimensions reflected his need to present fascism as pervasive and all-encompassing, the core substance not only of the state, but of each life within the state. Gentile acted on a Mussolini directive of December 1925: "that the schools should be inspired by the ideals of Fascism." He oversaw the creation of a curriculum in which six-year-old primary-school students learned to read and write by copying simple fascist slogans from specially produced primers: "Long live our DUCE, our Chief, and the founder of Fascism! Long live Italian Rome!" As students progressed, the slogans became more complex and fascist-slanted history lessons were introduced. Education became indoctrination.

Outside of school, most children were involved in age-specific fascist youth activities as part of the ONB, the Opera Nazionale Balilla, named after Gian Battista Perasso, familiarly called the Balilla, a Genoese youth who started an uprising against Austrian troops in 1746. Boys and girls aged six through eight enrolled in the Figli della Lupa (Children of the Wolf—meaning the wolf who suckled the mythical founders of Rome, Romulus and Remus). From membership in the Figli, boys went on to the Avanguardisti and Giovania Fascisti (Young Fascists) and girls to the Piccole Italiane and Giovani Italiane. At twenty-one, a young man became a Fascista and a young woman a Donna Fascista, party members. The only other youth organization permitted to coexist with the ONB was the Azione Cattolica, often called the Catholic Boy Scouts, but not affiliated with the Boy Scout movement begun by Britain's Lord Baden-Powell.

Fed on propaganda and catch phrases since childhood, it was natural to slip into an adult life similarly bathed in fascist slogans. These appeared in popular publications of all kinds, on wall calendars, and on posters plastered in every conceivable public space. Some slogans were of a general nature—*Credere, obbedire, combattere* (Believe, obey, fight) and "If I advance, follow me; if I stand still, drive me forward; if I retreat, shoot me"—but many others were bound specifically to Mussolini. These included an endless series of quotations from his speeches and, most important of all, the ubiquitous slogan, "*Mussolini ha sempre ragione*," Mussolini is always right.

Mussolini aimed at two objectives. The first was to bring Italy to the point at which the adjectives *Italian* and *fascist* would become synonymous; the second was to establish a personal dictatorship, one built on a cult of personality, which came to be called *mussolinismo*. It was important, Mussolini believed, for the people to see Italian government, culture, and conquest as the emanations of his personal, overmastering, and infallible will.

The fascists made widespread use of film and radio for propaganda purposes, although never with the pervasive brilliance shown by Josef Goebbels, propaganda minister for Adolf Hitler. By 1930, the Fascist Party directly controlled—with financial ownership stake—sixty-six percent of Italy's newspapers. Other papers received a daily communiqué from the government, instructing them on the official line that they were obliged to adopt in key stories. Opposition papers, having been declared illegal, had been entirely suppressed by 1930.

Within the limits set by party ownership and official instructions, free discussion in the press was not entirely squelched, especially where subjects peripheral to politics were concerned. Writers and editors debated hotly over issues in the arts, literature, and science. It was an aspect of Mussolini's genius that he profused Italian life with the fascist message, yet never to the total exclusion of incidental free discussion. In this way he avoided creating the impression that the Italian people were, in truth, his prisoners.

> *Mussolini installed his office in the Palazzo Venezia, a building whose grandeur he deemed suitable to fascism. Mussolini chose as his office the cavernous Hall of the Mappamondi, so called because the first world globe ever created was installed in the room. The Duce's desk was at one end of the hall, the door at the other. To greet honored guests, Mussolini would rise from his desk and meet the visitor halfway. Subordinates and functionaries, however, were obliged to run—not walk—the thirty-five feet from the door to his desk. Once arrived before the Duce's desk, ordinary callers were expected to stand, arm upraised in the Roman salute, until Mussolini returned the salute and offered the visitor a seat. Often, he allowed many minutes to pass before he returned the salute, and, often, he declined to invite his guest to be seated.*

Fascist indoctrination was not just the product of a stream of propaganda. Parallel with the positive messages were the ever-present consequences of dissent. After November 1926, most institutional forms of dissent—opposition parties and the opposition press—were made illegal. Dissenters no longer had to be prosecuted for their opinions, but now simply for breaking the law. Those found guilty could be imprisoned for long terms, but a guilty verdict was by no means necessary to imprison someone. On the orders of a tribunal presided over by the fascist prefect of a given district, an individual could be detained indefinitely by an order of *confino*. Such orders were usually issued at the request of the OVRA, the Organizzazione Vigilanza Repressione Antifascismo, the government secret police. Those served with a *confino* were interned on various islands that had facilities built for the purpose. These were, in fact, concentration camps—yet without the horrific features of those Hitler established. Internees lived in modest cottages and, except for having to report for a twice-daily roll call, they could move about freely on the island. Moreover, each internee was given an allowance—at first it was five lire a day, then ten—while, back home, their wives were paid two lire a day and an additional lira for each child.

Mussolini's purpose in the *confino* was not to punish, but to isolate, to take a bad influence out of circulation. Not that the picture was always so rosy, however. The guards on these islands were, after all, Blackshirts, very capable of brutality and torture.

For all that it took away, fascism did provide certain benefits, albeit mostly superficial ones. Fascism emphasized physical fitness—Mussolini looked upon his countrymen as prospective soldiers and workers, whom he wanted healthy—and an organization called the Dopolavoro ("after work") was founded to provide free recreational activities. Children who were members of the fascist youth movement were given a month-long summer holiday free of charge, either at the seaside or in the mountains. Education, as we have seen, was rigidly standardized by the fascist government, but that government also saw to it that everyone received an education, thereby greatly increasing Italy's rate of literacy. Finally, Mussolini introduced a policy by which wounded veterans were guaranteed work for the asking.

There is also no doubt that fascist laws prohibiting virtually all strikes and mandating a nine-hour workday improved Italian productivity. Mussolini claimed to have done much more than this, however. Fascism, he said, had wholly revitalized and resurrected a moribund economy. This was a typical exaggeration, but it is also true that Italy fared no worse under the onslaught of the worldwide Great Depression than did any other industrialized nation. Unemployment during the early 1930s was very high, but no higher than in Britain, Germany, or the United States.

Mussolini took three major steps to mitigate the effects of the Great Depression. First, on August 13, 1930, he rescinded laws forbidding emigration from Italy. During the 1920s, he had fretted over Italy's declining birth rate, and he put into place a system of monetary inducements to encourage large families. He also saw to it that most emigration was barred. Now, however, the program to promote reproduction was held in abeyance, and anyone who wanted to leave Italy was free to do so. Second, Mussolini initiated an extensive program of public works. In this, his thinking was similar to Franklin D. Roosevelt in his New Deal. Like Roosevelt, Mussolini embraced the economic theories of the great British economist J. Maynard Keynes, who proposed that governments should be able to spend their way out of a depression by employing large numbers in public works projects. The most spectacular of fascism's Depression-era projects was the draining of Rome's infamous Pontine Marshes. For centuries, these unhealthy swamps had bred malaria, endemic to Rome and known locally as Roman Fever. Draining them is one of a handful of indisputably worthwhile features of Italy's fascist legacy.

The centerpiece of Mussolini's economic strategy was a concept he called the Corporate State. Throughout the 1920s, Mussolini had presented fascism as the champion of capitalism and the implacable foe of communism and socialism. But in a speech to the Chamber of Deputies on November 14, 1933, he suddenly pronounced the "capitalist method of production" outmoded. The fascist alternative to communism, socialism, *and* capitalism was the Corporate State, through which fascism would direct all production. An act of March 20, 1930, created a National Council of Corporations, which was assigned to direct the activities of twenty-two individual corporations, each devoted to a particular form of industrial or economic life. Only one minor corporation, the Corporation of the Stage (regulating the film and theater industries), was set up in 1930. No other corporations were created until the end of 1934, and it was 1935 before the first of them, the Corporation for Cattle-Breeding and Fisheries, actually began to function.

The problem was this: Despite the law and despite Mussolini's 1933 speech, no one really knew exactly what the corporations were supposed to do. In fact, the Corporate State never became much more than smoke and mirrors; like so much else in fascism, it was a show. Mussolini portrayed himself as a man of action, and fascism was predicated on always taking swift and decisive action. In practice, however, it was usually enough to talk about action and to set up the framework for action. Actually implementing the plans and building on the framework were of secondary importance. Evaluating any results was of even less consequence.

Mussolini was always intent on giving the appearance of *doing*. In publicity pictures for the Pontine Marsh project, he posed with pick and shovel. He often involved himself in directing the daily minutiae of agencies and departments many, many levels below the proper responsibility of a head of government. He was anxious always to create the impression that he was omnipresent and involved in all aspects of Italy's life. As valuable as this show was for the sake of propaganda, it led to highly unproductive micromanagement. Most officials and bureaucrats were actually reluctant to do their jobs, for fear that the Duce would not approve. Individual initiative, invaluable in any complex organization and especially in a government, was stifled. Instead of getting things done and done efficiently, Mussolini's go-getter pose—a favorite fascist slogan was "A *noi!*"—frequently produced official paralysis amid a great show of activity.

This was compounded by another paradox of Mussolini's fascism. Even as he sought to create a personal dictatorship and a cult of personality, he constructed about him an enormous, unwieldy, and wholly inefficient bureaucracy. Not that the inefficiency of the fascist bureaucracy much mattered to Mussolini, for the purpose of the bureaucracy was less as an instrument of government than as a means of distributing patronage positions, providing a place for the employment of fascists. In this it was parallel to fascism itself, which existed less as a political ideology than as a means of acquiring and maintaining power.

If Mussolini had a driving need to amass personal power, it was not so that he could live like a king. If anything, for a man of his position, his personal life was rather modest. It was 1929 before Rachele and their five children (daughter Edda, nineteen; Vittorio, thirteen; Bruno, eleven; Romano, two; and Anna-Maria, two months) came to live with Mussolini in Rome. The family took up residence at Villa Torlonia on the Via Nomentana, donated to them by Prince Giovanni Torlonia. Certainly, it was an elegant home, and, added to it in 1930 was a country house presented by the town council of Forlì, the castle of Rocca delle Caminate, in Emilia, quite near where Mussolini had grown up. Yet none of this was extravagantly opulent. The Duce could have had much more.

He worked hard, rising at six, exercising, drinking a glass of orangeade or grape juice, then indulging his passion for horseback riding. After a shower and a breakfast of fruit, milk, and bread, he set off for the Prime Minister's office and was at his desk promptly at eight. At two in the afternoon he came home for lunch—typically spaghetti with tomato sauce, vegetables, and fruit, lots of fruit. He did not return to his office until six, spending the afternoon at home reading newspapers and books. From six to nine, he was back at the Prime Minister's office. Supper at the Villa Torlonia was after nine and, for Mussolini, Spartan, consisting of broth, vegetables, and fruit. He was in bed by 10:30 and insisted on not being disturbed unless there was very bad news. As for other news, even the best of it could wait until morning.

Except for his daughter Edda, always his favorite, Mussolini was rather distant with his children. He even once admitted that he was not a very attentive father, and one of his modern biographers, Denis Mack Smith, notes that others observed he habitually spoke to his children "as though they were a public meeting." Edda caused him some anxiety when she fell in love with a Jew, the son of an army colonel. Mussolini warned her about mixed marriages, and although he was not at this time rigid in his anti-Semitism, he would almost certainly have forbidden a marriage, if only to avoid offending his new ally, the Church. Luckily for the Duce, Edda soon turned from this young man to an industrialist's son. There was no religious issue here, but the young man's father turned thumbs down on the prospect of marriage when he discovered that Mussolini lacked sufficient fortune to ante up a hefty dowry. Edda ended up marrying Count Galeazzo Ciano, the strikingly handsome son of an admiral, who was a steadfast fascist. Mussolini was delighted, and the wedding took place on April 23, 1930.

Mussolini worked hard always to counterpoint the image of a gentle, loving family man to his steely, strutting, chin-out-thrust image as a fascist leader. He did much the same where foreign dignitaries were concerned. Most were impressed by the charming, smiling, soft-spoken manner he adopted in private, a welcome contrast to his strident public persona. Foreigners, it seemed, earnestly *wanted* to see Mussolini in the best possible light, and they accepted the charming self as real and the swaggering, bullying self as mere play-acting for public consumption.

Foreign officials were also pleased by Mussolini's refusal to embrace and encourage fascism outside of Italy. The attitude of established politicians in such countries as the United States, France, Belgium, Spain, Hungary, and especially Britain was ultimately condescending. Fascism was very well suited to "nations such as Italy," by which they meant nations and peoples who did not possess a tradition of democracy or who, it was felt, were somehow "not ready for" democracy. With such countries a man like Mussolini could work miracles. But fascism was not appropriate for the "more developed" states, and, ultimately, the leaders of most of Europe and the United States were as anxious to keep fascism away from their doors as they were to exclude communism. When Mussolini announced in March 1928 that "Fascism is not an article for export," diplomats and statesmen the world over breathed a collective sigh of relief.

But the decade of the 1930s would bring with it many lessons about the impermanence of pronouncements and pledges from totalitarian leaders, no matter how earnestly such declarations were made. By the early 1930s, Mussolini was engaged in secret—and sometimes not so secret—communication with developing fascist movements in France, most notably the Action Française of Charles Maurras and Léon Daudet; in Hungary; in Croatia; and in Belgium, where Léon Degrelle had founded the Rexist movement. He also communicated with the new National Socialist Party of Hungary and was very interested in a group called the Russian Fascists, which had been formed in exile by Konstantin Rodzaevsky in Harbin, a city in Japanese-occupied Manchukuo (Manchuria).

Most disturbing and increasingly less secret were Mussolini's links to England's Sir Oswald Mosely. Unlike most incipient fascist leaders in other countries, Mosely was by no means an outsider. He was an established politician and the son-in-law of no less a figure than Lord Curzon. It was, in fact, the Corfu crisis (Chapter 16, "Bombing Corfu, Killing a Critic"), in which Mussolini out-maneuvered Curzon, that kindled Mosely's admiration for the Duce. Whereas Curzon and even British politicians more friendly to Mussolini—Winston Churchill and Austen Chamberlain, for example—took it for granted that Mussolini's political philosophy and dictatorial methods were eminently unsuited to a democratic nation like England, Mosely began to see fascism as precisely what the country needed, especially with himself as the leader of the party. He visited Mussolini several times in Rome for advice.

Mosely had started his political career as a conservative, but soon left for the Labour Party and, in 1931, departed Labour to create his own New Party in 1931. The next year, he transformed this into the British Union of Fascists (BUF), which, in the years leading up to World War II, became highly vocal and visible. Boosted by the advocacy of the London *Daily Mail*, the party's membership reached a peak of forty thousand in 1934, meetings and parades of British Blackshirts, arms upraised in the Roman salute, became commonplace, and the BUF's increasingly strident anti-Semitism led to violence at many demonstrations. (BUF activities were significantly curtailed by the Public Order Act of 1936, and the party was banned entirely in May 1940 by emergency wartime regulations; Mosely and other British fascists were interned for the duration of the war.)

By the fall of 1932, Mussolini had radically changed his tune from "Fascism is not an article for export" to a prediction (or, depending on one's political orientation, a promise, declaration, or threat) that all Europe would become fascist "or fascisized" within a decade's time. Yet there was one up-and-coming fascist-style leader Mussolini was slow to embrace and, when he finally did, did so with marked ambivalence. Born in Austria in 1889, Adolf Hitler was only six years younger than Mussolini, but his rise to power was much slower. His political consciousness had been crystallized in the trenches of World War I. A lackluster youth, feckless art student, and general drifter, Hitler had proved to be a good soldier. He served with distinction, was decorated four times, and was seriously wounded, but (like Mussolini) never rose above the rank of corporal. Hitler remained with his regiment after the war, until April 1920, serving as an army political agent and joining the German Worker's Party in Munich in September 1919. In April 1920, he left the army to go to work full-time for the party's propaganda section. With postwar Germany in violent ferment, Hitler seized the moment to transform the German Worker's Party by August 1920 into the *Nazionalsozialistische Deutsche Arbeiterpartei*, commonly shortened to NSDAP or Nazi party, beginning with no more than seven members, including himself.

Hitler competed with many other German agitators, malcontents, and desperate men as a street-corner orator, loudly assaulting Germany's enemies, especially the communists and Jews, as well as the nations that had forced upon the German people the ignominious Versailles treaty and the German politicians who had betrayed the nation by signing it. Hitler contacted Mussolini briefly in 1922, before the March on Rome, and again in November of that year, after its success. He wanted Mussolini's counsel on how to effect a fascist-style revolution in Germany, and, in 1923, he specifically sought help with mounting a march on Berlin.

Mussolini kept young Hitler at arm's length. It is not known whether he gave Hitler any advice, and certainly he did not help him personally or directly; nevertheless, money was sent from Italy to the Nazi party, presumably with Mussolini's knowledge and probably at his direction. Still, there was plenty about Hitler to give Mussolini pause. To begin with, his arrest after the ill-conceived Munich Beer Hall Putsch hardly portended a political triumph. When *Mein Kampf* was published in 1925, Mussolini found it boring, calling it in 1930 a "tome that I have never been able to read." He dismissed it as a collection of clichés. There was also the prospect of German union with Austria, which Hitler advocated from the beginning, and which certainly posed a danger to Italy.

Yet after his release from prison—he served only nine months of a five-year sentence—Hitler rapidly consolidated his party and his power. After forging an alliance with the Nationalist Party headed by industrialist Alfred Hugenberg, the Nazis increased the number of seats they held in the Reichstag, the German parliament, from twelve to one hundred seven, thereby becoming the second largest party in Germany. Hitler did not confine his party's activities to the Reichstag, but went on to create the SA—the *Sturmabteilung,* or Brownshirts—as a paramilitary organization that beat down the opposition in the streets of Germany. In this Mussolini's Blackshirts had clearly inspired him, and he made no secret of this to the Duce. During the period of his rise, Hitler broke down Mussolini's standoffishness by a continual barrage of flattery. Hitler, who, in 1926 had been unable to obtain so much as an autographed photograph of Mussolini from the Italian embassy in Berlin (Chapter 17, "Making the Trains Run on Time"), made a special point of telling Mussolini that he displayed his bronze bust in Nazi party headquarters at Munich. Mussolini now not only authorized contributions to the Nazi election campaign fund, but, against the advice of his own Foreign Office, permitted Hitler to send his Brownshirts to Italy for training.

Hitler ran for president of the German republic in 1932. He narrowly lost to Paul Hindenberg, the aged hero of World War I, but the elections had gained the Nazis two hundred thirty Reichstag seats, thirty-seven percent of the vote, making it the largest party represented. Hindenberg, who detested Hitler, had no choice but to form a coalition government with him by appointing him *Reichskanzler* (Reich Chancellor, or Prime Minister) on January 30, 1933.

Now that Adolf Hitler and the Nazis were established facts of German life—at least in part thanks to the example and support of Benito Mussolini—the Duce had to deal with this new power. Mussolini believed that territorial expansion was a necessary expression of "national vitality," and he also knew that a policy of expansion meant fighting wars—for him yet another expression of national vitality. Potentially, as Mussolini saw it, Germany would be a great ally in what he believed and intended would be the coming war of expansion. But Germany was also potentially a terrible opponent, especially if a union between Austria and Germany were concluded. Another drawback to the new Nazi regime was its embarrassingly vehement anti-Semitism. Mussolini had flirted with such a policy himself, hoping to scapegoat the Jews by identifying them with the Bolshevik movement (Chapter 9, "Man of Destiny"), but he quickly abandoned that line. Now France and especially Britain, nations Mussolini by no means wanted to alienate, objected to Hitler's anti-Semitism and called on Mussolini to join them in forming a united front opposing this policy.

One of many bronze busts made of Mussolini by well-known sculptors of the day; thousands of copies of some were mass-produced. Hitler exhibited one at Nazi party headquarters in Munich.

(Image from ArtToday)

As usual, Mussolini found it natural to adopt a dual, even contradictory, stance. He assured the British and the French that he deplored the Nazis' anti-Semitic extravagances and that he would prevail upon Hitler to restrain his party. At the same time, Mussolini effectively talked his allies out of taking any direct action against Hitler and the Nazis. In this, he fed and fostered the growing mood of passivity and appeasement in the corridors of the British and French governments. The same attitude prevailed in October 1933, when Hitler threatened to leave the Disarmament Conference held among the members of the Four-Power Pact: Britain, France, Italy, and Germany. To the British ambassador in Rome, Sir Ronald Graham, Mussolini admitted that Hitler was dangerous, a "dreamer," and that his chief lieutenant, Hermann Goering, was a former insane asylum inmate. Such a remark would suggest that now was the time to take a firm hand against a nation led by so volatile a pair; but, no, Mussolini cautioned, to take military action against Germany, to invade the Rhineland, would bring "world chaos." Again, Mussolini persuaded his British and French allies to compromise, to appease Hitler by allowing Germany at least some of the arms it wanted.

Despite Mussolini's prototype appeasement policy, Germany withdrew not only from the Disarmament Conference, but from the League of Nations. Mussolini was furious, and he resolved to take steps to prevent any union between Germany and Austria. He decided that it was in Italy's best interest to have an independent, nonsocialist, but anti-German Austria, which would be pliable on the issue of the South Tyrol, the Italian-Austrian frontier. Accordingly, he supported Engelbert Dollfuss, the Christian Democrat who formed an Austrian government in 1932. Mussolini counseled Dollfuss to create a fascist state, lest Hitler preempt him and the Austrian Nazis take control. Mussolini agreed to provide Dollfuss with military support if Germany invaded Austria. Thus emboldened, in September 1933, Dollfuss was able to pass a motion in parliament to send itself into indefinite recess, thereby clearing the way for him to govern by decree. Using this power, in February 1934, Dollfuss acted against the heart of Red influence in Austria, the socialist city council of Vienna. He decreed its dissolution, thereby triggering four days of street fighting in which the Socialist Party was crushed.

Mussolini was pleased that Dollfuss was following the program he recommended, but he also recognized that the instability created by the fighting in Vienna opened up the possibility of a German invasion. He therefore persuaded France and Britain to issue with Italy a guarantee of Austrian independence. When the Austrian parliament reconvened in April 1934, it deprived the socialists of their seats and voted supreme powers to Dollfuss and his new government. Only the Austrian Nazis dissented.

Amid the Austrian crisis, Hitler decided that it was time for a face-to-face meeting with Mussolini. They met in Venice on June 14 and 15, 1934. Hitler wore a civilian suit, whereas Mussolini was arrayed in one of his bemedalled military uniforms. Side by side, Hitler appeared as a little man and Mussolini as robust giant—at least such was the impression the journalists took away from the meeting. In fact, Hitler, though slight of build, was a bit taller than the Duce at something over five-foot-five, but everyone was so accustomed to seeing Mussolini as a strongman that Hitler came off badly by comparison.

Little was definitively settled at the meeting, as the two dictators warily felt each other out, Hitler endeavoring more than Mussolini to appear genial. This may well have been the result of his genuine admiration for the Duce, who he insisted on regarding as something of a mentor, although it was a role Mussolini had by no means sought. They discussed Austria, and they both agreed to support the Dollfuss government. Hitler assured Mussolini that he contemplated no *Anschluss*—union—of Germany with Austria. (Thus one dictator lied to another.) In return, he asked Mussolini to break away from the Franco-British guarantee of Austrian independence. To this request Mussolini was noncommittal. Other topics remained matters of outright disagreement: Hitler's decision to stay outside of the League of Nations, the relation of the German government to the Catholic Church, and the Nazi policy with regard to the Jews.

Hitler returned to Germany from the meeting with a declaration that it had been a great success, and he expressed his continued admiration for Mussolini. For his part, the Duce was decidedly lukewarm. Hitler was something of a blowhard, he felt, and had a most annoying habit of quoting *Mein Kampf* at great length. Doubtless this would have been tedious under the best of circumstances, but Mussolini made it worse by insisting on excluding interpreters from the meeting. He prided himself on his fluency in German, a language he had failed to master sufficiently to earn one of the teaching credentials he had sought in 1907 (Chapter 4, "Angelica and Rachele"). The language barrier would continue to create problems for the two dictators, as Mussolini stubbornly refused to employ an interpreter. In any case, if Mussolini was genuinely unimpressed with Hitler or feigned such an attitude, he nevertheless linked himself to Hitler immediately after the Venice conference. In a speech at the Piazza San Marco, after Hitler had departed, Mussolini spoke of "Hitler and I" and, speaking for both, he pledged their determination "not to alter the political map of Europe or the world, or to add to the anxieties which are already disturbing all countries from the Far East to Far West."

Chapter 20

Another Lion in Abyssinia

Toward the end of the nineteenth century, Italy, having only recently become a unified kingdom, contracted the same itch that already afflicted Germany, France, and, paramountly, Britain: the desire for a colonial empire. On May 2, 1889, Italy concluded the Treaty of Uccialli with Menelik II, emperor of Abyssinia (modern Ethiopia), which was so ambiguously worded that it caused the Italo-Ethiopian War of 1895–96. Italy believed the treaty gave it a protectorate over Abyssinia, whereas Menelik II believed no such thing.

In 1895, Italy invaded the Ethiopian district of Tigre, to which Menelik responded by sending into the field an army that defeated two thousand four hundred Italians at the Battle of Menkele. This prompted Italy to dispatch twenty thousand men to Abyssinia, who were met at the Battle of Aduwa on March 1, 1896, by an Ethiopian force of eighty thousand. In a disastrous battle for Italy, more than six thousand five hundred of its troops were slain and another two thousand five hundred taken prisoner. Humiliated, Italy concluded the Treaty of Addis Ababa on October 26, 1896, by which it recognized Abyssinian independence in exchange for being permitted to cling to the coastal colony of Eritrea. A few years later, in 1900, Italy agreed to further reductions in its Eritrean holdings.

The stain of Aduwa remained on the Italian national psyche for decades. In February 1934, Mussolini informed Gen. Emilio

De Bono that he intended to expunge it by conquering the country that was now generally called Ethiopia. Not only would this restore the honor of Italy, but, added to Italian Somaliland and Libya (acquired from Turkey by the Treaty of Lausanne in 1912), it would become the basis of the new Roman Empire Mussolini spoke of with increasing frequency. Besides, Ethiopia was ripe for the taking. Except for Liberia, it was the only African country that was not a colony or protectorate of some European power, and it was woefully poor, backward, and underdeveloped.

There was one problem. At the moment, Italian relations with Ethiopia were quite friendly. As early as 1924, Ethiopia's emperor, Haile Selassie, the "Lion of Judah," had sought Italian aid in economic development. The two nations might well have nurtured a mutually beneficial relationship, but that is not what Mussolini wanted in 1934.

So before the end of the year, he fabricated the necessary provocation to war. By an Italo-Ethiopian treaty of 1928, the border separating Ethiopia, Italian Somaliland, and British Somaliland was to be surveyed and settled by a joint commission of representatives from all three nations. In November, British and Ethiopian officials were surveying the frontier at Walwal. The Italian contingent arrived in military strength, including aircraft. It was intended as an unmistakable threat to the other officials, and the British contingent decided to make a prudent withdrawal. The Ethiopians, however, stood their ground. According to the Italians, they didn't just stand, they attacked, killing a number of troops. This (the Italians reported) provoked an Italian counterattack, with ground forces and aircraft. More than a hundred Ethiopians died.

Although the Ethiopians denied that they had attacked, Mussolini demanded an apology and the punishment of those officers responsible for what he continued to insist was an act of war. Both Britain and Ethiopia called for international arbitration, preferably by the League of Nations. The Duce rejected these suggestions, protesting that Italy would not negotiate with a barbaric country where slavery still existed. Mussolini ordered Italian diplomats in Somaliland and in Geneva to refuse all negotiation with representatives of uncivilized Ethiopia and, indeed, to walk out on any meeting to which Ethiopians were even admitted.

Mussolini now had the ingredients of a war. Did he dare take the final step? What were the dangers?

Might Britain intervene? No, Mussolini decided, that was not likely. No one in post–World War I England wanted to fight, especially on behalf of a distant African country without economic or political interest to the British Empire. What of France? This was a somewhat different case. It had contributed heavily to the construction of a railroad from the French colonial port of Djibouti to Addis Ababa, Ethiopia's capital. But Mussolini was certain that France would accept his assurance that he had no intention of interfering with the railroad.

The only unknown in the diplomatic equation seemed to be Germany. If Italy were to wage war on Ethiopia, Mussolini resolved, it would do so this time with overwhelming force. That meant sending most of its army and air force against tribesmen with few modern weapons. At all costs, another Aduwa must be avoided. But would Adolf Hitler take advantage of the absence of the bulk of the Italian armed forces to invade and annex Austria? Mussolini put himself in Hitler's place and decided that the Führer was not yet ready to make such a move. Britain and France, in addition to Italy, were pledged to protect Austrian independence. Hitler was in no position to take on all three nations.

Mussolini always thrived on extravagant poses and reckless statements. Yet his aggression, while certainly dangerous to Italy and to the world, was never entirely heedless. Before he made an irreversible move against Ethiopia, he wanted to ensure Italy's diplomatic position in Europe. Accordingly, when France's new foreign minister, Pierre Laval, made a diplomatic call in Rome on January 5, 1935, Mussolini was determined to exploit to his advantage Laval's sympathetic right-wing orientation. Mussolini was eager to give Laval certain assurances—mainly a pledge to renounce any claims to French rights in Tunisia and acquiescence to a planned Franco-Soviet defensive pact—in exchange for a secret agreement on Ethiopia. Over the course of a four-day conference, France agreed, in a secret document, that "Italy has preponderant interests on all the territory of Ethiopia," except, of course, for the Addis Ababa–Djibouti railroad. Beyond matters concerning the railroad, France pledged not to interfere with whatever Italy might do in Ethiopia. Publicly, at a great diplomatic reception, Laval toasted Mussolini for having "written the finest page in the history of modern Italy."

In the meantime, the League of Nations ineffectually and desultorily deliberated the complaint Ethiopia had lodged against Italy. The only step the League took was to embargo the shipment of arms—both to Italy and Ethiopia. While this may have seemed equitable to the diplomats, it actually had very little impact on Italy, which had a more or less self-sufficient arms industry, but it did mean that nonindustrialized Ethiopia could now obtain no weapons with which to defend itself. The League had thus collaborated in the African nation's doom.

Mussolini shipped out the first contingent of troops to Africa in February 1935, but in March Hitler threw him a curve. In the first of a series of bold and deliberate breaches of the Treaty of Versailles, Hitler announced that Germany was reinstating compulsory military service. Mussolini's original fears that Hitler might move against Austria while the Italian army was in Ethiopia were suddenly revived. Worse, while Britain formally protested Germany's breach of the Versailles document, it did not call off a major diplomatic meeting with Hitler. The apparent rapport between Britain and Germany sent waves of anxiety through France and Italy, whereupon Mussolini called for a three-way summit among Italy, France, and England, at Stresa on Lake Maggiore. The meeting was especially timely, since British opposition to the Franco-Soviet pact, coupled with the new British cordiality toward Germany, seemed to portend the dissolution of the Franco-Anglo-Italian united front against Germany.

Mussolini was genuinely concerned about growing German militarism, and he wanted the Stresa conference to repair at least the appearance of a united anti-German front, but his primary anxiety at the conference concerned how Britain would respond to his plans for Ethiopia. He did not raise the topic himself, but waited for the British to do so, which, he assumed, they surely would.

But the British delegation did no such thing. No one in either the British nor the French delegation so much as mentioned Ethiopia. *Still* Mussolini trod softly. When the three powers composed their final communiqué expressing their unity against German aggression, Mussolini insisted a phrase expressing opposition to "any unilateral repudiation of treaties which may endanger peace" be edited to make it more precise, specifying opposition to "any unilateral repudiation of treaties which may endanger *the peace of Europe.*" Dotting the i's and crossing the t's, Mussolini carefully left the door wide open to the endangerment of Ethiopian peace—after all, Ethiopia was in Africa, not Europe. When Britain and France accepted his amended language, Mussolini saw the removal of yet more potential obstacles to his Ethiopian expedition. Accordingly, in a May 14 speech to the Italian Senate, he committed Italy to action in Ethiopia, declaring that it was necessary to safeguard Italy's interests in Africa if the nation were expected to play its role in keeping the peace in Europe. That this rationale was nonsense—Ethiopia was hardly at Italy's backdoor—must have occurred even to the Duce, but all that really mattered is that it *was* a rationale, however lame.

The European democracies were a frightened lot in the 1930s. They were afraid to offend one another, lest the anti-German alliance fall apart, and they were afraid to act against either Italy or Germany, lest they somehow weaken an anti-communist ally. Both of these fears now worked in Mussolini's favor. Diplomats who took a strongly anti-German stance did not want to act in any way that might drive Italy closer to the German camp. Diplomats whose concern was more anti-communist than anti-Hitler were likewise prepared to tolerate Italian aggression against Ethiopia, if that would help preserve the prestige of the fascist regime and maintain it as a bulwark against communism.

Yet just when Mussolini seemed assured of the support of the British government in his bellicose stance against Ethiopia, he suddenly shifted his ground. For he now wanted more than the conquest of Ethiopia. He saw that Britain was trying to manipulate the situation so that whatever Mussolini did in Ethiopia would look as if it had the sanction of the League of Nations and the British government. What Mussolini wanted was to act against Ethiopia in *defiance* of the League and Britain. His aim was to make a power play at the expense of both. As Mussolini saw it, diplomacy was a zero-sum game. There always had to be a winner and a loser, and he did not want either the League of Nations or Britain to appear in any sense as if they had won something as a result of Italian action.

Thus Mussolini refused all possibility of compromise. When Britain's ambassador to Rome, Sir Eric Drummond, warned that Britain might have to sacrifice its friendship with Italy for the sake of the League of Nations, Mussolini replied that he had committed too many troops and too much money to back away from Ethiopia as a result of a diplomatic solution. The matter would be settled by war—and if that meant a breach in Anglo-Italian relations, then that was the price that had to be paid.

Pursuing a course it would take with the other rising bully of Europe, Adolf Hitler, Britain backed down from Mussolini's threat. It now proposed that Ethiopia cede a large part of its territory to Italy in exchange for a piece of British Somaliland, which would compensate Ethiopia by giving it a valuable outlet to the sea. Moreover, Britain would finance the construction of port facilities in this territory.

Mussolini rejected the proposal, arguing that the proposed port would strengthen Ethiopia economically and give it ready access to the importation of arms. These grounds may have been vaguely reasonable, but they had been given in bad faith. Mussolini's real reason for rejecting Britain's offer—his only reason—was that it would deprive him of the opportunity of taking Ethiopia by force of arms. And when the League of Nations approved an offer to Italy of even more Ethiopian territory, plus a mandate and exclusive economic rights over *all* of Ethiopia, Mussolini, astoundingly, refused again. At this, Britain briefly rattled its saber, threatening to close the Suez Canal to Italian warships, thereby preventing the passage of troops to Ethiopia. Mussolini did not miss a beat in replying: Close the canal, and the Italian navy would force it open.

Britain and the rest of Europe knew only too well how a world war could begin over a seemingly local issue in a remote part of the planet. To save Ethiopia, even to save face, Britain was not prepared to start a new European war. After some debate and delay, Prime Minister Stanley Baldwin instructed Foreign Secretary Samuel Hoare: "Keep us out of war, we are not ready for it." Hoare grumbled about the prime minister's "indifference" to the plight of Ethiopia and about a "pusillanimous surrender to the Italians," but he did as he was ordered—which was to do nothing.

While the League of Nations stood idly by, Italy continued to ship troops to Eritrea, on the frontier with Ethiopia. By the end of August 1935, an Italian army of fifteen thousand stood ready, among them Mussolini's sons: Vittorio, age eighteen; and Bruno, underage at sixteen, but allowed to serve because his father wanted it so. Daughter Edda's husband, Count Ciano, also served, like Vittorio and Bruno, in the air force.

As the troop build-up approached critical mass, Mussolini began his own propaganda offensive, aimed at answering the question of why he was about to fight Ethiopia. The answer, given with the Duce's characteristic jut of jaw, was to make the world safe for civilization. Ethiopia was a barbaric state, ineligible for any serious consideration in international affairs. War against such a people was a mission mandated by civilization.

On September 11, Hoare stunned the League's General Assembly by issuing a strong promise that Britain would support and help enforce any sanction the League of Nations voted against Italy. Laval, on September 12, was equally surprising in affirming France's intention to enforce sanctions. But it was all a show. Hoare and Laval had secretly met before either addressed the General Assembly and had agreed that neither France nor Britain would go to war against Italy. The "Stresa front"—the anti-German coalition of the World War I allies—was too valuable to sacrifice for the sake of Ethiopia. The most drastic sanction Britain contemplated was a ban on importation of a certain limited list of Italian goods. Nevertheless, for the sake of appearances, Britain dispatched a substantial fleet to the Mediterranean. Mussolini pretended to be unimpressed. Informed by Ambassador Drummond that the ships had entered the Mediterranean, Mussolini replied that Italy would decide whether they would be allowed to leave the Mediterranean. But as the crisis continued toward the end of September, a nervous Hoare authorized Drummond to assure Mussolini that England regarded Italy as a friend and ally and would act only if the League of Nations agreed on a collective response. Mussolini was confident that the League would never authorize anything of the kind, and he therefore took Hoare's message as a green light for invasion.

On September 29, 1935, Mussolini issued his orders to Gen. De Bono: "No declaration of war. I order you to begin the advance in the early hours of 3 repeat 3 October."

On the eve of the advance, October 2, Mussolini addressed the crowd from the balcony of the Palazzo Venezia: "Let Heaven hear your shouts of encouragement to our soldiers, who are waiting in Africa, so that they are heard by our friends and enemies in every part of the world, the cry for justice, the cry for victory!"

On the next day, Gen. Emilio De Bono directed the invasion, with generals Rodolfo Graziani and Pietro Badoglio as his field commanders. Italy had brought to Africa a large force with modern weapons, including assault aircraft. It is an exaggeration to say, as was sometimes reported, that the Ethiopians opposed these instruments of modern war with nothing more than spears and knives. But it is a fact that they were pitifully underequipped by comparison with the Italians. Mussolini anticipated a rapid victory.

The people of Italy rose in a tumult of support for the invasion, with spontaneous celebrations and rallies everywhere. Although the Pope had expressed grave reservations before the invasion, saying privately that for a civilized nation to seize another country was "deplorable," he and the Church threw their full support behind the Duce once the invasion became an accomplished fact. As the churches of all warring nations have done for time out of mind, the Church of Rome now declared that God was on "our" side. The Duce would surely be blessed and victory was absolutely assured.

Partially roused from its stupor, the League of Nations sanctioned Italy as an aggressor on November 18, 1935, banning importation of all Italian goods and the exportation to Italy of a limited list, which did include raw materials essential to war. Modest though they were, the sanctions, especially those on Italian imports, had an immediate impact. Sending a large army so far afield was expensive, and even with the benefit of advanced weaponry, the Italian advance, under De Bono's inept leadership, bogged down within six weeks of the initial invasion. The Depression-wracked treasury groaned under the demand for cash, and without the prospect of export revenues, the economic picture was looking bleak.

All over the world, including in the United States, people of color protested the invasion of a black country by the people of a white country. To be sure, there can be no doubt that the same racism that lay behind all European imperialist adventures on the "Dark Continent" played a powerful part in the war. Yet if the war elicited outrage from the world's black population, it moved white politicians and diplomats remarkably little. To the degree that they were concerned about the "Ethiopian crisis" it was not for the sake of a black African country, but as a threat to world peace and to the disintegrating prestige of the League of Nations. Mussolini's demands—for half of Ethiopia, with a trusteeship over the other half, and for the total disbanding of the Ethiopian army—seemed far too much for the League of Nations to accept.

> *Racism was an important part of fascism. Any form of brutality was justifiable against the Ethiopians, members of an inferior race. Fascist law forbade interracial sexual relations and marriage, and, in Libya, Italian Somaliland, Eritrea, and Ethiopia, strict segregation laws were enacted and rigidly enforced.*

Mussolini's special emissary to Britain, Ezio Garibaldi, pressed the issue on Ramsay MacDonald (no longer in Parliament, but still a government official), asking him if England was prepared to "set the world on fire" for the sake of helping the League of Nations to "save face." MacDonald effectively answered yes, but England's foreign secretary, Samuel Hoare, had a different answer. He met with Pierre Laval and, on December 7, formulated the Hoare-Laval plan, which gave to Mussolini almost exactly what he demanded. This stirred a whirlwind of protest among the British press, people, and House of Commons, forcing Hoare's resignation—but not before the plan had been presented to Mussolini. Realizing that it would certainly be rejected by the British government and Ethiopia, Mussolini decided to seize the initiative by rejecting it first. The war would go on, then, and so much the better that it would go on in defiance of the League of Nations and the entire world.

As craven and outrageous as the Hoare-Laval plan was, some contemporaries came to believe that, had the plan been accepted, subsequent history would have been very different. Italy's breach with France and Britain might not have occurred, the Fascist-Nazi alliance might not have been concluded, and, therefore, Hitler might never have moved so aggressively into a new world war. Perhaps. But this speculation assumes that both Mussolini and Hitler were statesmen who always acted from rational motives—an assumption hardly warranted.

As Italy's gold reserves dwindled, Mussolini appealed for personal sacrifice, asking Italians to contribute to the war effort their gold wedding bands and other gold jewelry, which would be melted down to ingots. It would be but the first—and, as it turned out, the least—of the many material and spiritual sacrifices the Duce and fascism would exact from the people of Italy. Mussolini had a sacrifice of his own to make: He fired De Bono as commander-in-chief in Africa. The incompetent De Bono was replaced by the abler Badoglio, to whom Mussolini now sent more supplies and reinforcements, bringing the Italian army in Africa to two hundred thousand and the number of aircraft to an impressive four thousand. Badoglio made good use of these augmented forces, destroying two Ethiopian armies early in 1936 and raining bombs on inadequately prepared defenses. The new commander created a worldwide recoil of horror when he sent aircraft repeatedly and deliberately to bomb hospitals and when he ordered ground forces to use mustard gas on a large scale. Both of these tactics were flagrant violations of all international conventions on the rules of what was termed "civilized warfare."

The fascists were entirely unapologetic. The Ethiopians, after all, were "barbarians," and the rules of civilized warfare did not apply to them. To air force pilot Vittorio Mussolini—who participated in the attacks on hospitals—aerial bombardment was "magnificent sport" and "exceptionally good fun." He compared to the blooming of a rose the sight of Ethiopian cavalry blown up by an on-target bomb.

After De Bono's bumbling, the major Italian breakthrough, under Badoglio, came at the Battle of Lake Ashanga on April 9, 1936. This was followed by the fall of Addis Ababa, the Ethiopian capital, on May 5. Italian forces now ravaged Ethiopia. Addis Ababa was sacked, and, in an especially shocking act, the archbishop of the Ethiopian Coptic Church was executed and Coptic monks murdered.

Three days before the fall of the capital, Haile Selassie had fled and, in June, with great and moving dignity, he appeared personally before the League of Nations to plead for intervention. "I ask the fifty-two nations, who have given the Ethiopian people a promise to help them in their resistance to the aggressor, what are they willing to do for Ethiopia? And the great Powers who have promised the guarantee of collective security to small States on whom weighs the threat that they may one day suffer the fate of Ethiopia, I ask what measures do you intend to take? Representatives of the World, I have come to Geneva to discharge in your midst the most painful of the duties of the head of a State. What reply shall I have to take back to my people?"

In the flesh, standing before the world tribunal, Haile Selassie appeared to be anything but a barbarian. Yet the time for intervention was long past, and the League was powerless. By declining to take definitive steps against Italian aggression earlier, the British and French had hoped to save the League of Nations by avoiding a split with Italy and an Italian showdown with the League. Now it was all too apparent that the delay and inaction had themselves destroyed the League of Nations by revealing just how ineffectual and even irrelevant it was.

Ethiopia's emperor Haile Selassie is pictured here in 1943, arriving for a wartime conference aboard the USS Quincy on Egypt's Great Bitter Lake, two years after he had been restored to the throne following the British victory over Italian forces in Ethiopia.

(*Image from the National Archives and Records Administration*)

Back home in Italy, on May 9, thanks to Mussolini, Vittore Emmanuelle III was proclaimed King of Italy *and* Emperor of Ethiopia. After fifteen hundred years, Rome was again an imperial power, even if its imperial realm was nothing greater than an impoverished people suffocated by poison gas and blown apart by aerial bombs.

Chapter 21

Franco's Ally

People the world over were moved by the eloquent dignity of Haile Selassie's address to the League of Nations in June 1936. True, neither the League nor the rest of the world came to the rescue of his country, but his message nevertheless touched the international conscience. Nevertheless, while many felt sympathy for Haile Selassie and the people of Ethiopia, few, it seemed, pondered the implications of the conclusion of the emperor's speech: "And the great Powers who have promised the guarantee of collective security to small States on whom weighs the threat that they may one day suffer the fate of Ethiopia, I ask what measures do you intend to take?" The "they" in this sentence is ambiguous. Does it refer to the "small States" or the "great Powers"? In any case, spoken to representatives of nations, the majority of which prided themselves on the high level of their Christian civilizations, the speech and the plight of Ethiopia should have called to mind the words of Jesus recorded in the Gospel of Matthew: "Verily I say unto you, Inasmuch as ye have done it unto one of the least of these my brethren, ye have done it unto me."

But they did not. Morally, the "great Powers" did not feel attacked by what Italy was doing to Ethiopia. Even less did they feel attacked in any literal sense. They failed to grasp that allowing Mussolini to invade and possess one of the least among the world's nations was an invitation to him—and to others, in Japan and Germany—to attempt the same against them, great as they were. It would not be many years before this actually happened.

It was, in fact, already under way. For while the League of Nations fecklessly focused on Mussolini in Ethiopia, Adolf Hitler, on March 7, 1936, sent his troops into the Rhineland. This was not only a breach of the Treaty of Versailles, an agreement thrust upon an unwilling Germany, but also a violation of the Treaty of Locarno, into which Germany had freely entered in 1925. By the terms of the Locarno pact, the Rhineland was to be held inviolate as a demilitarized zone, a sacrosanct buffer to prevent a future world war. Anthony Eden, in 1936 British foreign secretary, asked his taxi driver what he thought of German troops in the Rhineland. "I suppose Jerry can do what he likes in his own back garden, can't he?" came the answer. Diplomats should have known better than cab drivers, but just as the world permitted Mussolini to take Ethiopia, so it now winked at the first goose steps in Hitler's march toward war.

In May 1936, Italy was intoxicated by its victory in Ethiopia. On the streets, the greetings people conventionally exchanged were replaced by the question "*A chi l'Abissinia?*" and the response, "*A noi!*"—"To whom does Abyssinia belong?" "To us!" But Benito Mussolini, at this time, was in an agony of anxiety, not over the horrific world he was creating with the bombing and gassing of men, women, and children, but over the health of his daughter, six-year-old Anna Maria, his youngest child.

At first it seemed to be whooping cough, which was serious enough, but then it became clear that Anna Maria had contracted polio. Mussolini once confessed to being a neglectful father, and people said that he spoke to his children as if addressing a meeting, but the critical illness of a child transforms even the most distant of parents. At first, her doctors thought Anna Maria was doomed to die and then they believed she would survive, but be paralyzed. Through it all, during the months of May and June, Mussolini moved his office to the room next to hers, but he found it almost impossible to work. When the good news reached him in June that the League of Nations was preparing to lift its economic sanctions, his only response was a wish that "they" would leave him in peace at his child's bedside.

On June 20, Anna Maria's physicians pronounced the child out of danger; she would neither die nor be paralyzed. And now

Mussolini could appreciate the other good news that was forthcoming. Austria became the first nation to recognize Vittore Emmanuelle III as emperor of Ethiopia, and Hitler's Germany followed closely as the second. Despite his misgivings, Mussolini planned to move Italy into alignment with Germany, gradually. However, sooner than Mussolini had anticipated, the two nations found themselves allies in a foreign war.

The lifting of League sanctions against Italy was announced on July 15, 1936, just two days before a military uprising broke out in Spanish Morocco and in Spain itself. For years, Spain had been in the process of tearing itself apart. On one side were the Roman Catholic Church, the military, the landowners, and the prosperous business interests; on the other side were urban blue-collar workers, agricultural workers, and many of the educated middle class. The extremes of each of these classes were represented on the far right by the falange, a party inspired by Mussolini's fascism, and, on the far left, by anarchists. But between these extremes was a bewildering array of political parties, whose ideologies ranged from monarchism to liberalism to socialism and communism. By the 1930s, a rancorous national debate had escalated to assassinations and random acts of terrorist violence and reprisal.

Although Mussolini had never been to Spain, such a political landscape was very familiar territory. He watched the developments carefully. In 1932, when Gen. Sacaneli Sanjurjo secretly contacted the Italian ambassador to Madrid, Raffaele Guariglia, asking Italy's support for the military coup by which he planned to overthrow the liberal government, Mussolini ordered Guariglia to encourage Sanjurjo secretly, but to avoid any public announcements. The coup, staged in August, failed. But two years later, as general strikes were called in Valencia and Zaragoza, and as street fighting broke out in Madrid and Barcelona, Mussolini invited Spanish general Emilio Barrera and other right-wing extremists to a secret meeting in Rome. Mussolini promised them money and arms to back a coup, which, however, the general never attempted.

But a new right-wing leader was emerging. Gen. Francisco Paulino Hermengildo Teodulo Franco-Bahamonde—better known more simply as Francisco Franco—earned a potent reputation among rightists for his swift suppression of a bloody uprising among miners in Asturias. Increasingly, Franco appeared as a strong and decisive leader against a background of faltering republicanism and the menacing rise of the left. When the elections of February 1936 brought to power leaders of the leftist Popular Front, Franco was exiled to a remote military post in the Canary Islands. The new leftist government deluded itself into believing that Franco's isolation had effectively put him on ice, but he made use of his remote location to organize a military-conservative coup without fear of interference from the government. Unwittingly, the leftists had done him a favor.

On July 17, 1936, at Franco's direction, military garrisons throughout Spain suddenly took over the garrison towns. Within a matter of days, the right-wing rebels were in control of Spanish Morocco, the Canary Islands, and the Balearic Islands (except Minorca), as well as parts of the Spanish mainland, including Seville and other cities. The forces of the republican government counterattacked, and soon the nation was divided roughly north and south. Thousands were killed in the early fighting, although even more—perhaps fifty thousand on each side—fell not in battle, but were executed, murdered, or assassinated.

Franco assumed overall command of the fascist, or nationalist, forces; his forces were collectively referred to as *falangistas*, Falangists. On July 21, he sent a special emissary to Mussolini to ask for military aid; in particular, aircraft to transport his Moorish troops from Spanish Morocco to the mainland. Mussolini replied with best wishes for Franco's success, but he declined to intervene in an internal war—unless some foreign Socialist government intervened in support of the left wing. Franco then turned to Hitler, who was untroubled by Mussolini's scruples and, on July 26, transported Moroccan troops on *Luftwaffe* planes.

There was talk among French, British, and Italian diplomats of adopting a formal nonintervention policy with regard to the Spanish Civil War, so that neither side would receive outside military aid. But, toward the end of July, the French government sent aircraft and other military aid to the republican forces; Mussolini responded by sending airplanes and other materiel to

Franco at the beginning of August. Before the month was out, he was shipping massive quantities of supplies to Franco, and then he transported Italian troops and aircraft to Majorca.

Mussolini may have had a strategic but nonideological motive for intervening in the Spanish Civil War. With Franco as an ally, Italy, in the event of war with England, would be in a position to take the British stronghold of Gibraltar and, with it, dominate the western end of the Mediterranean. However, there is no reason to doubt the ideological motive the Duce explained to his wife: that a republican victory in Spain would mean the establishment of Bolshevism in Spain, which would inevitably spread to France and, of course, would then menace Italy, not to mention the rest of Europe. In 1954, President Dwight D. Eisenhower would put forth a similar rationale to justify intervening against communist insurgents in Southeast Asia. "You have a row of dominoes set up, you knock over the first one, and what will happen to the last one is the certainty it will go over very quickly." This "domino theory" helped propel the United States into a decade-long war in Vietnam.

As Mussolini now saw it, the Spanish *Civil* War was really an international conflict, a contest between fascism and the forces of international anti-fascism, paramountly socialism and communism. Nor was he alone in this view. World War I had damaged an entire generation. Many of those who escaped death or physical wounds nevertheless emerged from the war maimed in spirit, disillusioned, the traditional values of their prewar reality shattered. The American expatriate writer, art collector, and cultural den mother Gertrude Stein called those who had come of age in the war a "lost generation." Morally and spiritually adrift, some in this generation saw the Spanish struggle as a cause at long last worth fighting for. Like Mussolini, they saw it as an international contest between fascism and anti-fascism, but, unlike him, the overwhelming majority of these young Americans, Frenchmen, Britons, and others sided with the left. As the war ground on, while Germany and Italy contributed to the fascists, the Soviet Union, along with volunteers from other nations, propped up the republicans.

Workers haul a giant block of marble destined to be carved into an equestrian statue of Benito Mussolini in Rome.

(*Image from ArtToday*)

Mussolini and his admirers were never very successful in articulating a clear-cut fascist ideology, despite the fact that the Duce kept a cadre of prominent Italian scholars busy with a project of developing and nailing down a fascist political theory. They labored, but they never got very far. Surely, in his own mind, Mussolini knew why this was so. He knew that fascism was always less a cogent political ideology than it was a stance, a pose, a method, and a means for acquiring power. That he put professors to work in a heroic effort to fabricate a full-blown ideology suggests that he regarded the absence of such an intellectual dimension as a weakness, perhaps even an Achilles heel. The Spanish Civil War suddenly addressed this flaw by elevating fascism—on the stage of world history, no less—to the status of a leading ideology, a worthy opponent of communism and socialism, the left-wing movements that never lacked for ream upon ream of political theory. Now people all over the world would have to speak of a "contest" between "great forces," fascism versus communism, fascism versus socialism. Of course, it was important to Mussolini that Franco and the fascists win the Spanish Civil War, but the mere fact that such a war was being fought was already a victory for Benito Mussolini.

> Some forty thousand foreign volunteers served in republican military organizations, and about half that number enlisted in ambulance corps and other noncombatant support units. Although it was officially neutral in the war and forbade the export of arms to Spain, the United States did not bar volunteers from enlisting to fight. The most famous of these was Ernest Hemingway, whose 1940 novel For Whom the Bell Tolls draws on his experience in the Abraham Lincoln Brigade, a unit made up of Americans.

As important as he thought the Spanish Civil War was, Mussolini approached it, as he approached most ideological issues, pragmatically. During the first three weeks of August 1936, he had sent a large quantity of supplies to Franco. He over-optimistically concluded that this would be sufficient to turn the tide in the fascists' favor, and, on August 21, he therefore agreed with France's socialist Prime Minister Léon Blum on a nonintervention policy. But the resulting nonintervention pact concluded among Britain, France, Germany, Portugal, the Soviet Union, and Italy soon broke down amid Soviet accusations of Portuguese, Italian, and German violations. In the fall of 1936, when Carlo Rosselli, an Italian socialist who had escaped from *confino* in the Lipari Islands, created a unit of anti-fascist refugees like himself and then dubbed it the Garibaldi Brigade, Mussolini was outraged. This, plus the redoubled intervention of the Soviets, moved the Duce to make a major commitment to the Spanish fascists.

It also pushed him into the arms of Franco's other principal supporter, Adolf Hitler. In September 1936, Mussolini expressed his approval of the idea of establishing a "Rome-Berlin Axis," a formal political and military alliance with Germany. The cause of international fascism had completely overridden Mussolini's misgivings about Germany's designs on Austria. On September 29, Franco established a government in Burgos, with himself as generalissimo and head of state ("*el Caudillo*"). In November, both Hitler and Mussolini recognized the Burgos government as *the* legal government of Spain. Both also increased the volume of aid to Franco, but while Hitler sent aircraft, flight crews, and technicians, Mussolini poured in not only air force units, but ground troops as well. By the early spring of 1937, fifty thousand Italian soldiers were fighting in Spain.

Spain had known many civil wars in its past, all exceptionally brutal. Before the intervention of foreign nations and foreign volunteers, the war begun in 1936 had been typically savage. Now that Spain had become an international battleground, the war was even more bitter, cruel, and intense: a killing machine. For most of the Italian troops, their baptism of fire came with the attack on Malaga in February. That republican stronghold fell to Franco's nationalists on February 8, whereupon the Italians took part in the slaughter of some four thousand republican prisoners of war. However, the next month, the Italian army was badly defeated at Guadalajara, in large part at the hands of the hated Garibaldi Brigade. The defeat caused a temporary rift in Spanish-Italian relations, as Franco blamed it on the Italian troops and Mussolini pinned it on Franco. To a stunned Italian public, Mussolini promised vengeance within two weeks, and when this was not forthcoming, he simply told the Italian people that, in actuality, Guadalajara had been a fascist victory.

Mussolini did exact some measure of vengeance for Guadalajara when assassins—almost certainly agents of OVRA, the Italian secret police—ambushed Carlo Rosselli and his brother Nello in Bagnoles, France, on June 9, 1937. Both men were stabbed to death.

Whatever else the Spanish Civil War meant to Germany and Italy, it was an opportunity for them to sharpen the swords of modern warfare. In particular, it gave the German *Luftwaffe* and the Italian air force an arena in which to rehearse the techniques of aerial bombardment of civilian populations. On April 26, 1937, the little town of Guernica was bombed out of existence by

German aviators in a campaign to which Italian airmen also contributed. The following year, it was Italian pilots who devastated Madrid and Barcelona, inflicting in these air raids far more death and destruction than any aerial attacks of the Great War. Bruno Mussolini flew twenty-seven missions over Spain, but when Franco's agents discovered that Soviet pilots were specifically gunning for the son of Mussolini, the generalissimo insisted that he return to Italy. He had served valiantly, but it would not help the fascist cause if some communist shot him down.

To the dismay of the Italian people, victory did not come quickly in the Spanish Civil War. By the end of 1937, the war had clearly become intensely unpopular and demoralizing on the home front. Despite a turn of popular opinion even against himself, Mussolini seemed not to care. He now saw the Spanish war as preparation for a much greater conflict, a great war of Italian conquest, and if Italians suffered in Spain, so be it. For they needed to be pounded into warriors as an armorer beats into deadly sharpness the blade of a saber. Was the war cruel? Mussolini deliberately made it crueler. He ordered Italian pilots to bomb more and more civilian targets with the sole object of demoralizing the enemy. Franco himself was mortified and outraged by what he considered Italy's terrorist tactics, tactics so unconscionable they would only damage the fascist cause. Mussolini was unconcerned, however, and he even suggested that biological warfare—germ warfare, as it was then called—be employed in Spain.

International public opinion, which for so many years had been highly favorable to Benito Mussolini, now turned against him. He did not care. If anything, he believed that it was just as well that the nations of the world should hate Italy, for to hate it was to fear it, and to believe that fascists were capable of employing any and all methods in waging war. As a gesture of contempt for the rest of the world, Mussolini withdrew Italy from the League of Nations in December 1937.

The war ground on through 1938, a costly war of attrition for Italy as well as for Spain, but by early 1939, the republicans were on the run. On March 5, the republican government fled into French exile, and by the end of the month all republican armies had either disbanded or surrendered. Spain was now a fascist nation, anywhere from five hundred thousand to a million soldiers and civilians lay dead, and Italy had forged an alliance with Nazi Germany, had created a new ally in fascist Spain, and, most of all, as Mussolini saw it, had triumphantly defied the entire world.

Chapter 22

A New Manifesto and
a New Mistress

Historians, as everyone knows, enjoy the gift of keen hindsight. From the perspective of eighteenth-century England, it was possible for Edward Gibbon to behold clearly and in its entirety the decline and fall of the Roman Empire. To Romans actually living during those centuries, whatever was happening must have seemed, at least most of the time, no more dramatic than business as usual. To recent historians looking back to 1939, it is clear that Italy was precariously poised on a steep and rocky precipice, its toes curling over the edge.

To Benito Mussolini, however, Italy in this year occupied firm footing atop its loftiest mountain since the Roman Empire at its greatest height. Italy had collected much of the territory it had wanted as a result of the First World War. It had acquired an African empire—adding Ethiopia to Libya (annexed from Turkey in 1912) and Italian Somaliland (wrested from the British after much diplomatic wrangling). In Spain, it had helped create Europe's second fascist state by prevailing in the "great contest" fought between fascism and communism/socialism; and, as we will see in the next chapter, it forged a "Rome-Berlin axis," and, after annexing Albania, hammered out a "pact of steel" with Germany. As Mussolini must have seen it, Italy had never been a greater or more powerful nation—at least not since the days of imperial Rome.

Such was the geographical view. Both Mussolini and Hitler saw national greatness and power principally in terms of geographical expansion. The bigger the octopus, the greater the octopus. Yet, for both dictators, there was always also another dimension to empire.

To the Italian people, Mussolini offered an economic rationale for conquering Ethiopia. He spoke of creating a colony there of ten million Italians, although he never explained just what work such a large colony would occupy itself with or how the entire enterprise would turn a profit. The other publicly expressed rationale for invasion was the duty and obligation of civilized countries to bring the benefits of civilization to the remaining dark and barbaric places in the world. It would be easy simply to dismiss both of these motives and to see Mussolini's conquest of Ethiopia in much the same light as his conquest of Italy itself: as an irresistible manifestation of the Duce's personal will. And as far as this explanation goes, it probably gets closer to the truth than the others. Yet there is also an element of truth to the myth of civilizing the barbaric. Scratch ever so lightly the surface of that ludicrously high-sounding rationale and you expose the deep core of racism beneath it.

From our historical perspective, it is hardly a revelation that racism lay at the core of Nazism and fascism alike. It is a curious thing about imperialist expansion, whether in the name of Hitler, or Mussolini, or Queen Victoria, that the imperialist both covets and despises what he acquires. Mussolini biographer Jasper Ridley observes that the career of Mussolini "moved from nationalism to imperialism and from imperialism to racism." As Mussolini the young socialist would have understood, such a progression is all too typical of human political nature. It is, in fact, the essence of world history. But Mussolini—the mature dictator, not the callow socialist—like Hitler, made no apologies for this progression and, on the contrary, saw it as both unavoidable and laudable.

When victory in Ethiopia did not immediately end the guerrilla resistance to Italian occupation, Mussolini found it easy to order his new viceroy of Ethiopia, Marshal Rodolfo Graziani, to execute without trial any guerrillas he captured. On June 8, 1936, Mussolini gave Graziani additional instructions: Make use of poison gas in a vigorous campaign of "terror and extermination" to crush the rebellion. Target rebels, target their supporters, and target their *suspected* supporters. The numbers killed were of no consequence. If anything, the more, the better.

As for the colonists sent to Ethiopia, they were, as a matter of official policy, to be inculcated with the conviction of their innate superiority over the black race. The object was not to coexist with the native population, but to dominate it. On April 19, 1937, pursuant to fascist policy, Vittore Emmanuelle III issued a decree making it a crime, punishable by five years' imprisonment, for any Italian to have sexual relations with a black inhabitant of East Africa. One colonist was foolish enough to appeal to the king for an exception, asking his permission to marry an Ethiopian woman. When the permission was denied and it was subsequently discovered that he had had sex with her in any case, the man was sentenced to thirteen months in prison.

While the issues of sex and marriage were of greatest concern in the policy regarding Ethiopia, laws were also enacted to enforce a segregation even more complete than that which existed in the American South of this era. Blacks and whites were not merely seated separately in public transportation, they rode separate trams; restaurants did not assign separate tables or rooms, but blacks and whites ate in separate restaurants. As Mussolini put Italians to work in Rome, building public works and monuments to the state, so he set Ethiopian laborers to cut a grand boulevard—suitable for fascist processions—through the heart of Addis Ababa. Only whites were allowed to drive or walk along this thoroughfare. Blacks were restricted to a narrow parallel street. In regard to labor, no white person could work for a black employer.

Typically, the flip side of the racist coin is demeaning paternalism, and fascist racism was typical in this regard. On February 19, 1937, during a celebration of the birth of a son to Prince Umberto, Marshal Graziani oversaw the distribution of charitable goods to the destitute of Addis Ababa. Not everyone was grateful. Two Eritrean nationalists hurled a number of bombs at Graziani and his attendants, wounding the marshal and thirty others. The two would-be assassins were quickly gunned down, but Graziani ordered much more. Italian troops ransacked native neighborhoods, burning down, on the spot, any house in which weapons were found.

For Guido Cortese, secretary of the Fascist Party in Addis Ababa, even this was not sufficient retribution. Acting independently of Graziani, he called on all fascists to take to the streets. *Squadristi* raked the city, slaughtering Ethiopians in their houses over a span of two days and three nights. At last, on February 21, Graziani roused himself from a hospital bed to order a halt to the action. The marshal reported to Mussolini that a thousand Ethiopians had been killed and a thousand houses burned. Eyewitness journalists estimated the death toll at three times this number.

Mussolini accepted Graziani's report without comment, but when even full-scale terrorism like this failed to suppress the guerrilla warfare that persisted in Ethiopia, the Duce ordered mass deportations to "internment camps." These were not the relatively pleasant compounds of the *confino*, the island camps to which Italian dissidents were sent (Chapter 19, "Enter Hitler"), but squalid concentration camps. Thousands of men, women, and children were sent on interminable death marches to these remote camps. Those who survived the march faced a brutal, disease-ridden subsistence in places that anticipated the nightmare death camps Hitler would soon build in Europe.

Even today, apologists for fascism and some historians freely acknowledge fascist racial policies, but point out that they were never as extreme as those of Adolf Hitler. Fascist action in Ethiopia argues that at least against black Africans, Mussolini's racist policies could be as extreme as Hitler's. It is also true that, as Mussolini and Hitler drew closer together politically, the Führer and his inner circle expressed concern that fascism was getting out of step with the extreme right—and with Nazism in particular—because it lacked a strong element of anti-Semitism. Hitler avoided personally speaking to Mussolini on this issue. Strange as it may seem, he did not want Mussolini to feel that he was being pressured to change his views. Hitler also believed that any blatant attempt to meddle in the internal affairs of fascism and Italian government would only rouse Mussolini to resentment.

A popular portrait of Mussolini, presented in a full-dress uniform befitting an emperor.

(*Image from ArtToday*)

But there were others within Hitler's circle who found it impossible to hold their tongues. When Mussolini made his first visit to Hitler in Germany during September 1937, he was privately asked by some of Hitler's inner circle why he seemed so untroubled by the "Jewish menace" in Italy. Mussolini had flirted with anti-Semitism as a means of opposing Bolshevism (Chapter 9, "Man of Destiny"), but soon rejected it (Chapter 11, "An Enemy for Everyone"). Now, in 1937, anti-Semitism seemed like nothing more than an irrelevancy. Of what concern was a tiny minority—about fifty thousand Jews living in mainland Italy—when Italy had just taken into its new empire several *million* blacks? These people, Mussolini pointed out, not the Jews, constituted Italy's potential racial "menace."

How, then, to explain what happened less than a year later, when, on July 14, 1938, the *Giornale d'Italia* published an article called "Fascism and the Problem of Race"? This document immediately took on an independent life as the so-called *Manifesto on Race*, and it addressed specifically the "Jewish question." Through a sleight of tortured logic, the *Manifesto* identified the Italian people as members of the same Aryan race to which the Germans claimed membership. Inasmuch as the Jews were not Aryans, neither were they Italians. The implication of this statement was grave: For if the Jews were not Italians, they could—and should—be somehow disposed of.

> Although both Nazism and fascism had strong racist elements, the Germans and the Italians had trouble seeing eye to eye over racial matters. In October 1938, Dr. Rudolf Frerks, vice director of the Office of Racial Politics of the Nazi Party, met informally with Italian officials responsible for overseeing racial policies, including Guido Landra, head of the Office of Racial Studies at the Ministry of Popular Culture. Landra repeatedly had to remind Frerks that it was the ancient Roman heritage of the Italian race, not anti-Semitism, that lay at the heart of Italian racial policy. Furthermore, Landra expressed dismay over persistent German allegations that "Negro blood" was present in southern and central Italians. Landra wanted to create an Italo-German Academy of Racial Science to help iron out the differences between the two allies. He also set up a secret Italo-German Committee on Racial Questions, which met in December 1938.

Authorship of the *Manifesto* was publicly credited to a group of scholars in the Ministry of Popular Culture. According to Mussolini biographer Jasper Ridley, it was actually drawn up by a young anthropologist named Guido Landra, head of the Office of Racial Studies at the Ministry of Popular Culture, who wrote in compliance with specific instructions provided personally by

Mussolini. How, then, to account for this sudden change in Mussolini's concern over the Jews? Once again, those eager to prove that Mussolini was "never as bad as" Hitler usually ascribe the *Manifesto* and the fascist policy of anti-Semitism to Nazi pressure. Yet there is no evidence that any such pressure was brought to bear. Most chilling is an exchange Ridley points to that took place on August 30, 1938, between Mussolini and his son-in-law, Count Ciano. Mussolini offhandedly proposed that the Jews be rounded up and deported to the northern tip of Italian Somaliland. There, he told Ciano, they could support themselves with certain natural resources, including a shark fishery, "which has the great advantage that, to begin with, many Jews would get eaten." At this point, then, Mussolini was capable of dismissing the "disposal" of Jews as a joking matter.

If Mussolini's change of policy was not due to German pressure, then what *had* prompted it? The great chronicler of the rise and fall of Nazism, William L. Shirer, was always most impressed and horrified by the fundamentally banal quality of Nazi evil. A similar banality was at the heart of Mussolini's newly promulgated anti-Semitic policy. It did not arise from any profound epiphany, but was the product of Mussolini's feeling that fascist doctrine should be *consistent* with German Nazi doctrine and *consistent* with the doctrine of fascist movements in other countries. In Romania, the Fascist Iron Guard was anti-Semitic. In Hungary, the National Socialists were anti-Semitic. In England, Sir Oswald Mosley's Blackshirts were anti-Semitic. In France, the Action Française was anti-Semitic. Everywhere that fascism existed, anti-Semitism was a part of it.

Mussolini must have come to believe that, as the originator of fascism, he had better appear to be in step with the movement's worldwide manifestations. Besides, he no longer had a personal motive for avoiding anti-Semitism. Margherita Sarfatti, ardent fascist, art editor for *Il Popolo d'Italia*, and Jew, was no longer Mussolini's mistress. She had been replaced in Mussolini's affections by a much younger woman, Claretta Petacci.

(After the publication of the *Manifesto on Race*, an alarmed Sarfatti called not on Mussolini, from whom she must have felt frankly estranged, but Count Ciano. He assured her that Mussolini would never act against her. Well-versed in the value of the Duce's promises, Sarfatti immediately took ship for Argentina and did not return to Italy until 1947.)

Mussolini was fifty and Petacci nineteen when he met her in September 1933. It was an encounter of the most random kind. He was in his chauffeured automobile driving from Ostia to Castel Fusano. His car overtook and passed another. In it was a pretty girl, who caught the Duce's eye. He turned to look. Seated beside the driver, an air force lieutenant who was her fiancè, she impulsively waved to Mussolini. The Duce told his chauffeur to pull over and to signal the other driver to do the same. Apparently without deferring to the lieutenant, Mussolini struck up a conversation with the girl, who gushed her admiration, and who agreed to meet him in Rome.

Claretta Petacci lived in the capital with her family, which was presided over by Dr. Francesco Saverio Petacci, a prosperous physician and an officer in the army medical corps. In 1934, she did marry the driver of that car on the road to Castel Fusano, a Lieutenant Federici, but she also became the Duce's mistress— whether before or after the wedding is not certain. Not surprisingly, however, the marriage did not last long. She and the lieutenant separated, although divorce seemed out of the question, because Mussolini, as part of his rapprochement with the Catholic Church, had outlawed divorce in Italy. This notwithstanding, Petacci's resourceful brother, Maj. Marcello Petacci, managed to obtain for the unhappy couple a Hungarian divorce, which was recognized under Italian law.

Not that this freed Claretta Petacci to see Mussolini openly. The Duce seems to have been drawn to her more powerfully than to any other of his several prior mistresses. Yet there were two people even romance could not bring him to offend: the Pope and Rachele Mussolini. In the past, Mussolini had made no secret of his many romantic conquests. With Claretta Petacci, however, he was so discreet that even his wife, who generally knew everything, was ignorant of the affair. Petacci entered and left his office in the Palazzo Venezia by a secret staircase, and the lovers also arranged secret meetings in the various towns to which Mussolini traveled on official business.

Free of Sarfatti and other scruples, Mussolini pressed ahead with his new anti-Semitic policies. On September 1, 1938, all foreign Jews who had come to live in Italy, Libya, or the Dodecanese since 1919 were ordered to leave within six months. On September 2, Jews were barred from enrolling or teaching in Italian schools and universities; however, those currently enrolled would be permitted to complete their studies. Subsequent decrees over the next several weeks barred Jews from membership in the Fascist Party, from enlisting in the army, from employing more than one hundred workers, and from owning more than fifty hectares of land. No Italian could marry a non-Aryan, which meant that no Italian could marry a Jew. (The Fascist Grand Council even went beyond this prohibition in the case of civil servants and soldiers, decreeing that these individuals could not marry any foreigner, Jewish or not.)

By "Jew" was intended anyone who had two Jewish parents or a Jewish father, even if the person in question did not practice the Jewish religion. Children of an Aryan father and Jewish mother were deemed Jews if they practiced the religion, but were not considered Jewish if they converted to another religion before October 1, 1938. And there were other exemptions as well. Foreign Jews aged sixty-five and older were exempted from the order to leave Italy, as were those who had married an Italian before October 1, 1938. Most important, Jews who had fought in World War I, or in Libya, Ethiopia, or Spain were exempted from most (but not all) provisions of the anti-Semitic decrees. Also exempted were Jews who had joined the Fascist Party between 1919 and 1922 or in the last half of 1924, when the party was threatened by the aftermath of the Matteotti murder.

Although the Germans had not greatly pressured Mussolini into enacting anti-Semitic decrees, once he did enact them, they did not hesitate to find fault with them. German officials complained that the decrees included so many exemptions and instances of leniency that the entire fascist anti-Semitic policy seemed half-hearted.

Mussolini didn't care. What was important to him was that he had taken steps to introduce *some* form of anti-Semitism into Italian fascism, thereby bringing his government's ideology into line with others. He wasn't about to argue the details with Nazis, nor was he willing to bow to the many Italians (including some prominent fascists) who did not approve even of lenient anti-Semitic decrees. Both the Pope and Vittore Emmanuelle III expressed their disapproval of the anti-Semitic policy.

Like so much else that Mussolini said, did, and decreed over his long political career, his sudden embrace of anti-Semitism—at once perfunctory and yet in defiance of popular, papal, royal, and even some fascist opinion—is puzzling in its self-contradictory nature. It ceases to be puzzling, however, if one ceases to demand that fascism stand up as a cogent and complete political system. For fascism does not. Mussolini needed to look no further intellectually or philosophically to justify racism and anti-Semitism than the fact he saw others, in England, France, Hungary, Romania, and Germany, take for granted: As a rock is hard or water wet, fascism is anti-Semitic.

Chapter 23

Peace in Our Time and a Pact of Steel

Seeing Benito Mussolini as he was in September 1937, when, clad in the uniform of a marshal of Italy, he made his first visit to Berlin to meet with Adolf Hitler, it would have been difficult to imagine him as the socialist he had been at the turn of the century—unshaven, unwashed, his clothes shabby, his manner that of an outcast. No one can deny that he had come a long way: from anarchical socialist, with a professed allegiance to the proletariat and a complete rejection of nationalism, to fascist, wedded to the captains of Italian industry, virulently nationalist and imperialist. But in at least one important respect, Mussolini never changed. Mussolini the schoolyard bully, Mussolini the penniless political drifter of the early 1900s, and Mussolini the resplendent fascist Duce were all Mussolini the misanthrope.

Other than with his parents, his brother Arnaldo, his wife Rachele, his favorite daughter Edda, and perhaps Claretta Petacci, Mussolini formed no truly meaningful attachments during his life. Except for Petacci, his mistresses served their purpose and then were either allowed to drift off or were spurned. As for male friends, Mussolini once boasted that he had none. He was contemptuous of the masses. To be sure, he was not a mass murderer on a par with Adolf Hitler, at whose behest millions were killed. Whenever possible, Mussolini preferred to work his political will through assault and battery rather than homicide. But he was still capable of ordering murder and even mass murder; he actually expressed regret that more people had not been killed in the "Fascist Revolution," and he had no difficulty ordering aerial bombardment and poison gas attacks against thousands of Ethiopian civilians.

In most contexts, a resumé like this would constitute ample credentials as a hater of humanity. The context in which Mussolini operated, however, included the likes of Hitler, Stalin, and the most coolly bureaucratic killer of all, Japan's Hideki Tojo. By comparison to these dealers in mega death, Mussolini, murderer of mere tens of thousands, comes off as something of a moderate. Still, the point is made: Unlike most politicians, Mussolini was by nature a loner little attracted to other human beings.

Yet Mussolini *was* a politician, and as such, he found that, like it or not, he needed people or, at least, followers. Once he was established as Duce, however, he increasingly attempted to run the government single-handedly, putting his fingers in every department, usually with results that ranged from inefficient to catastrophic. Similarly, in the arena of international politics, Mussolini had a powerful impulse to go it alone. He liked the idea of defying the world, and he even relished the thought that other nations hated—and feared—Italy. But he also realized that a world power needed a powerful ally. Significantly, the "axis" with Germany came about because the rest of the world shunned Italy. In a speech made during his 1937 visit to Berlin, Mussolini declared that the Rome-Berlin Axis really began in the fall of 1935, when Italy, suffering the sanctions of fifty-two members of the League of Nations, found in Germany the one great nation that would stand by its side. Italy and Germany were fighting together in Spain, Mussolini continued, against the common enemy, Bolshevism, and, together, they would prevail, an unbreakable alliance of one hundred fifteen million people.

During Hitler's rise to power, Mussolini repeatedly reassured his countrymen he would never allow Germany to annex Austria. He encouraged Engelbert Dollfuss to form a fascist government for Austria, promising Italy's support (Chapter 19, "Enter Hitler"). The constitution Dollfuss promulgated on May 1, 1934, came close enough to making Austria an Italian satellite that many Austrians were appalled and alienated. This disaffection with Dollfuss gave Hitler an opportunity to muster pro-German Austrian sentiment, and, emboldened, Austrian Nazis staged a coup against the Dollfuss government on July 25, 1934. It failed, but it did result in the assassination of Dollfuss himself. The crisis prompted Mussolini to send troops to the Brenner Pass, the Austro-Italian frontier. Almost exactly two years later, however, on July 11, 1936, Mussolini agreed in principle that Austria should be deemed "a German state," and on November 1, Italy and Germany formally concluded the Rome-Berlin Axis.

Mussolini told members of his government that his agreeing to the idea of Austria as a German state was only a matter of form, a bone he had to toss to Germany for diplomatic reasons only and that Hitler had assured him he had no intention of annexing the country in the foreseeable future. Secretly, however, Mussolini warned Austria's new prime minister, Kurt von Schuschnigg, that Italy would not intervene if Hitler invaded Austria. Mussolini clearly anticipated what Hitler called *Anschluss*, the union of Germany and Austria.

It came on March 13, 1938. German troops invaded Austria, imprisoned Schuschnigg (he remained a prisoner until the end of World War II), and proclaimed the *Anschluss*. Neither Austria nor Italy resisted. Speaking four days later to what was doubtless an anxious Chamber of Deputies, Mussolini simply shrugged off years of Italian opposition to Austrian union with Germany. Germany, he pointed out, was an ally—Italy's only reliable ally, and a mighty one at that. Together, Italy and Germany were invincible, and if Germany wanted Austria, Mussolini declared his determination to do nothing that might harm the Rome-Berlin Axis. Besides, it was clear that a vast majority of the Austrian people favored *Anschluss*, and, the dictator pronounced with straight-faced piety, it was folly to oppose the will of the people.

Ever since the involvement of the futurists in fascism, back in the early 1920s (Chapter 13, "New Legions"), *speed* had been a vaunted feature of the movement. When Cesare Mori could not push hundreds of Mafiosi through trial and conviction quickly enough to suit Mussolini (Chapter 18, "Assassins, Workers, Mafia, Pope"), the Duce urged him to adopt a "rhythm more in keeping with the times, in other words, more Fascist." Now, watching Adolf Hitler, Mussolini could only envy the velocity at which this man moved.

Austria fell to him in March 1938. Immediately, he prepared next to invade and annex the German-speaking Sudetenland of Czechoslovakia. When Hitler visited Rome on May 3, 1938, amid six days of parades, banqueting, and speeches of mutual congratulation, Mussolini promised Hitler that Italy would not interfere with a German invasion of Czechoslovakia.

In the meantime, a new player had arrived. In May 1937, Neville Chamberlain replaced Stanley Baldwin as prime minister of Britain. Chamberlain rationalized what had been for some years the British approach to Mussolini as well as Hitler, and he gave this hitherto nameless policy a name: "active appeasement." To preserve the peace of Europe, Chamberlain proposed a foreign policy of determining what Hitler wanted and then giving it to him. Some in British government, paramountly Winston Churchill, saw this policy as defeatist and dishonorable. In the end, it was just that, but Chamberlain's intention was to behave toward Germany in such a way as to conserve military resources to fight what he saw as the far more serious threat posed by Japan and, most interestingly, Mussolini's Italy.

When Hitler made known his intentions regarding the Czech Sudetenland, Chamberlain responded by warning him against aggressive action. When Hitler stood firm, Chamberlain caved. The prime minister traveled to Berchtesgaden, Hitler's Bavarian chalet, and, in essence, proposed to give Hitler all that he demanded. When he demanded nothing less than the immediate cession of the Sudetenland, Chamberlain agreed, but asked Hitler to delay invading Czechoslovakia until he could persuade Paris and Prague to agree to the cession.

At first, France objected, and the French government appealed to Franklin D. Roosevelt for support. But the temper of the times in the United States was resolutely isolationist, and France, having no wish to stand alone against Germany, agreed to hand the

Sudetenland to Hitler. At first, too, the Czechs proposed to fight. That the Czech people should object to the dismemberment of their nation greatly annoyed Chamberlain, who remarked, "How horrible, fantastic, incredible it is that we should be digging trenches and trying on gas masks here because of a quarrel in a far-away country between people of whom we know nothing."

Chamberlain failed to grasp many things. He failed to grasp that there was really no such thing as "appeasing" a Mussolini or a Hitler. They would never be sated in their hunger for conquest. He also failed to grasp that Czechoslovakia, far from being an obscure little country, was the strategic keystone of Europe. Its geographical location was critical, and it already contained a major arms works as well as thirty army divisions. In their headlong rush to avoid war by sacrificing their sworn ally, the French and British sent ministers to Czechoslovak president Edouard Beneš to tell him that their governments would not honor the Treaty of Versailles and other agreements pledging to protect Czecho-slovakia. If Beneš did not consent to cede the Sudetenland to Germany, France and Britain would stand aside as Hitler invaded and destroyed the country. Without alternative, Beneš yielded, and Chamberlain, now reduced to a kind of messenger boy, flew to Germany on September 22 to tell Hitler. The Führer's reply stunned Chamberlain. Hitler declared that he did not trust Beneš to do as he promised, so unless his demands were immediately accepted, he would invade in six days.

Through this crisis, Mussolini was both calm and delighted. He did not believe that a war would actually break out, but he was confident that Chamberlain, by all his shameless truckling to Hitler, had forever sacrificed the prestige and credibility of Britain—and that suited the Duce perfectly. To the Italian people, Mussolini spoke of Czechoslovakia as an agglomeration of nation-alities and races that "could not" survive as a nation. He also remarked that the Czechoslovak military was cozy with Moscow and that, under these circumstances, Hitler's proposal to wait six days before invading was moderate and generous to a fault. Finally, to an audience at a meeting in Padua on September 24, Mussolini delivered the coup de grace, reminding his listeners that it had been none other than Edouard Beneš who presided over the General Assembly of the League of Nations when it sanctioned Italy over Ethiopia.

On September 28, the British ambassador, through Count Ciano, transmitted a letter from Chamberlain asking Mussolini to persuade Hitler to postpone the Czech invasion for twenty-four hours. Mussolini telephoned Hitler, who agreed, inviting him, Chamberlain, and French premier Édouard Daladier for a conference at Munich the next day, September 29, 1938.

The eleven-thousand-square-mile Sudetenland was populated by about eight hundred thousand Czechs and some two million eight hundred thousand people of German ancestry. It contained most of Czechoslovakia's industry, the core of its communications network, its military outposts, and its natural defenses. By the early evening of September 29, the Sudetenland was presented to Germany, in return for Hitler's promise that he would now make no further territorial demands in Europe. Mussolini and Ciano drew up the papers, which were signed at about two on the morning of September 30. No Czech had been permitted to participate in the conference, but a Czech representative was allowed to wait for news at Chamberlain's hotel. By 2:15 he was told.

The Munich Conference (left to right): British Prime Minister Neville Chamberlain, French Premier Édouard Daladier, Adolf Hitler, Benito Mussolini, and Mussolini's foreign minister (and son-in-law), Count Galeazzo Ciano.

(Image from ArtToday)

Later in the morning, Hitler and Chamberlain signed a document promising never to go to war with each other, and Chamberlain turned next to Mussolini, expressing his desire to improve Anglo-Italian relations and thanking him for the role he had played in preventing a second world war. From Munich, Chamberlain flew back to London, waved a scrap of paper in the air, and announced that he had brought from Herr Hitler "peace for our time."

> *From outside his office at 10 Downing Street, on September 30, 1939, Prime Minister Neville Chamberlain, holding up for all to see his agreement with Hitler countersigned by Mussolini, spoke:*
>
> My good friends, this is the second time in our history that there has come back from Germany to Downing Street peace with honor. I believe it is peace for our time. I thank you from the bottom of our hearts. And now I recommend you go home and sleep quietly in your beds.

On his return to Rome from Munich, Mussolini was greeted by adoring crowds and, personally, by the king himself. "Duce! Duce! Duce!" rang in his ears. The Munich agreement, he said a few days later, meant the "end of Bolshevism in Europe, the end of communism in Europe, the end of Russian political influence in Europe." What he did not say—aloud—was that he believed it also spelled the end of democracy in Europe. Emboldened by Chamberlain's capitulation to Hitler, Mussolini, through Ciano and via the British ambassador, informed Chamberlain that if Anglo-Italian relations did not dramatically improve, he would be forced to conclude a full military alliance with Germany against Britain and France. What would prevent this from happening was England's full diplomatic recognition of Italian sovereignty over Ethiopia. Chamberlain replied to this ultimatum without a trace of indignation. Instead he asked for a quid pro quo. Withdraw at least some troops from Spain, and British "public opinion" would likely be moved to accept official recognition of Italy's rights in Ethiopia.

Believing that a fascist victory was almost at hand in Spain, Mussolini easily decided to withdraw ten thousand of the thirty thousand Italian troops still fighting. In return, on November 16, 1938, Britain officially recognized Vittore Emmanuelle III as "King of Italy and Emperor of Ethiopia." On January 11, 1939, Chamberlain paid a state visit to Mussolini in Rome, where the Duce assured him that, while the Berlin-Rome Axis would remain in force, it need not get in the way of Anglo-Italian friendship.

Chamberlain's "peace for our time" endured for a very brief time indeed. On March 15, 1939, German troops left the Sudetenland, invaded the rest of Czechoslovakia, and entered Prague. Hitler unilaterally declared a German protectorate over the entire nation. To Chamberlain, it was a slap in the face, a blatant violation of the Munich agreement. He wrote to Mussolini, asking him to intervene. Some historians believe that Mussolini himself was greatly disturbed by Hitler's failure to inform him, his Axis partner, of his intention to invade all of Czechoslovakia. If this was the case, Mussolini did not let on. Instead, he publicly supported Hitler's action, and he declined Chamberlain's request for intervention.

British Prime Minister Neville Chamberlain (right) during a state visit to Mussolini in Rome, January 11, 1939.

(Image from National Archives and Records Administration)

Yet it is difficult to believe that, at some level, Mussolini, founder of fascism, did not resent being relegated to the role of junior partner in the alliance with Germany. On April 7, 1939, Italian forces invaded Albania. As Hitler neglected to advise Mussolini of his intentions toward Czechoslovakia, so Mussolini did not tell Hitler what he was about to do in Albania. Hitler accepted Italy's Albanian adventure as graciously as Mussolini had accepted the German invasion of Czechoslovakia. He offered his congratulations to the Duce on his glorious victory.

Actually, it had not been entirely glorious. Before he risked invasion, Mussolini had first tried to buy off Albania's King Zog. He offered a sum of money in exchange for the king's acceptance of Italian occupation. When Zog refused, Mussolini invaded. Except at the town of Durrës, Albanian resistance was feeble, and Mussolini's troops overran the country within twenty-four hours—the kind of rapid victory perfectly suited to the fascist self-image. Zog, his wife, Queen Geraldine Apponyi, and their infant son Skander fled to Greece and, from there, to London. On April 12, the Albanian parliament voted to unite the country with Italy, making Vittore Emmanuelle III "King of Italy and Albania, Emperor of Ethiopia."

Feeling that he was now truly the equal of Hitler, Mussolini authorized Count Ciano to conclude with Germany's foreign minister, Joachim von Ribbentrop, precisely the agreement he had promised Chamberlain he would never make: a full-scale military alliance aimed squarely against Britain and France. Signed on May 22, 1939, it was christened by Mussolini "The Pact of Steel." Hitler saw it in less poetic terms, as neither more nor less than the recipe for a war he desperately wanted. Laying plans for the invasion of Poland, a nation Britain and France had pledged to defend, he now swore: "I'll cook them a stew they'll choke on."

.

Part Six

Spoils of War

Chapter 24

To March with Germany?

"Pact of Steel" was Mussolini's phrase. His first thought had been to call the alliance with Germany "The Pact of Blood," but he quickly rejected that title. Perhaps it seemed a bad omen. After all, this was not the conventional kind of defensive military alliance nations routinely concluded, but an explicitly offensive agreement. If either nation *started* a war, the other was obliged to join in. Perhaps, too, Mussolini realized that a "Pact of Blood" would be too difficult for the Italian people to swallow. For while Mussolini rushed headlong into a military alliance with Germany—letting the Germans write the text of the pact and not so much as deigning to consult his own military advisers on its terms—a tide of anti-German feeling swelled among the Italian people.

Or perhaps it was that the phrase "Pact of Blood" rang too loudly with the truth.

Truth had never meant much to Mussolini. To this inveterate journalist, *words* were always important—"steel" instead of "blood;" "fascism," not "Bolshevism"; "Aryan" rather than plain "Italian"—but *truth* was just so much smoke. Mussolini lied and lied easily, often saying the opposite of what he meant. But a lie is conscious and deliberate. Far more dangerous was Mussolini's even greater capacity for self-deception.

Having just signed a pact obliging him to go to war, Mussolini pretended he had—or deceived himself into believing he really had—an army of more than one hundred fifty divisions (in excess of two million men), with state-of-the-art equipment, including modern tanks, ready to fight immediately. Backing this tremendous force was a reserve, he said, of no fewer than twelve million troops, who could be quickly mobilized. The truth was that he had only ten divisions ready to field, understrength at that, perhaps one hundred sixty thousand men in all. Their equipment was obsolete or obsolescent. Nor were any of these divisions armored in any modern sense; the Italian army had World War I–vintage armored cars, but no tanks. Airplanes had always been a passion of Mussolini's. He had an aviator's license, and two of his sons were air force pilots. But the Duce, who added minister for aviation to his many offices, had neglected the air force as thoroughly as he had neglected the other services. It was described as "irremediably out of date."

Prime Minister Mussolini inspects a new Fiat pursuit plane about 1928. Early on, he encouraged the development of Italian military aviation, but ultimately neglected it. The result was that, on the eve of World War II, the Italian air force was equipped with hopelessly outmoded aircraft.

(Image from the author's collection)

It was with the signing of the Pact of Steel that Mussolini seems suddenly to have become aware of the shocking insufficiency of his military forces—this despite the fact that he had put himself in overall command of the army, air force, and navy. He should have known better. Rattling his saber since the mid 1930s, he should have been re-arming, preparing for the war he was helping to make inevitable. Instead, he seems to have contented himself with the fiction that he was a military prodigy, that he was in charge, and that if he said one hundred fifty divisions were ready to fight, then those divisions would somehow materialize.

The crisis of the Italian military on the brink of war—a skeletal army, an outmoded air force, a navy its own sailors referred to as the "cardboard fleet"—is a stunning illustration of the inefficiency of totalitarian government founded on a cult of personality. The Duce was the nation's sole decision-maker. The Duce was also its sole administrator. Government was entirely centralized. A bulky bureaucracy was in place, but it existed mainly to employ loyal fascists, not actually to run the government. Mussolini was paranoidly parsimonious with authority. What precious little he delegated from time to time, his functionaries were always reluctant to exercise, lest their actions meet with the Duce's disapproval. For if the Duce was tight-fisted where authority was concerned, he was prodigal in meting out blame. Therefore, few officials ever ventured to rock the boat. Fascist centralization killed initiative. In the military, it was not the best officers and bravest soldiers who rose to command, but the most compliant, the quietest, what some called the "empty uniforms." Often, the entire government was paralyzed, waiting for word from the Duce.

Mussolini's capacity for rationalization and denial were monumental. Unlike that other wishful thinker, Neville Chamberlain, Mussolini did not believe Hitler had been "appeased" by the Sudetenland or even by the occupation of all of Czechoslovakia. Although Hitler kept secret from Mussolini his intention of invading Poland, the Duce understood all along that Poland was, indeed, Hitler's next target. Mussolini also understood that the invasion of Poland would bring a general war—one that, this time, England and France surely could not avoid fighting.

Thoroughly unprepared for such a war, Mussolini had nevertheless agreed to fight it. He persuaded himself of two fictions: first, that a war would come, but that he could delay Italy's entry into it until the nation was better prepared and only if it appeared that Germany was winning. Second, he believed that while Germany took Poland, Italy could attack some combination of Greece, Turkey, Romania, or Switzerland and enjoy German support in doing so. His primary thought was to obtain territory in the Balkans, which would supply ample raw materials for the manufacture of armament and materiel. How he could reconcile the objective of delaying Italian entry into the war with the objective of obtaining German support for a campaign in the Balkans, let alone against Switzerland, he did not say.

In contrast to Hitler, who was wedded to the German military and conceived conquest in strictly military terms, Mussolini, even on the verge of war, desperately grasped at the vaguest of alternatives to military conquest. He told Count Ciano and others that he planned to use the impending war to spread disruptive anti-Semitism and revolution throughout the British and French colonies. He said that he would also throw Italy's support behind independence movements in Alsace, Brittany, Corsica, and Ireland. As for the great wild cards in this war, the United States and the Soviet Union, Mussolini claimed to have little concern. He believed the United States would remain resolutely neutral. As for the USSR, in an especially stupefying instance of denial, Mussolini suggested that its intervention on the side of the democracies would actually aid the Italian-German cause by undermining England and France with communism.

By 1943–44, as the war turned against Germany, Hitler's generals would discover that the Führer, too, was capable of gross self-delusion, but in 1939 Adolf Hitler was sufficiently realistic to avoid engaging in the idle speculations and flights of fancy with which Mussolini contented himself. Since coming to power, Hitler had directed the rearmament of Germany in defiance of the Treaty of Versailles, and he had militarized the Rhineland in breach of the Treaty of Locarno. He had tested the democracies by annexing Austria and the Sudetenland, then by taking all of Czechoslovakia.

Now, preparatory to invading Poland, he was not about to dismiss, as Mussolini so blithely did, the Soviet Union. The ideological justification of the Pact of Steel, as well as the earlier, 1937, Anti-Comintern Pact (among Germany, Japan, and Italy) was, of course, the creation of a united front against the great Soviet threat. But when the USSR's Josef Stalin, observing Hitler in action, approached the Führer with a proposal for a nonaggression pact, Hitler brushed ideology aside and jumped at the offer. On August 23, 1939, Nazi Germany and the Soviet Union, modern history's great ideological antagonists, stunned an already reeling world by signing a pact pledging not to go to war with one another. A secret protocol annexed to the pact went much further: Stalin gave his blessing to Hitler's invasion of Poland—and even agreed to provide assistance—in exchange for Hitler's agreement not to interfere with a Soviet invasion of Finland.

News of the Hitler-Stalin pact, which Germany withheld from Italy until it was signed, had an extraordinary effect on Mussolini.

Ever since signing the Pact of Steel, the Duce had been alternately assailed by fears of fighting a disastrously premature war and euphoria over the prospect of the glorious spoils such a war would cast at Italy's feet. He perversely avoided meeting with Hitler to discuss Italian war readiness, but he did send a secret message to the Führer telling him that he would prefer postponing war, only to conclude with an assurance that, this preference notwithstanding, Italy was "one hundred percent ready" to go to war.

Having thus given Hitler the green light, Mussolini thought better of it a few days later and, in a panic, dispatched Count Ciano to Germany with a message spectacularly contradicting the assurance the Duce had just sent. Ciano was instructed to inform Hitler and his foreign minister Ribbentrop that Italy was *not* prepared for war and would not be for another four years—or, perhaps, seven or eight! Ciano flew to Berlin and spoke his piece. Without flinching, Hitler and Ribbentrop listened, then replied that the war would not, under any circumstances, be delayed. With supreme confidence, they assured the Duce's emissary that neither Britain nor the Soviet Union would intervene in the Polish invasion, and that Italy could have Greece and Yugoslavia—without (and this was the real deal maker) even having to contribute to the principal fighting.

Ciano was thrilled. The purpose of his mission instantly dissolved, and he reported to Mussolini the wonderful news: Italy would enjoy the fruits of conquest without the associated labors. But the *gerarchia*, the senior fascist advisers Mussolini sometimes heeded and sometimes ignored, were not impressed. Some of the *gerarchia* plucked up the courage to tell the Duce that a war now would bring disaster upon Italy, regardless of what Hitler and Ribbentrop said. They pointed out that Germany had violated the Pact of Steel by deciding to invade Poland without consulting Italy. This gave Mussolini the perfect excuse for renouncing the alliance.

Gerarchia *was an important word in fascism. While roughly equivalent to the English "hierarchy," it connoted an almost mystical elite, the inner circle of a fascist meritocracy. Some of the* gerarchia *held official posts in the government or military, while others were nothing more than highly placed Fascist Party members. Mussolini relished the myth of an all-knowing inner circle, but, typically, he distanced himself from the* gerarchia *and ignored their advice. Mussolini had used the word* gerarchia *as the title of one of fascism's early journals.*

In the past, such an expression of doubt and disagreement would have brought a tirade from Mussolini and, most likely, the immediate dismissal of the naysayers. Now, however, the Duce admitted that the *gerarchia* might be right. He confessed to them that he was greatly disturbed by Hitler's treatment of him as the junior partner in the Pact of Steel. Mussolini left the meeting with his *gerarchia* apparently determined to denounce the alliance.

But he did nothing. It was as if he found it impossible to stand up to Hitler. Perhaps he feared the Führer. Perhaps he felt he could not afford to lose face with him. Perhaps what he feared most of all was an accusation of cowardice.

Over the next several days, Mussolini agonized indecisively until, finally, on August 21, he resolved to inform Hitler personally that he wished to withdraw his offer of full military support. On the verge of composing this message, word of the Hitler-Stalin Pact reached him.

The rational response to this news would have been instantly to denounce the Pact of Steel. Hitler had breached the Pact of Steel by making a major agreement—virtually an alliance—with a mutual ideological enemy without informing, let alone discussing, the matter with Mussolini. Instead of angrily denouncing the alliance, however, the Duce greeted the news of the Hitler-Stalin pact as Italy's salvation. In an instant, his quite rational misgivings evaporated. If an alliance between Germany and Italy was formidable, how much more so an alliance among Germany, Italy, and the Soviet Union? There was no longer any need to send a message of doubt to Adolf Hitler. Mussolini was euphoric.

But not for long. Within days, the Duce resumed his oscillation between enthusiasm for the war and dread of it. On August 26, as the hour of the invasion approached, Hitler pushed Mussolini for a commitment. Unable to tell the Führer no, Mussolini replied that, yes, Italy was ready to join Germany—provided Hitler send a crash shipment of some seventeen thousand trainloads of war materiel. So extravagant was this figure that it was clear to the Führer it was intended not as a realistic demand, but as an excuse to avoid fighting. His patience at last exhausted, Hitler accused Mussolini of what he most dreaded to be accused of: cowardice.

But even Mussolini was now beyond caring much about being called a coward. Frantically looking for a way out of war, he offered himself as a mediator between Germany and Britain. Both sides rejected him. Facing reality, Hitler ceased browbeating his wavering ally and, instead, implored him at the very least to keep any intention of Italian neutrality a secret. This, at least, would maintain Britain, France, and Poland in a state of anxiety. Mussolini agreed to keep mum, then promptly communicated to London his pledge that Italy would never start a war against either France or Britain. From Hitler's perspective, this was, of course, a betrayal, but Mussolini saw it as the ultimate form of neutrality: Do not choose sides until you see which side will win.

At 4:30 on the morning of September 1, 1939, with no declaration of any kind, the heavy, hawklike *Stuka* dive-bombers of

Adolf Hitler's *Luftwaffe* swooped down on targets all across Poland. Simultaneously, a German battleship "visiting" the port of Danzig opened fire on Polish fortifications, and the *Wehrmacht*, the superbly trained and magnificently equipped German army, stormed across the Polish frontier. World War II had begun.

Later that morning, Benito Mussolini addressed his cabinet. Hitler, he said, had "treacherously" violated the Pact of Steel, and, therefore, Italy would not join Germany in its invasion. The journalist-turned-dictator refused to call this policy what it was, neutrality, because that was a distastefully nonfascist term. Instead, he instructed the cabinet—and, subsequently, the press—to refer to it as "nonbelligerency."

The cabinet had been long accustomed to expressing approval for everything Mussolini proposed. Now its enthusiastic round of applause was doubtless a spontaneous and genuine product of profound relief. Perversely, the response displeased Mussolini. The "proper" fascist attitude in this situation was regret—for real fascists crave battle—and when the Duce heard talk of a planned *popular* celebration to be staged outside his Palazzo Venezia office, he angrily vetoed any such demonstration as the work of the "usual peacemongers."

Chapter 25

Mountains and Deserts

Mussolini was relieved to be out of the war—for now—and throughout the autumn and winter of 1939 and into the early months of 1940, he resisted powerful pressure within the fascist hierarchy to join the hostilities. The pressure came not from the *gerarchi* as an official body, but from two of the most rabidly aggressive fascists: Roberto Farinacci and Giovanni Preziosi. Farinacci, secretary general of the Fascist Party, was always an extremist, who, in the early days of fascist power, had advocated the summary execution of the party's moderates. Preziosi was the party's leading anti-Semite.

Within days of the September 1, 1939, invasion of Poland, Britain and France declared war on Germany. Farinacci joined Preziosi in pinning responsibility for the war on Jews in those countries, and, on December 7, 1939, Farinacci proposed in a Fascist Grand Council meeting that Italy immediately enter the war on the side of Germany. Mussolini replied that the time was not yet right. Farinacci did not argue directly with Mussolini, but, in February 1940, wrote the Duce that "honorary Jews" within the party—including Italo Balbo and Emilio De Bono—were responsible for holding Italy back from taking its rightful place at Germany's side.

Mussolini continued to resist the pressure for war, but he by no means steered a strictly neutral course. He launched a propaganda campaign in support of the Germans while studiously avoiding attacks on Britain or France. Privately, to U.S. Under-Secretary of State Sumner Welles, whom President Roosevelt had dispatched to Europe in a hopeless attempt to mediate among the belligerents, Mussolini said that the British and French insistence on restoring Czech and Austrian independence was unreasonable. Unless the Allies backed down from this position, the war would continue. He did not fault Germany in any way.

Because Mussolini did not behave strictly as a neutral head of state, Britain and France could have found justification for attacking Italy. But they had their hands full with Germany, and the official Franco-British line avoided so much as even criticizing Italy. At times, British diplomats and the press even went out of their way to dissociate fascist policy from Nazi doctrine and, with the Hitler-Stalin pact in place, lumped Nazism together with Bolshevism as godless twins opposed to Christian civilization. (Italy, in contrast, was a good Catholic country.)

Despite having congratulated Hitler on the pact with Stalin, and despite drawing confidence from the thought of an Italian-German-Russian alliance, by January 1940 Mussolini was advising Hitler not to forget that fascism and Nazism were fundamentally opposed to Bolshevism. Hitler delayed responding to this reminder for two months, then suggested that it was Stalin, not he, who was bending his ideology, becoming less dogmatically a communist. Significantly, Hitler did not let on to Mussolini that he would soon betray his pact with Stalin by invading Russia.

Disappointed in and suspicious of Mussolini as he must have been, Hitler remained friendly and understanding. On March 18, when Mussolini met with him at the Brenner Pass, the Duce assured Hitler that Italy would enter the war—at the right moment. He had delayed only because he had been fully confident that Germany could annihilate Poland without Italian aid and that, in fact, Italy was at present more useful to Germany as a non-belligerent than as an active ally. Hitler seemed to accept this vague argument, but one has to wonder what Mussolini felt listening to himself. For no sooner did he return to Rome from his meeting with Hitler than he sat down to draw up a secret memorandum to Vittore Emmanuelle III on Italy's war aims.

Mussolini prided himself on his grasp of military strategy and world power politics. Moreover, he had successfully propagated the myth of his omniscience: "Mussolini," the most familiar propaganda catch phrase went, "is always right." Nevertheless, his analysis of the war situation was a remarkable combination of bull's-eyes and shots wildly off the mark. He believed that a negotiated peace was impossible, because France and Britain would never renounce their demands for the independence of Austria, Czechoslovakia, and now Poland. But he lacked full confidence in Germany, believing, as the French did, that the great chain of fortifications along France's frontier with Germany, the Maginot Line, was impregnable and that, therefore, the Germans would not dare make a definitive offensive thrust on the Western Front. The battle lines, Mussolini wrote, would be drawn at sea and in the east, in the Balkans or the Caucasus.

How would Italy fit into all this? Mussolini wrote that to remain neutral would deprive Italy of any significant place in the postwar world. Of course, to fight against Germany was out of the question; therefore, to enter the war would mean making an alliance with Germany. Mussolini identified the British as Italy's chief opponents, because British control of Gibraltar and Suez effectively confined Italy to the Mediterranean. However, Mussolini did not think it possible to take the offensive directly against Britain. Instead, he outlined a timid, temporizing, and distinctly unfascist campaign of almost pure defense. Believing the collapse of the French army highly improbable, he called for a defensive stance on the Franco-Italian border and a defensive stance in Libya. Only in marginal areas, against lesser powers—Yugoslavia or Greece in the Balkans, British Somaliland and the French at Djibouti in Africa—should Italy attack. On the all-important topic of just when the nation should enter the war, Mussolini remained silent.

It is a generally accepted maxim of military strategy that wars are not won by defense alone, and Mussolini's commanders should therefore have taken alarm at the Duce's almost exclusively defensive war plans. There is no evidence that they did anything of the kind. As for Hitler, in stark contrast to Mussolini, his war plans knew no defense. They were thoroughly aggressive, and when, on May 10, 1940, he launched an end run around the Maginot Line, through Belgium and Holland, rendering France's great defensive fortress chain useless, the war picture changed radically. In England on that very day, Winston Churchill replaced the now pathetic figure of Neville Chamberlain as Britain's prime minister. A few days later, Churchill wrote to Mussolini, hoping to reaffirm Anglo-Italian friendship. Emboldened by Germany's *Blitzkrieg* advance through the West, Mussolini replied that Anglo-Italian friendship had ended when Britain took the lead in sanctioning Italy for its actions in Ethiopia. As Britain entered the war to honor its treaty obligations to Poland, so Italy, Mussolini declared, intended to honor its obligations to Germany.

Mussolini stopped just short of declaring war, but with Germany sweeping through France, he suddenly realized that if he hesitated much longer, the war would be over—and Italy would have cheated itself out of its position in the postwar world. He told his generals on May 26 that he would declare war on Britain and France on June 5. The generals asked for a few additional days, so the declaration came on June 10. As the people of Italy had earlier cheered Mussolini's decision to be a "nonbelligerent," they now cheered his decision to stand shoulder to shoulder with the remarkable, unstoppable Adolf Hitler.

On June 11, Vittore Emmanuelle III officially appointed Mussolini commander-in-chief of the combined Italian armed forces. With France already falling to Germany, Mussolini ordered an invasion of southern France; for an offensive against a collapsing nation was quite feasible. For their part, the British were not slow to take the war to Italy. RAF bombers attacked Turin, inflicting light damage. By way of revenge, Italy's air force pounded the British naval base at Malta, as well as the civilian areas of the island. Among the Italian pilots flying missions against Malta was Bruno Mussolini.

By mid-June, the Germans were in Paris, and Marshal Henri Philippe Pétain, the commander who had risen to heroic stature in World War I by vowing at Verdun that the Germans "will not pass," handed France to Hitler. Mussolini flew to Munich on June 18 to meet with the Führer and carve out his share of France. He informed Hitler that he wanted Nice, Corsica, Tunisia, and Djibouti, thank you very much. Hitler replied only that he had not yet decided on the peace terms he would impose on France. There was nothing Mussolini could do but agree to await his decision.

In the meantime, Italy, which had been steadily building up its army, now had a large number of troops in Ethiopia and Italian Somaliland—one hundred ten thousand, under Amadeo Umberto, Duke of Aosta—and an even greater number in Libya, two hundred thousand commanded by Italo Balbo. These forces clashed with British units while the Italian generals prepared to make major moves against Egypt, the Sudan, and British Somaliland.

In one of these early exchanges, on June 28, Balbo was shot down and killed by Italian antiaircraft gunners, who mistook his squadron for a flight of British aircraft. Mussolini's cool response to the news of Balbo's death suggested to many that he was relieved finally to be rid of an immensely popular man who always loomed as a potential rival. This may or may not have been the case, but that the overall commander of two hundred thousand troops risked his life by flying combat missions showed the poor judgment that Mussolini actively encouraged. A hands-on micromanager himself, Mussolini urged (sometimes ordered) top commanders and party officials to show themselves in the front lines, expose themselves to fire, and generally risk their lives. The able and aggressive Balbo was replaced by the far less capable and overly cautious Marshal Rodolfo Graziani.

In the meantime, amid anxiety over Italy's share of France and anxiety over the impending invasion of Egypt, Mussolini faced a crisis closer to home. In August, Claretta Petacci was rushed into surgery to treat an acute attack of peritonitis, caused either by a miscarriage or a botched—illegal—abortion. On the day of the operation, August 27, 1940, while the war situation was critical, Mussolini rushed to Claretta's home to await the outcome of her surgery. His distraction continued over the next several days when she failed to recover immediately from the operation and seemed close to death. But, by early September, she had regained her health.

On September 13, Graziani launched the Italian invasion of Egypt and made encouraging advances through early December, until, on December 9, the British Western Desert Force, a mere 31,000 men, ripped through a vulnerable gap in Graziani's line, then advanced westward, chewing up each major Italian fortification along the way. By the middle of the month, Graziani's much larger army—*four times* the size of Western Desert Force—had been pushed out of Egypt. It was a devastating and humiliating defeat.

Nor was the news from the Balkans better. Gen. Sebastiano Visconti-Prasca led an army of one hundred sixty-two thousand Italians and Albanians from Albania into Greece, only to be stoutly resisted in the mountains by about one hundred fifty thousand Greeks under Gen. Alexander Papagos. The highly effective Greek defense was followed by a Greek counteroffensive during November 22 through December 23. The Albanian contingent of the Italian forces mutinied, and the Greeks rolled over the remaining Italians in an advance into Albania. The Italian army lost huge quantities of materiel and was pushed all the way to the Adriatic. As they fell back on their naval base at Valona, the British bombarded it, just as they had heavily bombarded the naval base at Taranto, on the heel of the Italian mainland itself, during the night of November 11–12. The disaster complete, Marshal Pietro Badoglio was forced to step down as Italy's chief of staff.

Italian aircraft destroyed on the ground during the doomed Egyptian invasion.

(*Image from National Archives and Records Administration*)

> *Under the command of the remarkable Maj. Gen. Richard N. O'Connor, Britain's Western Desert Force advanced in two months five hundred miles against the far larger Italian army, destroying nine Italian divisions, taking a total of one hundred thirty thousand prisoners, and capturing massive numbers of vehicles and heavy guns. Considering the magnitude of the achievement, British casualties were remarkably light at five hundred killed and 1,373 wounded.*

Reeling from these early catastrophes, Mussolini met with Hitler at Hitler's Berchtesgaden retreat on January 19, 1941. Perhaps looking for something useful to do with the Duce, Hitler asked Mussolini to meet with Francisco Franco to persuade him to bring fascist Spain into the war. The two dictators converged on February 12 at Bordighera on the Italian Riviera. Mussolini made the case that, despite Italian setbacks, Germany and Italy would surely win, and Spain's participation would bring victory that much more swiftly. Franco replied by expressing his gratitude for the aid Germany and Italy had given him during the civil war, and he assured Mussolini that he had complete confidence in the valor of Italian arms, which surely would overcome the present reverses; however, he claimed that Spain was still so devastated by the effects of the civil war that embarking on another war was impossible at this time.

But Franco left the door open, albeit just a crack. He was concerned, he told Mussolini, that Hitler's arrangements with the Vichy government of France would curtail Spain's colonial aspirations. Like the desperate salesman he was, Mussolini endeavored to get his foot into that not-quite-shut door. He asked: Suppose Germany satisfied Spain on the colonial score? Franco replied that Spain would, in that case, enter the war—but he resolutely refused to say when, and thus Mussolini was given a taste of the medicine he himself had earlier administered to Hitler.

In the early months of 1941, Italy was the target of intensive British bombardment from air and sea. Genoa was badly hit on February 9, and even Mussolini's own daughter, Edda, became a victim. Working for the Italian Red Cross, she was bound for

Albania when her hospital ship was attacked and sunk by British bombers. She and the other nurses made it safely into rafts and were rescued. But it must have been painfully clear to Mussolini that not only was he unable to protect Italy from attack, his own daughter had nearly been sacrificed.

At the end of 1940, the only bright spot in the Italian military picture was East Africa, where Italian forces had made good headway against the British in British Somaliland. However, on January 19, 1941, the British mounted an invasion of Ethiopia and Eritrea. Simultaneously, British forces moved against Italian Somaliland. Progress was steady, as Italian and native forces folded, yielding ground. On April 4, Addis Ababa, the Ethiopian capital through which Mussolini had cut a triumphal boulevard for the exclusive use of Italian whites, fell to the British.

On May 5, Haile Selassie was returned to his throne. Prime Minister Churchill (whose nation had done nothing to help the emperor in 1935) wrote to Haile Selassie on May 9: "Your Majesty was the first of the lawful sovereigns to be driven from his throne and country by the Fascist-Nazi criminals, and you are the first to return in triumph." Britain, reeling under the German *Blitz,* deserted by France, facing one disaster after another, was nevertheless able to achieve victory against Italy and restore the emperor Mussolini had removed. Italy, allied to a juggernaut that claimed one victory after another, had known in its first year of war nothing but ignominious defeat. For Mussolini, it was a painful paradox.

Chapter 26

Home Front and Russian Front

"Mussolini is always right." Less than a year into the war, that catch phrase of the "fascist revolution" had become a mockery, the man on the street's dismally sarcastic response to each fresh piece of bad news. On March 28, 1941, the battleship *Vittorio Veneto* was severely damaged by British warships off Cape Matapan, Greece. Named for the victory that allowed Italy to think of its disastrous experience in World War I as a triumph, the *Vittorio Veneto* was the pride of the fleet. If the symbolism of the beating it took was profoundly depressing to the Italian people, even more devastating was the effect of what happened over the next few days. Three of Italy's thirteen destroyers were sunk, as were five of its eight aircraft carriers, with the loss of two thousand four hundred Italian sailors.

On June 10, 1941, the anniversary of his entry into war, Mussolini reviewed Italy's war status in an address he delivered to what had formerly been the Chamber of Deputies, an elected body, and what was now the Chamber of the Fasces and the Corporations, a body appointed by Mussolini himself. The loss of Ethiopia he dismissed as merely a passing episode in what had become a great "vendetta" between Italy and Britain. The Italian defeat in Greece he interpreted as a victory—as, in fact, it was, albeit not one achieved by the dismal performance of the Italian army, but by the army of Italy's ally, Germany, in spite of Italy's failure. While it was true that the Italian people had endured much sacrifice, Mussolini admitted, he assured the Chamber that Britain could not prevail, because it had no purchase on the European continent, and the United States would never enter the war.

Privately, Mussolini recognized how poorly his armed forces were performing. He fixed the blame not on himself as commander in chief, but to some extent on incompetent and cowardly generals, and even more on the Italian people. As the war ground on, Mussolini increasingly came to believe that Italy was losing because its people were insufficiently disciplined, insufficiently tough, and insufficiently courageous. Well before World War II ended, Benito Mussolini, once worshiped nearly as a god, was the most hated man in Italy. From the Duce's point of view, however, the feeling was mutual.

Misery on the home front came not only from the endless litany of military losses and the anguish of families who had sent their sons to die, but it was also the result of the war's impact on the economy. Always concerned first and foremost with appearances, Mussolini had resisted implementing any program of food rationing. For one thing, he wanted the people to feel that there was no need for panic or alarm, that the war would have really very little effect on their daily lives. He also wanted to demonstrate to the world the economic strength of fascism. Whereas even the capitalist democracies required strict rationing and suffered severe shortages, fascist Italy had plenty.

The trouble was that it did not. Food stocks quickly dwindled, and Mussolini secretly negotiated shipments of cereal from Germany. When supplies reached a critically low level, Mussolini belatedly instituted rationing, but, at this late hour, he had to do so on an emergency basis. Suddenly, Italians found their daily bread ration slashed to an infinitesimal one hundred fifty, then one hundred, grams per person—essentially a daily pinch of bread crumbs.

Not that rationing, when it came, did much good. The black market thrived in Italy as it did nowhere else. So did a cottage industry in the printing—by the million—of counterfeit ration cards. With the black market came runaway inflation. To control it, Mussolini formed a price and wage committee with himself at its head, but, like virtually every other fascist institution in wartime Italy, price and wage control proved entirely ineffective. More than seventy-five percent of the nation's agricultural output went directly into the black market.

Statistics like these fueled Mussolini's growing contempt for the people he led. Faced with economic disaster, he began talking like the socialist he once had been, threatening to collectivize land and nationalize certain industries. Probably in response to this kind of leftist rhetoric, Count Giuseppe Volpi, the prominent industrialist who headed the semi-official fascist industrial confederation, assured Mussolini that Italian industry could outperform both Britain and the United States. It was an instance of the denial of reality as spectacular as anything Mussolini himself had ever fabricated, and even he didn't accept it.

Then came June 22, 1941. On that day, in violation of the nonaggression pact, Nazi forces crossed the Soviet frontier and invaded Russia. Hitler had not informed Mussolini.

In a memoir, Rachele Mussolini recalled that her husband, who was told of the invasion within hours after it began, called it a terrible mistake. It is possible that he thought so. Certainly, he had taken comfort in the thought of an alliance not just with Germany, but with Russia as well. Yet, whatever he may have thought, he immediately wrote to Hitler to congratulate him on having once again taken the lead in the struggle against Bolshevism.

Nor did Mussolini stop at mere congratulation. Now, at the nadir of Italy's military fortunes, he begged Hitler's permission to send an Italian expeditionary force to Russia. Understandably, the Führer did not express great confidence in the capability of the proposed force, but Mussolini assured him that these troops would fight very well because, at long last, they were going up against the hated Bolsheviks. Mussolini assigned command of a contingent of two hundred thirty thousand troops to Gen. Giovanni Messe, and the first units of this group embarked on June 25, 1941.

Mussolini had great expectations that the Russian adventure would redeem Italy's honor and morale, because he was clearly hitching the Italian wagon to a rising star. So far, the Russian campaign was going spectacularly well for Germany. The great Soviet air force, largest in Europe, had been all but wiped out—on the ground—in the first twenty-four hours of the invasion. Hitler's troops were brushing aside all resistance. Indeed, by early August, Italians, on the coattails of their German allies, were halfway to Moscow.

> The Soviet air force may have been the largest in Europe, but it was not necessarily up to date. What figured even more importantly in Germany's success was the element of surprise combined with a dearth of leadership among the Soviets. Throughout the 1930s, Stalin, always paranoiac, purged the Red Army (air force included) of top-level officers. This is a major reason the Red Army folded before the German advance—many of the field-grade officers had been executed by Stalin! The telling point is that the planes were destroyed on the ground. Command was so nonexistent that no one ordered a creditable counterattack.

Feeling buoyed at last, Mussolini was suddenly hit by the news that his son, Bruno, a twenty-two-year-old air force pilot, had been killed in a training exercise near Pisa. Although devastated by his loss, the Duce carried on and personally visited the Russian front in company with Hitler on August 28. Mussolini had himself photographed with his general, Messe, four hundred miles inside Soviet territory. He was confident that this picture would make a profound impression at home.

Two things no dictator can afford: to lose a war and to look ridiculous. In The Great Dictator, *a unique 1940 masterpiece of visual political satire, Charlie Chaplin (left) played a version of Adolf Hitler and Jack Oakie (right) portrayed Mussolini.*

(*Publicity still from the author's collection*)

But the news from Russia began to turn bad in November, as Red Army counterattacks checked the German-Italian advance some forty miles outside Moscow, just as the brutal Russian winter began to set in. By this time, Mussolini as well as the Italian people were feeling increasing resentment and distrust of their German allies. Mussolini now blamed Hitler for bogging down in Russia, and he even seemed to take a perverse pleasure in news of multiplying reverses on the Russian front. Throughout Italy, there was grumbling at the numbers of Italian civilians Mussolini had allowed to be drafted, not into the Italian army, but into the German workforce. The Duce sent a total of three hundred fifty thousand workers to German war plants, and it became clear that Hitler valued Italians far more as slaves—which is how they were treated in Germany—than as soldiers. Complaints were filtering back from these conscripts about how they were kept near starvation and housed in worse conditions than prisoners of war. As for

Mussolini, throughout the war, he had been building up the fortifications along the Austro-Italian border—hardly the gesture of a loyal ally.

But, again, Mussolini's spirits were lifted by the news he received on December 3, 1941, from the Japanese ambassador in Rome, that Japan would, within days, declare war on the United States. When the attack on Pearl Harbor came on December 7, Mussolini was elated. He dismissed the United States as an inconsiderable military power, and he rejoiced that Germany and Italy were now to be joined by Japan, creating a combined military force of a quarter-billion men. The Duce predicted that the entry of the United States and Japan would extend the war for as much as five years—a fact that, for some reason, delighted him.

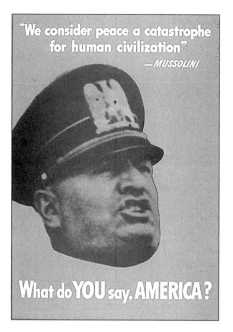

An American propaganda poster from World War II.

(Image from National Archives and Records Administration)

Indeed, as 1941 ended and 1942 began, things began to look up for what was now the Rome-Berlin-Tokyo Axis. By spring, the Germans and Italians, after enduring a record-cold winter, made new advances on the Russian front, and in mid June the Italian navy sank five British ships in a battle in the Mediterranean. Mussolini, very much out and about, insisted on piloting his own plane over the Mediterranean while the battle was in progress. Shortly after this, he visited the North African front, staying in Libya for twenty days. He believed that his appearance on the front lines was a "gift" greatly treasured by the troops and nearly magical in its effect on them; however, each extended absence from Rome sent the government deeper into chaos. Mussolini had built his administration entirely around himself, and, without his physical presence, the bureaucratic machinery ground to a halt. Worse, immediately after returning from Libya, on July 19, Mussolini fell ill with severe stomach ulcers, doubtless aggravated by constant anxiety combined with a diet that now consisted almost exclusively of fruit and milk.

The Duce's condition worsened in the fall as the Russian front began to turn decisively against the Germans and Italians, who were stalled at Stalingrad, and as British general Bernard Law Montgomery fought Germany's vaunted "Desert Fox," Field Marshal Erwin Rommel, into retreat at El Alamein, Egypt. Rommel appropriated Italian vehicles to evacuate German soldiers, leaving the Italian troops behind to be captured. It was, he explained, his duty to save the "best soldiers." As it had earlier in East Africa, the Italian position in North Africa was rapidly collapsing. Hard on the heels of this catastrophe, the RAF launched a massive air raid against Genoa on October 23.

With the war going from bad to worse for Italy, Mussolini was being pressured by Hitler's SS chief, Heinrich Himmler, to begin deporting Italian Jews to Poland. As he became increasingly dismayed by Italian defeat, Mussolini's anti-Semitic rhetoric intensified. As in the earliest days of fascism, he spoke again of Bolshevism as a Jewish political movement and a Jewish plot to destroy Christian civilization. Italian Jews were rounded up and interned, but, through 1940, 1941, and 1942, none were deported.

Apologists for Italian fascism claimed—and some still claim—that Mussolini was not aware of the Holocaust, the Nazi program not merely to deport Jews, but to exterminate them. It is true that, in October 1942, when Himmler visited Mussolini in Rome, he assured the Duce that deported Jews received humane treatment. Subversives were sent to concentration camps, to be sure, but cooperative Jews were put productively to work in pleasant surroundings, while the elderly were actually given care in rest homes. Mussolini did not challenge Himmler on these points, even though his own Foreign Office had informed him, two months earlier, that the Germans were gassing Jews in Polish camps.

If anything, the great majority of Italian people opposed drastic action against the Jews. Italian troops occupying southern France actually blocked French officials from carrying out the Vichy government's orders to deport French Jews. In Athens, the Italian officials in charge of the Axis occupation of Greece refused to enforce German decrees that Jews wear a yellow Star of David as identification. Early in 1943, no less a figure than Joachim von Ribbentrop, Hitler's foreign minister, personally complained to Mussolini about the failure of Italian troops to carry out deportations. Mussolini apologized and assured Ribbentrop as well as Hitler himself that he would personally see to it that such "sentimental humanitarianism" toward the Jews would come to an end. But he seems never to have issued to his commanders any orders to this effect.

It is hard to believe that Mussolini actively wished to rescue Italy's Jews. More likely, he just didn't want to be bothered one way or the other. Of far greater concern to him were signs of disintegration on the home front—a general strike in Milan's war-production plants in March 1943—and the accelerating collapse of Italian and German positions in North Africa. In April, Mussolini proposed to Hitler that the two of them make a separate peace with Stalin, so that they could direct their entire war effort against the United States and Britain. Hitler refused. The next month, German and Italian forces in North Africa fell back on Tunis, where they were trapped by U.S. and British forces on the ground and, on the Mediterranean, by the Royal Navy off the Tunisian coast. In a single stroke, one hundred fifty thousand Axis troops were taken prisoner.

> In May 1943, Mussolini authorized his general in Tunisia, Giovanni Messe, to surrender. Subsequently, he fabricated the myth that Messe was a traitor and coward, whose surrender led to the invasion of Italy. Similarly, Mussolini authorized the surrender of Isola de Pantelleria, but subsequently protested to his German allies that the admiral in charge had disobeyed his personal and direct command to defend "to the last man" the island fortress off the coast of Sicily.

With North Africa secured, the Allies attacked Isola de Pantelleria, which lay between Tunisia and Sicily. Mussolini had often boasted that this island fortress was impregnable, but it folded on June 11, 1943, after only a week under continuous attack. It was the first piece of Italian national territory to be yielded to the Allies, and it brought forth calls from the fascist inner circle that Mussolini open negotiations with Britain and the United States. The Vatican, fearing that Italy was on the verge of revolutionary insurrection, had already offered itself as a mediator.

Mussolini, taken ill again with his ulcers during May and June, rejected any notion of surrender. Although in many places his countrymen were near starvation, Mussolini blithely claimed that food and other supplies were still abundant, and that Italy could easily hold out another three years. As for the Vatican, if it feared a revolution, he would personally authorize the formation of "execution platoons" to keep wavering Italians in line. He warned the people that if Italy surrendered, Churchill and Roosevelt would see to it that every Italian would be killed or enslaved and the nation stripped of its art treasures, its great factories, and its proud universities. Young men would be executed or castrated, and any children they may already have would be deported. In Il Popolo d'Italia, Mussolini put it even more directly: If Britain won, then Italy would be exterminated. The Duce therefore resolved to fight the war "to the last Italian"—now a favorite phrase. There would be no surrender.

On July 9 and 10, 1943, Sir Bernard Law Montgomery's British Eighth Army and the U.S. Seventh Army under George S. Patton landed on Sicily. Throughout the ensuing invasion of the island, Patton's forces were aided by members of the local Mafia, who cleared the roads of snipers, arranged "spontaneous" welcomes for the advancing troops, and furnished guides through the confusing mountain terrain. Twenty years ago, Mussolini had declared war on the Sicilian Mafia (Chapter 18, "Assassins, Workers, Mafia, Pope"), and now the Mafiosi were delighted to contribute to the defeat of a common foe.

German resistance to the invasion was both professional and tenacious, but the Italian forces on the island showed little stomach for a fight, and by August 17, the Allies were in possession of Sicily, and they occupied the town of Messina, since ancient times the stepping-off point for armies poised to invade the Italian mainland.

Chapter 27

Coup d'Etat

Some revolutionary movements—the American Revolution, the French Revolution, the 1917 Russian Revolutions, for example—develop over the course of many years. Others, including the "Fascist Revolution" of 1922, culminating in the March on Rome, are accomplished in the remarkable space of a few days. As Mussolini was thrust into power almost overnight, so he tumbled from it just as quickly.

The Italian people had greeted their nation's entry into the war, at a high point for their gallant ally Hitler, with enthusiasm. Well before the first year of that war was out, however, enthusiasm turned to dismay, dismay to despair, and absolute faith in the Duce to cynical mockery. With the Allied invasion of Sicily, commencing on July 9 and 10, 1943, the turn against the regime of Benito Mussolini was complete—not only at the level of the man and woman in the street, but also at the highest levels of the fascist government and party. With foreign troops now on Italian soil, Mussolini's ministers asked what he proposed to do. The Duce, miserably plagued by his ulcers, replied that he would "throw the invaders into the sea." He also reminded those who asked him what *he* proposed to do that *they* had all taken oaths to die for him, if need be. Those who had the stomach to press Mussolini for details of his planned defense were dismayed to discover what many of them had already suspected: There were no details because there were no plans.

At this point in time, the Duce was so sick, distracted, and distant that he seemed remarkably unconcerned about the enemy at the gates. Things would be fine, he insisted, once he had broken free of Hitler. But when would he make that break? Only after Italy had scored a military success!

To entreaties that he open negotiations with the Allies, Mussolini no longer replied with outright rejection, but with a vague promise to "think about it." Some officials suggested to him that the Fascist Grand Council, which had not been called into session since 1939, might be convened to remove some of the burden of command from him. Mussolini vaguely agreed to summoning the Council.

In the meantime, on July 19, Mussolini flew—acting as his own pilot—to Treviso for a meeting with Hitler at a quiet country villa in San Fermo, near the village of Feltre in the Trentino. Hitler himself had been contemplating the desirability of supporting a replacement for Mussolini—but who? In all of Italy there did not seem to be a viable candidate. Without an alternative to the Duce, Hitler determined to do whatever he could to prevent his otherwise useless ally from yielding to pressure to make a separate peace with England and America.

As usual in meetings between the two dictators, it was Hitler who dominated the discussion. Mussolini used to refer to the Führer's monologues as the "gramophone record." This time, however, the monologue was more pointed than usual, an acid-tongued catalogue of the failings of Italian arms. To the disgust of Mussolini's entourage, which included his chief of staff, Gen. Vittorio Ambrosio, the Duce was utterly passive. He meekly submitted to Hitler's proposal that Italy allow its army to be reorganized under a German commander, yet the instant the meeting was over, Mussolini repeated to his staff his firm intention of breaking free from Germany. At this, Ambrosio decided, then and there, to tender his resignation.

Hitler and Mussolini together: The smiles were for public consumption.

While Mussolini was at Feltre, news reached him that Allied aircraft had bombed Rome. It was a profound shock. For month after month, bombs had rained down on Turin, Genoa, Milan, and other major Italian cities and ports. But Rome had been spared, and the people had taken to assuming that the presence of the Pope in this "Eternal City" would keep the capital safe. The July 19 air raid did avoid the center of Rome and also stayed clear of the Vatican, concentrating instead on rail yards and industrial areas, but the point had been made. Nothing was sacred. Rome was a target, like any other.

The meeting of the Fascist Grand Council Mussolini had vaguely authorized before he left for Feltre was set to convene at

5 P.M., Saturday, July 24. As he made his way out the door of his borrowed residence, Villa Torlonia, Rachele Mussolini called to her husband: *Have them all arrested!* she advised. Count Dino Grandi, former ambassador to Britain and one of the councilors present at the meeting, had anticipated that Mussolini might be thinking of doing just that. Accordingly, he carried a hand grenade in his pocket and was determined to blow everyone up, himself included, if the Duce made a hostile move.

But Mussolini was as passive before the Fascist Grand Council as he had been before Hitler at Feltre. Grandi began the session by making a motion that command of the army, navy, and air force be removed from the hands of Mussolini and presented to the king. From five until after midnight and into the morning hours, the motion was discussed and amended, until it included not only taking the armed forces away from Mussolini, but reinstating the constitutional power and authority of parliament, the Grand Council, and all the ministers. At points in the discussion, the question was put to Mussolini: Was there any way to win the war? And, if not, how could peace be made so that further destruction might be avoided? The Duce made no answer to either question.

The meeting dragged on into the dark morning of July 25. Some councilors, both emboldened and disgusted by Mussolini's paralysis of will and spirit, blamed him directly and solely for the disaster that had befallen Italy. Others put the blame on the Fascist Party. Still others blamed neither Mussolini nor the party as such, but the nature of dictatorship, which must ultimately alienate the people. It was a very late hour for such critical self-examination.

As expanded by amendment, Grandi's motion was carried by a nineteen-to-seven vote before first light on July 25. Through the night, Mussolini had put up no fight. His abject surrender under attack was something even he could not explain to himself. Perhaps the explanation was as simple as this: Mussolini *wanted* out.

After the meeting, he returned to Villa Torlonia for a few hours' sleep, then left for his office. There he busied himself reading the usual reports, as if nothing had happened, and before noon he met with the Japanese ambassador. To him he announced that he would seek a separate peace with the Allies, unless Germany sent him more arms. A bit later, he was informed that some of those who had voted in favor of Grandi's motion now desired to recant their votes. The Duce replied that it was too late, that he would report to the king, and that the "traitors" would be dealt with in "the most energetic manner." With that, at two in the afternoon, he visited the Tiburtino section of Rome, which had borne the brunt of the July 19 air raid, and at three he returned to Villa Torlonia. At ten minutes to five, he departed for his meeting with Vittore Emmanuelle III at his residence, the Villa Ada.

> *Mussolini wrote his own (third-person) account of his downfall, focusing in greatest detail on the approximately twenty-four hours between 5 P.M., July 24, 1943, and 5:20 P.M. on July 25. Called* History of a Year, *it was published serially, subject to German censorship, in the Milan newspaper* Corriere della Sera *beginning on June 24, 1944. It appeared later as a pamphlet supplement to* Corriere della Sera *and then, in November 1944, as a book in a French translation issued by a Swiss press. Until the final collapse of the fascist regime, it was a best-seller.*

In his own account of his fall from power—narrated, curiously enough, in the third person—Mussolini wrote that, prior to his meeting with Vittore Emmanuelle III, he was "completely calm" and that he "thought that probably the King would relieve him of the command of the Armed Forces ... which he had for some time wished to give up. In other words, Mussolini arrived at the Villa Ada without any misgivings. His frame of mind might be called in retrospect positively naive."

The king, Mussolini reported, was "unusually excited, his face ... distraught." Leading Mussolini into the drawing room, he said: "My dear Duce, it can't go on any longer. Italy is in pieces. Army morale has reached the bottom and the soldiers don't want to fight any longer. The Alpine regiments have a song saying they are through fighting Mussolini's war." After singing "several verses"— apparently he knew them by heart—the king continued:

> *The result of the votes cast by the Grand Council is devastating. ... Surely you have no illusions as to how*

*Italians feel about you at this moment. You are the most
hated man in Italy; you have not a single friend left,
except for me. You need not worry about your personal
security. I shall see to that. I have decided that the man of
the hour is Marshal Badoglio. He will form a cabinet of
career officials in order to rule the country and go on with
the war. Six months from now we shall see. All Rome
knows about what went on at the Grand Council meeting
and everyone expects drastic changes to be made.*

According to Vittore Emmanuelle's later account, Mussolini
was dumbfounded and unprotesting. According to Mussolini's own
account, he was hardly struck dumb, but replied calmly:

*You are making an extremely grave decision. If you pro-
voke a crisis at a time like this the people will believe that,
since you are eliminating the man who declared war, then
peace must be at hand. You will strike a serious blow at
the morale of the Army. The fact that our troops—the
Alpine regiments or the others—won't go on with the war
for Mussolini is of no importance, provided they are willing to fight for you. The crisis will be claimed as a personal triumph by both Churchill and Stalin, especially the
latter, whose antagonist I have been for the last twenty
years. I am perfectly aware that the people hate me. I
admitted as much last night before the Grand Council.
No one can govern for so long and impose so many sacrifices without incurring more or less bitter resentment. Be
that as it may, I wish good luck to my successor.*

Both the king's account and Mussolini's agree on one fact: The
entire meeting, which ended the regime of Benito Mussolini,
lasted just twenty minutes.

A captain of the King's Guard approached the deposed Duce as
he stood in an anteroom. The captain announced that he had been
ordered to drive him home in a military ambulance. When
Mussolini protested that he had arrived in his own car, the officer
replied firmly, "It is an order, Duce."

They drove off at top speed, and it was quickly apparent to Mussolini that he was not being taken to Villa Torlonia. Instead, he was driven from one military barracks to another. At one stop, he was handed a letter from Marshal Badoglio. It informed him of Badoglio's appointment as prime minister and went on to say that he, Mussolini, would be taken to a secure place for his own protection.

Doubtless, Mussolini saw this operation for what it was, an arrest and imprisonment, but it was also true that he very much needed protection. Word of his dismissal spread rapidly, unleashing a torrent of pent-up popular rage against the fascist regime and against himself. As mobs of fascist bullies had once attacked anti-fascists in their homes, now the anti-fascists targeted the houses of prominent party members. Mussolini was held in several places until, on July 28, he was transported to the island of La Maddalena, off the Sardinian coast—the very prison to which Tito Zaniboni, the socialist deputy who had tried to assassinate Mussolini in 1925, had been confined (Chapter 17, "Making the Trains Run on Time"). Without explanation, his jailers set Zaniboni free a few days after Mussolini's arrival on the island.

As for Rachele Mussolini, she learned of her husband's arrest from an anonymous telephone caller. Fearing that she would be attacked by anti-fascist mobs, her friends begged her to leave Villa Torlonia. She heeded their advice, but did not go far, only moving out of the main villa to settle in at the doorkeeper's house close by. There, the wife of the doorkeeper, a woman named Irma, who worked as a chambermaid at Mussolini's offices in the Palazzo Venezia, offered a stream of comforting conversation. In the course of her unguarded speech, she let slip the name of Claretta Petacci.

Mussolini's wife had never before heard of this woman who had been her husband's mistress since 1933. She pressed poor Irma for information, and the chambermaid at last revealed all that she knew. That revelation put events in a new perspective for Rachele Mussolini. She thoroughly grasped that Benito Mussolini was no longer the Duce, and that was certainly bad enough, but she was far more devastated by the news that her husband had been unfaithful to her—again, and for so very long.

Chapter 28

Puppet in a Stork

In July 1943, there were approximately four million members of the Fascist Party in Italy, each of whom had taken a most solemn oath of personal loyalty to Benito Mussolini, for whom they pledged themselves to die, if necessary. News of the Duce's downfall spread rapidly, yet not one fascist raised a finger in protest. No leader rose up to organize resistance, to rescue Mussolini, to restore him to power. Even the Duce's own newspaper, *Il Popolo d'Italia*, did nothing more than delete Mussolini's name from the masthead and replace the customary front-page portrait of the Duce with a picture of Marshal Pietro Badoglio.

Among the fascist inner circle, the *gerarchia*, one man committed suicide, two others fled to asylum in the German embassy, and the rest threw themselves at the feet of the new prime minister. Badoglio was little interested in giving top positions to Mussolini's inner circle, however, although he did not arrest, persecute, or jail them, either. He appointed a cabinet not of fascists or anti-fascists, but of career civil servants in the hope of restoring some degree of function to the government. Badoglio also clearly announced that the war would go on.

Pietro Badoglio was far from being a brilliant man, and many contemporaries and some later historians have been even less kind in their judgment of King Vittore Emmanuelle III, at least one applying to him the word *moron*. Both Badoglio and the king were criticized, in 1943 and later, for failing to use the ouster of

Mussolini as an occasion to seek an immediate armistice with the Allies. Had they done this, some have argued, much of the costly Allied campaign in Italy, which lasted practically until the surrender of Germany, might have been avoided. At the time, however, it must have seemed to the king and his new prime minister that to break suddenly with Hitler would bring an immediate German invasion of Italy, which would only serve to complete the destruction the Allies had begun.

Indeed, Hitler, although he expressed regret at Mussolini's removal—and must certainly have been deeply suspicious of Badoglio—announced that he would keep his fingers out of the internal affairs of the country. This included refraining from intervention in Badoglio's failure (almost certainly purposeful) to enforce Mussolini's anti-Semitic decrees. As a result, almost immediately after Badoglio's appointment, many anti-fascist political prisoners were released, and Jews were set free from the internment camps. Communists, still deemed an imminent menace, were kept locked up. Doubtless Hitler was as fearful of driving Italy into an alliance with the Allies as Vittore Emmanuelle and Badoglio were fearful of provoking Hitler to invade. It was a standoff.

As for Mussolini, although held on the island of La Maddalena, he was not kept incommunicado. He was permitted to receive letters from his family, and they from him. Other communication also reached him, including a sixtieth birthday telegram (July 29) from Reichsmarschal Hermann Goering and a birthday gift from Adolf Hitler himself, a complete edition of the collected works of Friedrich Nietzsche—which, Mussolini wrote in his final memoir, *History of a Year,* he sincerely treasured and eagerly devoured. Mussolini received cordial treatment from his guards, whom he treated cordially in return, often passing the time in playing cards with them.

Hitler, of course, was correct to mistrust Badoglio. On the very day that he announced the continuation of the war, the new prime minister directed Raffaele Guariglia, Italy's ambassador to Spain, to contact the Allies through the British embassy in Lisbon, Portugal, in order to open peace talks with them. At the suggestion of the

British, the negotiations that followed took place in Tangiers, where, it was felt, they would attract less attention.

Not that there was anything to negotiate. For the Allied position was firm: Nothing less than unconditional surrender would be accepted. With this laid down on the table, the Allies stepped up their bombing raids against Italian cities, especially Turin and Milan, which had already been hit hard and often. Germany's foreign minister, Joachim von Ribbentrop, contacted Guariglia to obtain his assurance that he was not talking peace with the Allies. Absurdly enough, under the circumstances, Ribbentrop asked for Guariglia's "word of honor" on the topic. Guariglia swore that no negotiations were underway.

Ribbentrop's concern prompted the Badoglio government to worry that the Germans (or die-hard Italian fascists), suspecting that a separate peace was in the works, might attempt to rescue Mussolini and organize around him a pro-war opposition government. Besides, one of the conditions the Allies were demanding in return for a cease-fire was the delivery, into their hands, of Benito Mussolini. Accordingly, on August 28, Mussolini was suddenly and secretly moved from La Maddalena to an abandoned hotel atop the highest peak of the Gran Sasso mountains, near the village of L'Aquila, north of Rome. Here, it was felt, he could be more effectively guarded.

A little more than a week after Mussolini was moved, Marshal Badoglio announced, on September 8, 1943, that he had concluded an armistice with the Allies. Denouncing this as infamy, Hitler responded with greater alacrity than the Allies, who should have been better prepared. Before Allied troops could reach Rome, the German *Wehrmacht* occupied the capital and all of Italy north of the Volturno River. Vittore Emmanuelle III and Badoglio decamped and set up a government at Brindisi.

As the Führer had been swift in seizing most of Italy, so he was bold in his decision to rescue and resurrect Benito Mussolini. He assigned a daring paratroop commando, Otto Skorzeny, to locate and recover the Duce. Skorzeny did his work with remarkable speed, quickly determining Mussolini's whereabouts and immediately formulating a plan for his rescue. Although Mussolini was still guarded by Italians presumably loyal to the Badoglio government—men who might shoot the Duce sooner than allow his rescue—the Gran Sasso, like the rest of northern Italy, was controlled by the Germans. That was a major plus. But to reduce the risk of Mussolini's being shot, Skorzeny took along on the rescue mission a General Soleti, a high-ranking officer of the Italian police.

As Mussolini recounted in his *History of a Year*, September 12, 1943, dawned in thick fog on the Gran Sasso, but after noon, the sun broke through, and by two, it was a clear, crisp September day. He wrote in the third person:

> *Mussolini was sitting with folded arms in front of an open window when a glider landed about a hundred yards away. Four or five men in khaki uniforms got out, set up two machine guns, and then advanced toward the lodge. A few seconds later other gliders came down and the same maneuver was repeated. ... Carabinieri and policemen rushed out of the hospice with drawn arms and lined up against their attackers. Meanwhile Captain Faiola burst into the Duce's room and said:*
>
> *"Shut the window and stay where you are!"*
>
> *But Mussolini looked out the window and saw another larger group of Germans, who had taken possession of the funicular railway and were marching resolutely up toward the hospice with Skorzeny at their head. The carabinieri had already raised their guns to fire when Mussolini spied among the Germans an Italian officer whom he recognized when they drew nearer as General Soleti of the Police.*
>
> *Mussolini broke the ominous silence preceding the order to fire by a loud shout: "What are you doing? There's an Italian general! Don't shoot! Everything's in good order!"*

At the sight of the Italian general the guards lowered their guns. Mussolini was escorted to a Luftwaffe Fiesler F-156 Storch, a "Stork," a light, single-engine airplane designed to land on and take off from extremely short, unpaved fields. It was piloted by a German air ace named Gerlach.

"I knew all along that the Führer would give me this proof of his friendship," Mussolini reported that he said to Skorzeny.

Even with an ace at the controls, the take-off must have been harrowing. Troops pushed the plane back to gain a few more yards, the single prop kicked over, the plane, whose take-off speed was a mere thirty-six miles per hour, rolled down the stony field, and, "barely a yard from the precipice, with a jerk of the stick, it took off into the air."

The Stork flew Mussolini to an airfield at Pratica di Mare, where he was ushered into a military version of the Junkers JU-52 tri-motor Hitler himself used as his primary air transport. It took off for Vienna, arriving late at night. The Duce was lodged in the Continental Hotel and, at noon on the next day, boarded a train for Munich. From here, he flew to Rastenburg to thank Hitler, in person, for having rescued him. The Führer sent another plane to Rocca delle Caminate, the summer home outside of Forlì where Rachele Mussolini and two of the Mussolini children, Anna Maria and Romano, were now staying. The plane transported the Duce's family to him in Munich.

Despite the armistice, the Allies were somewhat undecided about just how to treat Italy. Was it a new ally or a defeated enemy? Many in Hitler's inner circle were not at all undecided, however, but firmly believed that Germany should now regard Italy as a conquered foe. Hitler had another approach. He decided to install Mussolini as the head of an Italian fascist government to oppose the government set up by Badoglio. He believed that by keeping Italy divided against itself in this way, the position of the Allies in the country would be weakened. Besides, whatever Mussolini's shortcomings, he was a like-minded dictator, and Hitler was loath to allow the downfall of an ideological comrade-at-arms. It would set a potentially fatal precedent.

As for Mussolini, the man who, after Feltre, had talked about making a break with Germany, who complained that Hitler patronized him as a junior partner and subjected him to tedious lectures, he now felt nothing but gratitude. Was it apparent to him that he was now not even a junior partner, but a puppet of the

Third Reich? Perhaps. But, if so, it did not seem to matter. Better a living puppet than a dead dictator.

Mussolini did whatever Hitler told him to do, beginning with a broadcast from Munich to a radio audience of millions in which he declared that King Vittore Emmanuelle III and Marshal Pietro Badoglio had treacherously betrayed Italy to its enemies. For the salvation of the nation, he, Benito Mussolini, would now preside over a new Italian Social Republic and would lead it to victory alongside its ever-faithful German allies.

Mussolini begged Hitler to let him return to Rome and govern from there, the ancient capital. The Führer's advisers protested that, in Rome, Mussolini would only get in the way of the real government, the government of German occupation. It is a measure of how hollow Hitler realized—or intended—the restoration of Mussolini to be that he instantly agreed with his generals. Explaining to Mussolini that Rome was uncomfortably close to the front lines, he instructed the Duce to set up his government at Salò, on Lake Garda, near the northern Italian frontier. The parliament could meet in nearby Verona.

The Allied and Nazi leaders were not the only people confused by shifting allegiances. Shortly before the Mussolinis left Munich for the Villa Feltrinelli, in Gargnano, designated as the Duce's new residence and office, Count Galeazzo Ciano arrived. Mussolini's former foreign minister and present son-in-law was, as of mid September 1943, a man without a country. In the fateful July 24 and 25 meeting of the Fascist Grand Council, he had voted against his father-in-law, but he now discovered that this fact had given him no place in the Badoglio government. His vote against Mussolini was not sufficient to erase his history as a high fascist official, let alone as a member of the Mussolini family. He decided, therefore, to join Mussolini up north in the hope that blood was thicker—thicker than what? Did Ciano really expect Mussolini to forgive and forget?

If he did, he was not alone. Remarkably, another five of the seventeen members of the Grand Council who voted against Mussolini fled the south in the hope of finding refuge in German-occupied

Italy. (The other dozen Council members decided either to tough it out among the southern anti-fascists or to make for Spain, where Franco offered asylum.) Those who came north badly misjudged Mussolini. The Duce readily accepted the recommendation of the hard-core fascists surrounding him at Salò that Emilio De Bono, Giovanni Marinelli, Luciano Gottardi, Carlo Pareschi, Tullio Cianetti, and Ciano be tried by the Italian Social Republic on charges of high treason. On October 17, 1943, Galeazzo Ciano, husband of Edda Mussolini, was extradited from Germany to the Italian Social Republic to await trial with the others.

In the meantime, Mussolini pressed forward with the formation of a new government, a government without a king and, astoundingly enough, a government based on a new constitution drafted not by a longtime prominent fascist, but by a comrade from Mussolini's early socialist days. Nicola Bombacci had been a leading member of the Italian Communist Party after World War I and had often tangled with fascists in the Chamber of Deputies. When Mussolini began rounding up and arresting communists after the March on Rome, Bombacci fled to Moscow, but was expelled from the Soviet Communist Party in 1927 when he became a member of the Left Opposition. He decided to risk living in Mussolini's Italy rather than Stalin's Russia, and his old friend the Duce saw to it that, as long as he promised to remain politically inactive, he would not be bothered. When Bombacci wrote a long, thoughtful letter of condolence to Mussolini on the death of his brother Arnaldo in 1931, the two actively renewed their friendship. Moved by patriotism during the Ethiopian War, Bombacci applied for membership in the Fascist Party and, sponsored by his friend, was accepted. It was to him that the Duce now turned for his constitution.

Hitler and the other Nazis gave little thought to the constitution of the Italian Social Republic or who was writing it. They understood that whatever the constitution said or didn't say or the new parliament voted or didn't vote, Mussolini would do as he was told—or the German occupiers would do it for him. What they *were* concerned about was that the Italian Social Republic at long last begin taking action against Jews as befit a fascist regime.

Mussolini now agreed—for the first time—not only to declare all Jews enemy aliens, but to deport them to Polish death camps.

> *With the creation of the Salò republic, the Holocaust belatedly and tragically came in earnest to Italy. Even now, however, despite Mussolini's explicit orders, many Italians resisted cooperating with authorities in rounding up Jews. It was reported to Heinrich Himmler that, in Rome, for every Jew captured, eleven escaped, thanks to action by locals. In all, some seven thousand Italian Jews died in Polish death camps, a staggering number, to be sure, representing fifteen percent of Italy's prewar Jewish population—yet far less than anywhere else in Nazi-occupied Europe, except for Denmark.*

Mussolini did not hate Jews, but he apparently did not find it terribly difficult to harden his heart against them. Certainly, they, in their thousands, were less important to him than his son-in-law, and Edda was confident that her father would protect her husband. Her shock must have been profound when he made it clear that his duty prevented any such protection. As the Germans wanted Italy's Jews deported and disposed of, so they wanted the traitors of July 24 and 25 summarily executed, and, on this, the hard-line fascists were in complete agreement.

Realizing at last that her father meant to see her husband dead, Countess Edda Ciano fled to Switzerland, carrying with her diaries in which Ciano had recorded, over the years, any number of humiliating actions and pronouncements by Benito Mussolini. Her desperate hope was that she might now trade the diaries for her husband's life and, to this end, she contacted Heinrich Himmler. After consulting with the Führer, Himmler replied that there was no interest in such an exchange.

Of the six men found guilty of treason, five were sentenced to die. One, Cianetti, who had tried to rescind his vote the morning after it had been cast, was sentenced to a prison term of thirty years. The others were executed on January 11, 1944, each, Count Ciano included, given the special death reserved for traitors: Tied to chairs, each was shot in the back of the head. They would not be the last high fascist officials to suffer grisly execution.

Chapter 29

Prey of the People

L ife as Hitler's puppet was not easy. Mussolini was accustomed to having his orders obeyed. Now he was rarely in a position to give orders, and the Führer often failed even so much as to acknowledge Mussolini's many letters to him. Hitler knew what Mussolini refused to admit even to himself: that he, the Duce, was no longer head of a sovereign state. When the direction of Mussolini happened to coincide with that of the Germans, the Duce was still permitted to believe he was in charge. But when a dispute arose, the Duce was not argued with, but merely ignored.

Thus the leader of the Italian Social Republic found he could do little enough when Hitler's troops made harsh reprisals against his countrymen for anti-fascist resistance activity. The German policy in occupied Italy was the same as in any other *enemy* nation under occupation: For every German killed by an anti-fascist partisan, authorities shot many—twenty, fifty, or a hundred— hostages. No attempt was made to single out the guilty, anti-fascists or known resistance fighters. Instead, fifty, a hundred, or more Italian civilians were routinely plucked at random from the streets or from their homes and summarily executed.

Mussolini scored a victory of sorts against this reprisal policy after a March 23, 1944, partisan attack killed thirty-two SS men in Rome. Mussolini successfully prevailed on Hitler to reduce the reprisal ratio of Italian to German dead from fifty-to-one to ten-to-one. However, these three hundred thirty-five Italians (fifteen were added after another SS man succumbed to his wounds) were executed in the most unseemly and miserable way possible. Taken to the Ardeatine caves, an abandoned sandstone quarry outside of Rome, they were shot in darkness and in shame. Mussolini was outraged, not because the hostages had been killed, but because they had been killed shabbily, not like Italians, the Duce protested, but like Poles. It is significant that this protest on racist grounds had more effect on the Nazis than any of Mussolini's earlier objections. On August 21, 1944, Field Marshal Albert Kesselring, in charge of the military occupation of Italy, ordered that, from now on, all reprisals were to be carried out exclusively against partisan guerrillas and those deemed partisan sympathizers.

In practice, many German officers were none too careful about separating partisans from ordinary, unresisting citizens, but Mussolini had at least won the battle in principle, and that was greatly heartening to him. As for artisans, if anything, Mussolini was even more zealous in desiring their swift execution than the Germans were. He ordered Italian authorities to refrain from negotiation of any kind with guerrillas. They were to be shot wherever and whenever they were caught.

As bitter as Mussolini's resentment of German authority sometimes was, the alternative seemed to him unthinkable. He told the Italian people—and he likely believed it himself—that an Allied victory would mean the end of Italy as a nation. The Allied demand for "unconditional surrender" would bring, he said, enslavement to "Anglo-American Jewish capitalism."

While German resistance to the Allied invasion of Italy was fierce and effective, exacting a terrible toll on British and American forces, the Nazis, under unremitting attack, gradually yielded ground. Simultaneously, the Allied air forces steadily intensified the raids against the cities of northern Italy, which prompted Mussolini—who had never hesitated to bomb the men, women, and children of Ethiopia and Spain—to protest crimes against humanity. The German "Blitz" against London and other British cities, intensive bombing intended to demoralize the civilian population, had, if anything, only increased popular solidarity and determination to win through to absolute victory. In contrast, few citizens of northern Italy felt a patriotic attachment to the

Italian Social Republic, and instead of pulling together amid the Allied raids and the dwindling rations, they rebelled. In March 1944, general strikes were called in Milan and other great industrial centers of the north.

At the height of the strikes, some three hundred fifty thousand workers idled themselves, prompting Hitler to order the arrest of every fifth striker. The Führer's intention was to transport these men to Germany as slave labor, but Mussolini asked him to delay execution of his order to give him time to talk the strikers back to work. Probably because the arrest and transportation of tens of thousands of Italians presented logistical difficulties to an army under attack and in retreat, Hitler agreed to the delay. Mussolini broadcast a surprisingly eloquent and measured appeal to the strikers, explaining that they had been duped by communists, who had purposely coordinated the strike with the operations of the Anglo-American armies and air forces. Thus, the Duce explained, the strikers had been made the unwitting instruments of Italy's enemies. They were killing their countrymen.

Within a week of Mussolini's broadcasts, the strikes all across northern Italy ended.

Whatever feeling of triumph Mussolini derived from breaking the general strike was short-lived. On June 5, 1944, Rome fell to the Allied advance. The loss of the capital hit him hard in two ways. First, he had persuaded himself that Rome represented an absolute line, which would be defended so fiercely and effectively that the Allies would never be able to advance beyond it. Second, Rome was the heart of Italy, objective of the glorious march that had brought the triumph of Italian fascism. The Duce broadcast a pledge that the city would be retaken, repeating the vow Garibaldi had made in 1862: "Rome or death!" But the next day, June 6, brought, if anything, even worse news. The Allies had landed at Normandy. Occupied France was under invasion. From the very beginning of the war, even before Italy's entry, Mussolini had vehemently denied the possibility that Hitler's "Fortress Europe" could ever be breached. Now it had been.

For Mussolini, the handwriting should have been blazing on the wall. Yet, against all reason, he persisted in the faith that the Axis could never be defeated. On July 20, 1944, a bomb, planted by a cabal of German military officers, exploded in a conference room at Hitler's Rastenburg headquarters. Hitler was slightly wounded, but he was sufficiently recovered to meet with Mussolini for a routine war conference later that very day. Far from seeing this most recent—and very nearly successful—attempt on Hitler's life as further evidence of the disintegration of the Axis cause, Mussolini, for most of his life an avowed atheist, interpreted the Führer's survival as evidence of nothing less than divine intervention. Moreover, the Duce took bizarre comfort in learning that even Adolf Hitler could be betrayed, just as he himself had been. They were, at long last, equals.

By the end of 1944, all rational hope of an Axis victory had been extinguished, and Mussolini now grasped at irrational hopes. He assured a Milan audience on December 16, 1944, that Germany was on the brink of deploying new "wonder weapons" that would annihilate the enemy. In private, he turned from German invention to Italian, telling an associate that Guglielmo Marconi, the inventor of radio, had developed a "death ray," but, unfortunately, had kept it secret—and was now eight years in his grave.

Was he grasping at the thinnest of straws? Did he really believe the Germans were about to develop what he referred to as an "atomic device" or some newer, more powerful "V" weapon to replace the V-1 buzz bomb and the V-2 rocket? Or was this talk nothing more than evidence of emotional disintegration? By the fall of 1944, Mussolini suffered a series of attacks described as episodes of "nervous collapse" and "an absolute loss of energy and intelligence." He was perpetually sleepless and unable to eat.

Like Hitler, whom many of his inner circle now believed frankly mad, Mussolini declared his intention to wage war to the finish. As Hitler spoke of fighting to the last German, so Mussolini swore he would "fight to the last Italian." He evoked the ancient example of Thermopylae, which three hundred Spartans had defended to the death against one hundred thousand Persians in 480 B.C.E. And he raised the far more recent example of Stalingrad, which the German army had held at the cost of three hundred thousand men before finally surrendering to the Red Army on February 2, 1943. Incredibly, Mussolini ordered troops to prepare defenses at Valtelline, practically on the border with Switzerland. His commanders declined to carry out such a useless order, but they allowed him to believe that preparations for this last-ditch defense were underway.

While he continued to speak of "last-ditch" defenses and fighting "to the last Italian," Mussolini began to think of escape. One idea suggested to him was sailing to Japan in a submarine, another was flying to Argentina or Spain. These notions he rejected as impractical or ignominious. More appealing was the idea of seeking asylum in Switzerland, but preliminary inquiries revealed that the Swiss were not eager to have the likes of Mussolini in their midst and would very probably turn him over to the Allies.

Having run out of options, Mussolini left his quarters on Lake Garda to return to Milan. His German guards objected, but, at this stage in a losing war, they did nothing to prevent his leaving. On April 25, 1945, in a state of despondency, he agreed to meet with partisan leaders at the house of the archbishop of Milan. His hope, doubtless, was to find some alternative to absolute, unconditional surrender. In his talk with the partisans, he no longer made any pretense of saving Italy. His sole concern was his personal fate. He was told that he could rely on receiving a "fair trial," but there could be no assurances or guarantees beyond this.

At this point, Mussolini abruptly broke off the discussion. According to one account, he vaguely excused himself by reporting that he had just learned that Germany was about to make a separate peace with the Allies (this was not true), then quickly left the meeting. Another version says that he told the partisans he could not agree to surrender without first consulting the Germans, and he promised to return to the meeting within an hour, only to disappear. Whichever was the case, he left, and, with Nicola Bombacci, his comrade at arms from socialist days, most recently the author of the constitution of the Italian Social Republic (Chapter 28, "Puppet in a Stork"), he sped out of Milan in a car.

Again, there are differing versions of what he ultimately intended to do. One account reports that he meant to go to

Valtelline, where, he declared, thirty thousand loyal fascists were waiting to fight the final battle. It is quite possible that he was sufficiently deluded at this point to believe that in all Italy thirty thousand fascists loyal to him could be found, let alone that they were armed and concentrated at Valtelline. Another version of his departure from Milan holds that he intended to seek Swiss asylum, despite the unpromising prospects of this course of action; after all, he had nothing further to lose. Whatever his intention, he did leave Milan in the nick of time, for it fell to partisan control on the next day, April 26.

Mussolini drove as far as Lake Como. If he had really intended to take a last stand at Valtelline, it must have been now that he realized there was no one there to stand with him. On April 27, he and other Italians, including Bombacci, joined a convoy of about two hundred German soldiers who were driving toward the Swiss border, hoping, like Mussolini, to find asylum.

The whereabouts of Rachele, Anna Maria, and Romano Mussolini at this time are not clear. Either they were already at Como or soon would be. What is known is that Mussolini, shortly before he left Como, wrote to Claretta Petacci to tell her that he was trying to get to Switzerland with a German convoy. He urged her to escape Italy by any means possible. She decided not to try to flee on her own, but to join Mussolini, and she prevailed upon her brother Marcello to overtake the convoy in his fast Alfa Romeo.

Mussolini and the Germans, in the meantime, were driving up the west shore of Lake Como when they were intercepted at Musso by a large partisan force. The partisan commander told the German troops that he would permit them to continue on to Switzerland after he had inspected the convoy for any Italians. Mussolini had disguised himself with nothing more elaborate than a Luftwaffe helmet. It did not take the partisans long to recognize the man whose face had been the most familiar sight in Italy for more than two decades.

Mussolini, Bombacci, and other Italians removed from the convoy were taken to the town of Dongo. There Marcello and Claretta Petacci were waiting; for partisans had already intercepted the Alfa. Claretta refused to leave Mussolini's side, so, together, they were separated from the other prisoners. The couple was held under guard in a farmhouse at Giulino di Mezzegra. Nicola Bombacci and Marcello Petacci, along with the other Italian prisoners, were led to the Lake Como shore and shot dead.

> *Partisans arrested Rachele, Anna Maria, and Romano Mussolini in Como, but intervention by the United States Army saved them from harm. Rachele heard about her husband's death on a radio broadcast. After several months' internment, she, Anna Maria, and Romano were released. Mussolini's son Vittorio escaped to Switzerland. Benito Mussolini's battered corpse was recovered from the square in Milan where it hung by its heels, and the former Duce was subsequently buried in the family mausoleum in the cemetery of San Cassiano, Predappio.*

Although stories about the end of the lives of Benito Mussolini and his last mistress vary and conflict, what is most likely is that the Council of the Resistance, the chief partisan authority, decided that Mussolini should be immediately shot, despite explicit British and American instructions that he not be harmed. The Italian resistance could not tolerate the idea of relinquishing Mussolini to Anglo-British justice. This was not merely a matter of vengeance, but also because the majority of the partisan leadership was communist and well aware that however much the Americans and British hated fascists, they had little enough love for communists. The partisans did not trust the Allies to punish Benito Mussolini.

The actual order for Mussolini's execution was signed by Gen. Raffaele Cadorna, president of the Council of the Resistance and son of Luigi Cadorna, who had been Mussolini's commander in chief during World War I. Walter Audisio, a communist partisan commander, carried out the order. On April 28, in the afternoon, he fetched Mussolini from the farmhouse. Claretta Petacci, refusing to leave his side, went along. They stopped at a crossroads a short distance from the house. Audisio read aloud the death sentence pronounced by the Council, then ordered two members of the squad that had accompanied him to fire. Claretta Petacci died with the first shot. Mussolini was only wounded when his executioner's submachine gun jammed. A shot from a second weapon finished him off.

Partisans struggle to hold back the Milan crowd swarming around Mussolini's corpse (visible at bottom center) before his body, with thirteen others, was strung up by the heels on an iron fence.

(*Image from ArtToday*)

It was 4:30 in the afternoon. But Benito Mussolini, dead as he was, had not quite reached his end. His body—together with that of Claretta Petacci and those of the others who had been executed separately, fourteen corpses in all—was taken to the Piazzale Loreto, a large public square near Milan's Central Station. There they were all hung by their feet along an iron fence in front of a filling station. A mob, not unlike those that had so many times wildly cheered *Duce! Duce! Duce!* now converged on the hanging meat that had been human beings. The mob cursed, spat, beat, and kicked. Soon, the face of Benito Mussolini was all but unrecognizable. In their way, the execution and post-mortem battery were actions eminently fascist—summary, swift, and savage, carried out in a "rhythm," as the Duce himself would have said, "in keeping with the times."

The World of Mussolini: Who Was Who

Acerbo, Giacomo Member of the Fascist Grand Council; voted to oust Mussolini, July 25, 1943.

Albini, Umberto Member of the Fascist Grand Council and close confidant of Mussolini; voted to oust Mussolini, July 25, 1943.

Aloisi, Baron Pompeo Chief of Mussolini's first cabinet.

Attolico, Bernardo Fascist ambassador to Germany.

Audisio, Walter (alias Colonel Valerio) Officer of the Italian partisans who led Mussolini's execution.

Badoglio, Marshal Pietro Italian army commander named by King Vittore Emmanuelle III to replace Mussolini after the Duce's ouster on July 25, 1943.

Bakunin, Mikhail Russian anarchist revolutionary whom the young Mussolini greatly admired.

Balabanoff, Angelica Prominent Russian socialist, who served as Mussolini's mentor and mistress before World War I.

Balbo, Italo Early fascist leader; Mussolini colleague and potential rival; later Italy's Minister of Air.

Baldwin, Stanley British prime minister during 1923–24 and 1924–29.

Bastianini, Giuseppe Member of the Fascist Grand Council; voted to oust Mussolini, July 25, 1943.

Battisti, Cesare Socialist Party leader and editor in Trentino, when Mussolini was active in the party there.

Beneš, Edouard President of Czechoslovakia at the time of the Sudetenland crisis.

Bianchi, Michele Early national secretary of the Fascist Party.

Blum, Léon Leading French socialist and one of Mussolini's most vocal early opponents.

Bombacci, Nicola Longtime Mussolini comrade; a fascist convert from communism, he was tapped by Mussolini to write a constitution for the Italian Social Republic, the puppet government Mussolini created after his liberation by Hitler.

Bonomi, Ivanhoe Italian socialist leader, prime minister, and important opponent of Mussolini.

Cadorna, General Count Luigi Inept commander in chief of Italian forces through most of World War I.

Cadorna, General Raffaele Commander of Italian partisans opposed to fascism and German occupation; signed the order to execute Mussolini. Son of Luigi Cadorna.

Chamberlain, Sir Austen British foreign secretary in the 1920s and admirer of Mussolini; he was the half-brother of Neville Chamberlain.

Chamberlain, Neville As British prime minister from 1937–40, he used "active appeasement" in a misguided effort to avert war with Adolf Hitler's Germany.

Churchill, Winston Opponent of Neville Chamberlain's appeasement policy; served valiantly as Britain's wartime prime minister, 1940–45.

Cianetti, Tullio Member of the Fascist Grand Council, who voted to oust Mussolini, July 25, 1943, but then tried to rescind his vote.

Ciano, Count Galeazzo Mussolini's son-in-law (married daughter Edda) and foreign minister; as a member of the Fascist Grand Council, he voted to oust Mussolini, July 25, 1943, and was subsequently executed, with Mussolini's approval, for treason.

Ciano, Countess Edda *See* Mussolini, Edda.

Cipriani, Amilcare   One of Benito Amilcare Andrea Mussolini's three revolutionary namesakes; a Communard who fought with Garibaldi to liberate Rome in 1862.

Corridoni, Filipo   Mussolini's early socialist comrade.

Costa, Andrea   One of Benito Amilcare Andrea Mussolini's three revolutionary namesakes; organized the Bologna socialist uprising of 1874.

Croce, Benedetto   Prominent Italian philosopher and early supporter of Mussolini against bolshevism.

Curzon, George Nathaniel   British foreign secretary and early critic of Prime Minister Mussolini.

Dalser, Benito Albino   Mussolini's illegitimate son by Ida Irene Dalser.

Dalser, Ida Irene   Mistress who attempted legal action against Mussolini for alimony and child support; bore his son Benito Albino.

D'Annunzio, Gabriele   Celebrated Italian poet and novelist; his filibustering expedition against Fiume in 1919 upstaged Mussolini.

De Bono, General Emilio   Inept Italian commander in chief in the war against Ethiopia; a member of the Fascist Grand Council, he voted to oust Mussolini, July 25, 1943, and was later executed as a traitor.

De Nicola, Enrico   President of the Chamber of Deputies when Mussolini signed the Treaty of Pacification with the socialists in 1921.

De Vecchi, Cesare   With Mussolini, one of the first fascists elected to the Chamber of Deputies; an advocate of violence.

Diaz, General Armando   Replaced General Luigi Cadorna as Italian commander in chief during World War I; the victor of Vittorio Veneto.

Dolfuss, Engelbert   With Mussolini's encouragement, set up a short-lived fascist government in Austria; assassinated by the Austrian Nazis.

Drummond, Sir Eric   British ambassador to Italy before the outbreak of World War II.

Dumini, Amerigo   Fascist hit man who, with four others, murdered Mussolini's most prominent opponent, Giacomo Matteotti.

Facta, Luigi   Ineffectual liberal prime minister of Italy at the time of Mussolini's rise to power.

Farinacci, Roberto   Fascist extremist and consistent advocate of maximum violence.

Federzoni, Luigi   Fascist Grand Council member and a moderate voice within the party and government; he voted for Mussolini's removal as prime minister, July 25, 1943.

Finzi, Aldo   Prominent Jewish fascist, accused of impeding the investigation of the Matteotti murder.

Franco, General Francisco   Leader of the Spanish fascists and, with the aid of Mussolini and Hitler, victor in the Spanish Civil War.

Garibaldi, Giuseppe   Italy's national hero and radical revolutionary; his photograph decorated Mussolini's boyhood home.

Garibaldi, Peppino and Ricciotti   Grandsons of Giuseppe Garibaldi; supported intervention in World War I and were early supporters of fascism.

Gaspari, Cardinal Pietro   The Vatican official with whom the Mussolini government negotiated the Lateran Treaty in 1929.

Gentile, Professor Giovanni   Italian scholar appointed as Fascist Minister of Education; edited the *Enciclopedia Italiana*, produced under fascist auspices.

Giolitti, Giovanni   Liberal Italian politician and five-time premier; sought a coalition with the Fascist Party in 1921.

Giunta, Francesco   Fascist member of the Chamber of Deputies who earned renown by forcibly ejecting the socialist deputy Francesco Misiano from the parliament building.

Graham, Sir Ronald   British ambassador to Italy.

Gramsci, Antonio   Italian communist philosopher who wrote his most important works while a prisoner of the fascist regime.

Grandi, Count Dino   Foreign minister from 1929–32 and ambassador to Britain until 1939.

Graziani, General Rodolfo   Governor of Libya and Italian Somaliland, and viceroy in Ethiopia; appointed commander in chief of military forces of the Italian Social Republic.

Guidi, Rachele   *See* Mussolini, Rachele.

Haile Selassie   Emperor of Ethiopia deposed by Mussolini in the 1935–36 war and restored to the throne after the British victory in Ethiopia in 1941.

Himmler, Heinrich   German Reichsfuhrer-SS, head of the Gestapo and the Waffen-SS, Minister of the Interior, and architect of the Holocaust.

Hitler, Adolf   Founder of the Nazi Party and Führer of Germany, 1933–45.

Hoare, Sir Samuel   British foreign secretary who, with Pierre Laval of France, secretly negotiated a plan to deliver most of Ethiopia into Italy's hands.

Juárez, Benito   One of Benito Amilcare Andrea Mussolini's three revolutionary namesakes; president of Mexico who overcame the puppet emperor Maximilian I.

Kesselring, Field Marshal Albert   Leader of the German occupation of Italy following the Badoglio government's armistice with the Allies.

Laval, Pierre   French premier and foreign minister who formulated with British foreign secretary Samuel Hoare the secret Hoare-Laval plan to deliver Ethiopia into the hands of Italy.

Lenin, Vladimir I   Architect of the Bolshevik Revolution of 1917 and first leader of the Soviet Union.

MacDonald, Ramsay   British prime minister from 1931–35.

Malatesta, Errico   Italian anarchist; early Mussolini role model and later adversary.

Marinelli, Giovanni   Fascist Grand Council member implicated in the murder of socialist leader Giacomo Matteotti.

Marx, Karl   Father of communism and author of *Das Kapital*; young Mussolini carried in his pocket a medal stamped with his profile.

Matteotti, Giacomo   Courageous socialist opponent of Mussolini and the fascists; was beaten to death, probably at the behest of Mussolini.

Messe, General Giovanni   Mussolini's commander in North Africa.

Minzoni, Father Giuseppe   Outspoken anti-fascist priest murdered by fascists.

Misano, Francesco   Outspoken socialist opponent of the fascists who was forcibly ejected from the Montecitorio (parliament building).

Mori, Cesare   Fascist official Mussolini appointed to prosecute the Mafia in Sicily.

Mosely, Sir Oswald   Founder and leader of the British Fascist Party.

Mussolini, Alessandro   Father of Benito Mussolini.

Mussolini, Anna Maria   Mussolini's youngest daughter.

Mussolini, Arnaldo   Mussolini's brother; may have ghostwritten *My Autobiography* in 1928.

Mussolini, Bruno   Mussolini's second-oldest son.

Mussolini, Edda   Mussolini's daughter and eldest child; married Count Galeazzo Ciano.

Mussolini, Rachele (neé Guidi)   Wife of Benito Mussolini.

Mussolini, Romano   Mussolini's youngest son.

Mussolini, Rosa   Mussolini's mother.

Mussolini, Vittorio   Mussolini's eldest son.

Mussolini Mancini, Edvige   Mussolini's sister.

Nitti, Francesco Fausto   Italian premier during 1919–20; lived in exile during fascist years.

Petacci, Claretta   Mussolini's last mistress; she was executed with him on April 28, 1945.

Pius XI, Pope   Pope from 1922–39; during his pontificate, the Lateran Treaty with fascist Italy was concluded (1929).

Pius XII, Pope   Pope from 1939–58; criticized for his failure to speak out against the Holocaust and the fascist persecution of Jews.

Rafanelli, Leda   Exotic socialist radical who befriended Mussolini but, apparently, spurned his sexual advances.

Roosevelt, Franklin D.   President of the United States, 1933–45; Mussolini's hatred of him was intensely personal.

Rossi, Cesare   An accomplice in the murder of Matteotti, he wrote a 1945 account of the incident, clearing Mussolini of direct involvement in the crime.

Sarfatti, Margherita   Mussolini's Jewish mistress and cultural mentor; she was the art critic for his newspaper, *Il Popolo d'Italia*.

Sorel, Georges   French political philosopher, whose syndicalism was an important influence on Mussolini's early political thought, as was his advocacy of political violence.

Stalin, Josef   Second head of state of the Soviet Union and wartime nemesis of Mussolini.

Toscanini, Arturo   Famed Italian symphony conductor; an early member of the Fascist Party, he soon spoke out against its excesses, was beaten, and fled the country for the United States.

Vecchi, Ferruccio   Leader who presided over the first meeting of the Fasci di Combattimento, the birth of Italian fascism, in 1919.

Vittore Emmanuelle III   The King of Italy who appointed Mussolini prime minister in 1922.

Volpi, Albino   Accomplice in the murder of Giacomo Matteotti.

Wilson, Woodrow   U.S. president from 1913–21, instrumental in formulating peace after World War I, including the creation of the League of Nations.

Zamboni, Anteo   After attempting to assassinate Mussolini in 1926, he was lynched and literally torn to pieces.

Zaniboni, Tito   A socialist deputy who attempted to assassinate Mussolini on November 4, 1925.

Zog, King of Albania   Mussolini attempted to bribe him before invading Albania in 1939.

Appendix B

Suggestions for Further Reading

Berezin, Mabel. *Making the Fascist Self: The Political Culture of Interwar Italy.* Ithaca, NY: Cornell University Press, 1997.

Boswoth, R. J. B. *The Italian Dictatorship: Problems and Perspectives in the Interpretation of Mussolini and Fascism.* London: Arnold Press, 1998.

Collier, Richard. *Duce! A Biography of Benito Mussolini.* New York: Viking Press, 1971.

Fermi, Laura. *Mussolini.* Chicago: University of Chicago Press, 1961.

Gregor, James. *Young Mussolini and the Intellectual Origins of Fascism.* Berkeley: University of California Press, 1979.

Hartenian, Larry. *Benito Mussolini (World Leaders Past and Present).* New York: Chelsea House, 1988.

Hibbert, Christopher. *Il Duce: The Life of Benito Mussolini.* Boston: Little, Brown, 1962.

Knox, MacGregor. *Mussolini Unleashed: Politics and Strategy in Italy's Last War.* New York: Cambridge University Press, 1982.

Lyttle, Richard B. *Il Duce: The Rise and Fall of Benito Mussolini*. New York: Macmillan, 1987.

Mussolini, Benito. *My Rise and Fall*. Reprints *My Autobiography* (1928) and *History of a Year* (1945). New York: Da Capo, 1998.

Ridley, Jasper. *Mussolini: A Biography*. New York: Cooper Square Press, 2000.

Sbacchi, Alberto. *Legacy of Bitterness: Ethiopia and Fascist Italy, 1935–1941*. Lawrenceville, NJ: Red Sea Press, 1997.

Smith, Denis Mack. *Italy and Its Monarchy*. New Haven, CT: Yale University Press, 1989.

——. *Mussolini*. New York: Vintage, 1983.

Whittam, John. *Fascist Italy*. New York: St. Martin's Press, 1995.

Index

Index

British, 215-216
caporalmaggiore, 80
captured by allies, 302-303
Catholic Church, 190
Chamber of Deputies, 171, 271-272
Cheka, 167-168
childhood, 9-14
children, 41, 52, 79, 202, 224-225,
    269-270
Corfu, League of Nations, 165-166
corporal, 77
Corporate State, 200-201
cowardice, 260-261
cult of personality, 151
De Bono, Emilio, 211-212
death, final hours, 303-304
deputy seat in parliament, 123-124
destiny, 90-91
destruction, 47
dictatorship, 90, 152-153, 185, 234
drafts in Italy, 24
dual with Ciccotti, Ettore, 129-130
Duce, 282
editor, *Avanti!*, 51-56
election campaign for parliament, 124
end of Bolshevism, 249
escape, 301-302
Ethiopia, 211-218, 234-236
fall from power, 281
family, 243-244, 302
Fasci di Combattimento, 113-114
fascism, 67-68, 89, 98, 100-102, 114,
    120-122, 126-127, 137, 174-180,
    203-205, 228-229
    hierarchy, 263
    leadership, 132-136
    legion formation, 131-133
    takeover, 134-136
    violence, 128-129
Fascist Party, 289
fashion, 15-16, 55
fatherhood, 224
fiancées, 14
Fiat pursuit plane, 256
Fiume, 107-108
full-dress uniform, 237
gerarchia, 44-45
Germany
    alliance, 255
    Jews, 110-111
    militarism, 214-215
government, 161, 168
Gran Sasso mountains, 291
Great Depression, 199-200
health problems, 279
Himmler, Heinrich, Italian Jews, 278
Hitler, Adolf, 213, 261-264, 283
Hitler-Stalin pact, 259
Hitler's puppet, 297
humanity credentials, 244
ideologies, 65-66
Il Duce, 93-94
Il Popolo d'Italia, views on World War I,
    75, 85-89
illegitimate son, 185-186
impact of mother's death, 27
imperialism, 97
impersonal force, 151
imprisonment, 287, 290
influences of family, 8

injuries, 183
international conflict, Spanish Civil War,
    227
internationalism, 71, 95
interventionist movement, 69-70
Italian Social Republic, 297
Italo-Turkish War, speeches, 48-49
Italy, 272
    Ethiopia, 213-214
    government, 137-146
    international reputation, 161
    regiment, 26
Japanese ambassador, 284-285
Jews, 110-111, 238-239, 241-242
jobs, 16, 37-39, 42-44, 51
journalism, 97, 155-156, 255
Jubaland, 163
King of Italy, 222
La Lotta di Classe, 42-44
La Maddalena, imprisoned, 290
last-ditch defense, 300-301
Lateran Treaty, 191-192
Laval, Pierre, France, 213-214
laws, 189-190
League of Nations, 215-216, 231
lies told to mother, 19
lifestyle, 201-202
link to Massimo Rocca, 63-64
Mafia, 187-189
March on Rome, 140-145
marriage to Rachele Guidi, 35, 41, 79
Marx, Karl (influences of), 32-33
micromanagement, 201
military, 251, 257-258, 270, 287
misanthrope, 243
mistresses, 239-244
National Executive Committee, 50
nationalism, 38, 66, 70-71
neutrality views, 64
new government, 294-295
newspaper, 289
Nietzsche, Friedrich (influences of), 32-33
parliamentary system, 112
personality, 46-47, 202-203
politics, 125-126, 129-131, 244
    agenda, 208
    career, 108-109
    violence, 160-163
Pontine Marsh project, 201
power, 47, 55-56, 159-160
prime minister of Italy, 144, 146, 149, 154
prisoners of war, 278-279
prosecutions, 39-40
prototype, 209-210
public image, 202-203
racism, 234-239
radio broadcast, Italian Social Republic,
    294
railways, 180
rape, 46
Red Week in Milan, 56-57
reputation, 15-16
rescue mission, 291-293
rise of fascism, 122-123
rise of Italy, 233
Russian front, 274
self-contradiction, 46-47
sex, 14-15
shamelessness, 46-47
Sheridan, Clare, 152